RISK
IS STILL A FOUR LETTER WORD

GEORGE HARTMAN

Stoddart

Published in 2000 by Stoddart Publishing Co. Limited
34 Lesmill Road, Toronto, Canada M3B 2T6
180 Varick Street, 9th Floor, New York, New York 10014

Distributed in Canada by:
General Distribution Services Ltd.
325 Humber College Blvd., Toronto, Ontario M9W 7C3
Tel. (416) 213-1919   Fax (416) 213-1917
Email cservice@genpub.com

04   03   02   01   00   1   2   3   4   5

Canadian Cataloguing in Publication Data
Hartman, George E. (George Edward), 1949–
Risk is still a four letter word

ISBN 0-7737-6110-1

1. Finance, Personal. 2. Finance, Personal — Canada.
3. Investments — Canada. 4. Risk.
I. Title.

HG179.H377 2000   332.024   C00-930067-8

Cover Design: Bill Douglas @ The Bang
Text Design: Tannice Goddard
Graphs: Crowle Art

THE CANADA COUNCIL | LE CONSEIL DES ARTS
FOR THE ARTS | DU CANADA
SINCE 1957 | DEPUIS 1957

*We acknowledge for their financial support of our
publishing program the Canada Council, the Ontario Arts
Council, and the Government of Canada through the
Book Publishing Industry Development Program (BPIDP).*

Printed and bound in Canada

To Mom, Harold, Patricia and Elton

Contents

Foreword

I can't believe it has been seven years since George Hartman's fine work, *Risk Is a Four Letter Word*, was first released. Most financial books don't pass the test of time — this is a dynamic that often renders once-sensible advice worthless and that has many times humbled even the most intelligent among us. George's advice, though, seems even wiser and more relevant today, hence this new work, *Risk is STILL a Four Letter Word*.

There is no such thing as a riskless investment. And common sense would dictate that if there was, it wouldn't offer sufficient returns to justify buying it.

There's the rub.

Risk and reward are closely linked. For the most part, the higher an investment's perceived risk, the higher its potential reward. Therefore, attempting to eliminate or even to dramatically reduce risk may not be an investor's most prudent strategy.

Am I suggesting that an investor should wholeheartedly embrace risk? No. Although theoretically that approach may lead to fine long-term performance, when mixed with human nature, it often self-destructs. For with increased risk comes increased volatility. And with increased volatility comes increased stress. And with increased stress comes an increased number of emotional decisions. And that final increase leads to Canadians' favourite investment practice — "buy high, sell low" (or to my family's traditional version — "buy extremely high, sell extremely low").

So the answer, for most of us, can be found neither by shunning risk nor by marrying it. Instead we should court it — learn to accept it, work with it, and most important, strive to understand it.

How much risk is acceptable? How much is prudent? Of course, the answer differs for each of us depending on a number of factors, including our risk-tolerance level, the desired rewards and our time-frame.

How we best allocate our assets must take these factors into account as well as some others; for example, whether we want to actively or passively manage our money. That's what this book is all about. Not giving you a prescribed asset mix, but instead teaching you how to develop your own strategy, one you can understand, feel comfortable with, maintain and prosper from.

Asset allocation is not the same as market-timing. That's a good thing, because all empirical evidence indicates that accurate market-timing is a pipe-dream. Instead, George Hartman's approach to asset allocation teaches the judicious management of risk through diversification — a worthy objective for all of us.

DAVID CHILTON
AUTHOR OF
THE WEALTHY BARBER

Acknowledgements

This book is really a sequel to my first book *Risk Is a Four Letter Word*, so it seems appropriate to acknowledge some of the people who contributed to the success of the original and therefore underpinned the foundation for this one.

As I said in this space in the original version, after many years of lecturing on the subject of investing I assumed that putting the concepts I'd so often presented into written form would be a relatively easy task. I quickly learned that it was far from easy, and impossible to do alone. Books like this don't happen without the assistance and encouragement of many people.

I will always be grateful to David Chilton, author of the enormously successful *The Wealthy Barber*, who first showed how anxious people are for common-sense ideas about financial planning and investing. David's encouragement and criticism always seemed to come at precisely the right time. I am again honoured to have the foreword to this book written by David.

The initial idea for a book on this topic came from my exposure to another author and lecturer, Roger Gibson (*Asset Allocation: Balancing Financial Risk*), whom I have followed around like a devoted disciple at every meeting of the International Association for Financial Planning. Since then, countless other great commentators have shared their thoughts and insights to help shape mine.

Special mention needs to be made of the people at Stoddart Publishing Co. Limited who have waited so patiently for the follow-up to my first book. Managing Editor Don Bastian kept the light in the window and, when I said I was actually (finally!) going to proceed, assembled a great support team. Marnie Kramarich, who received the assignment of project leader, is a very gracious yet persistent taskmaster and exactly the type of person I needed to keep things rolling. Wendy Thomas was more than kind with her editing comments and Deborah Crowle's graphics brought simplicity to complex explanations.

Current and former business colleagues deserve special mention: Kim Sawyer and Jennifer Tait, who not only encouraged me but also covered for me when my attention was more on the book than on my job; Ken Stroud, who insisted I "had to do it," Bernie Baigent who kept asking "When?" and Paul Morford, whose unbridled enthusiasm energized me.

My most heartfelt thanks go to the thousands of financial planners and investment advisers and their clients across the country who have listened to my dissertations on managing risk and reward. Through dialogues with them, I have learned to differentiate between what is theoretical and what is practical.

Introduction

It's not whether you win or lose that counts,
but who gets the blame.
— WILL ROGERS, AMERICAN HUMOURIST

The past few years have been a remarkable and rewarding experience for me. The overwhelming success of my first book, *Risk Is a Four Letter Word — The Asset Allocation Approach to Investing*, has been beyond my most ambitious expectations. Thousands of people from coast to coast who have attended my workshop "How to Get a Piece of the Action . . . with Peace of Mind" have reaffirmed my belief, through their questions and feedback, that Canadians are indeed serious about achieving financial success and hungry for advice on how to do so.

My travels across the country have also been educational.

Separating the theoretical from the practical has become easier. Fuzzy concepts have given way to specific strategies, and emotions to reason. Unfortunately, during this same period I have heard tales of misery from too many investors. Some lost money through lack of knowledge or fear; others were overly aggressive and greedy. Some were afflicted with the "paralysis of analysis" — attempting to gather every scrap of information about potential investments before making the decision to join in and missing some great opportunities along the way. Others moved too quickly or too often — there was a lot of action but very little progress. Fortunately, I have also had the pleasure of meeting many winners. Often they were Main Street investors who thought and acted like Bay Street professionals. These were the folks who took time to create a plan. They realized that achieving financial success as investors is like building a business. It requires well-defined goals, a strategic plan and a strong support team.

Perhaps as instructive as anything else is the determination these people had to make their money work as hard for them as they did to earn it. That required them to personally take responsibility for what happened. Let's acknowledge that there are many well-trained financial planners, tax experts and investment professionals out there who can provide sound advice in their respective disciplines. In fact, you'll often see phrases like "Consult an expert" throughout this book. I emphatically encourage you to do so but not by abdicating responsibility for your money to your financial advisers so they can be blamed if things don't work out. The truth is that no one has a monopoly on insight or confusion when it comes to investing.

So how do we sort all this out? The answer lies in knowledge. The very fact that you are reading this book is encouraging. You have made the commitment to learn and understand some of the essentials of successful investing. And here is the good news — by learning a few basic truths about the way investment markets behave, understanding the nature of risk and reward and appreciating how asset allocation can be used to manage the tradeoff between those two, you can apply the same principles to your individual portfolio that professional money managers use for billion-dollar accounts. Above-average results can be attained by simply doing a few things right and avoiding serious mistakes.

So what should you expect from this book? Well, to begin with, it is a book about concepts — some are original, but many are borrowed, because after 25 years in the financial services industry, I can confidently say that when it comes to investing, everyone has an opinion. There is no shortage of books, brokers, bankers or bellhops who are willing to share with you their secrets for making money. People who wouldn't give directions to a lost tourist have no hesitation in striking up a conversation with a stranger on where the market closed. The subject of investing has universal interest and seems to be politically correct in almost any setting.

The evolution in thinking about investment strategy since my first book *Risk Is a Four Letter Word* was initially published in 1992 has also been fascinating. Back then "asset allocation" was of academic interest only to analysts and professional money managers. Today individual investors have greater knowledge, are better informed and want more involvement in the management of their financial affairs. Other factors such as the availability of comprehensive market data, the refinement of analytical tools and the widespread use of sophisticated personal computers have aided in the progression of our interest and aptitude.

Undoubtedly, however, the most significant contributions have come from breakthroughs in the theory of money management, which really began in the 1950s with the work of Nobel Prize–winner Harry Markowitz, who wanted to go beyond the traditional "don't put all your eggs in one basket" approach to managing investments. He asked, "How can we earn attractive returns without undue amounts of risk?" and "How much risk is necessary to achieve our goals?" Using mathematics to solve the puzzle, Markowitz discovered that it was possible to simultaneously minimize risks and improve returns by having a broadly diversified portfolio. Using historical investment performance, he created a "mathematically correct" or "efficient" portfolio. The scientific system to achieve maximum returns with the least amount of risk that Markowitz pioneered eventually became known as "modern portfolio theory."

The thrust of modern portfolio theory has been to shift the emphasis from trying to maximize returns to managing risk. The goal is no longer to try to beat the market, but rather to devise long-term strategies to move us toward our financial goals with the least amount of risk. Asset allocation does not try to outguess the markets so much as it intelligently works with them, allowing their inherent power to shine through.

I was weaned on modern portfolio theory, and as we progress in the following pages I will draw on its concepts but only to the extent that they help us understand asset allocation. My emphasis will be on developing a practical framework for making investment decisions that will give you confidence in the choices you have made and reduce the temptation to abandon your long-term strategy when markets begin to misbehave.

There are several things this book will *not* do:

- It will not tell you *what* to buy — There are literally thousands of investment opportunities available in Canada today, and I leave the prediction of what is going to give the best return over the coming year or the next five or 10 years to those who have greater ability than I to foresee stock market conditions, interest rate trends, international events, government policy decisions, political changes and investor psychology. Any one of these can have a significant impact on investment results.
- It will not tell you *when* to buy — Long-term trends are rela-

tively apparent and reliable. The dramatically increased volatility of markets in the short run, however, makes timing of investments, in my opinion, a game only for the extremely insightful
and brave. To be sure, investment results will be significantly
improved with accurate market timing but repeated studies have
proved that only a few very skilful investors will be able to practise it profitably.

• It will not tell you *how* to buy — There are no other products or
services with the diversity, number of distributors and variety of
ways to purchase as those found in the world of investing. Stockbrokers, mutual fund salespeople, insurance agents, financial
planners, banks, trust companies, credit unions, professional
associations, trade unions and direct sellers offer a myriad of
choices. I will provide some general guidelines, but the decision
as to how you acquire your investments must be based on your
own personal needs and preferences.

So if I am not going to tell you what to buy, when or how to invest,
where's the value in this book? I think it comes from providing
the knowledge and tools to help you develop and implement an
intelligent investment program. I hope to accomplish this by discussing the advantages and disadvantages of various investments
and their applications. More important, however, I want to
outline a process that you can use to build a portfolio that meets
your personal wealth accumulation objectives within a level of risk
that you find manageable.

Writing for an audience as diverse as the investing public presents a real challenge in determining what to include or emphasize.
As noted, investor knowledge and awareness are much higher
today than they were even 10 years ago. Consequently, I have
raised the level of sophistication of the topics slightly higher than
it was in *Risk Is a Four Letter Word*. My hope is that each chapter in *Risk Is STILL a Four Letter Word* will provide either new

information or new perspectives on familiar financial issues that will be important to both novice and experienced investors. It is important to restate here that this book is about a process to manage investment decisions successfully — not about making money. While the procedures discussed will not guarantee investment success, they will significantly increase the odds of building a portfolio that will stand the test of time.

1

If I'm So Smart . . . How Come I'm Not Rich?

It is only by understanding the emotions of others that an investor has a chance to produce superior results.
— SIR JOHN TEMPLETON, INVESTMENT LEGEND, FOUNDER OF TEMPLETON FUNDS

We have met the enemy . . . and he is US!
— POGO, COMIC STRIP CHARACTER

Sound contradictory? Perhaps, at first reading. But if we stop for a moment to think about what these two very savvy observers of human nature say, they both make great sense. Let's begin with the latter commentator first, Pogo — still one of my favourite philosophers! Certainly he is more widely read than most of the so-called sages, and as trite as the musings of a comic strip character may seem, I believe Pogo is right. Much of the grief we experience as investors is self-inflicted. It's not that we want to make it difficult to succeed in investing — it's just that we're human. That means we all have feelings, attitudes, desires, beliefs and biases and are capable of judging and second-guessing. Furthermore, each one of us comes to the investment arena with our own experience and varying degrees of ability to manage our emotions — and emotions certainly play a major role in investing. In fact, this is the truth upon which Sir John's and Pogo's remarks are based. If we want to be successful as investors, we have to understand what motivates *us* as well as how the emotions of others move investment markets.

We know, for example, that while, in the short run, investment markets (stock, bond, real estate, art or any other market) are totally unpredictable, in the longer term, they have a rhythm to them. Over time, they move up and down, partially in recognition of the fundamental value of the securities themselves, *but also according to how you and I feel about the future* — are we optimistic that prices will go higher or pessimistic that they will go lower? Obviously, when the feeling is good, we continue to invest and prices continue to rise. When the love affair wanes, however, the selloff starts and prices naturally decline, sometimes precipitously.

What causes the sentiment to change? Well, quite frankly, it is normally not the real value of the investments themselves. Generally, what was once a good investment has not suddenly and mysteriously gone bad. How do we know this? It's easy. If the stock market drops 10 or 15 percent in a short period of time, does this mean that the companies listed there are suddenly worth 10 or 15 percent less? Did their sales fall by that amount? Are revenues off by 10 or 15 percent? Are expenses up that much? Do they all unexpectedly find themselves in a dying industry? Of course not.

The price of a stock can fluctuate quite a bit during market ups and downs, but the core, underlying value of the enterprise itself seldom changes so dramatically. What changes is our perception of whether stock prices are generally too high or too low. When that sentiment shifts, the market reverses its direction. Knowing that this is what's going on allows us to construct a long-term strategy, *unique to ourselves*, that gives us confidence to ride out the plunges and temper our euphoria at market peaks, thereby resisting the "call of the crowd" to try to outsmart the markets. That's why Sir John Templeton was so right in saying that understanding other people's emotions is critical to investment success. Mark Twain put it a little less subtly when he said, "Let us be thankful for the fools. Without them, the rest of us could not succeed."

GREED AND FEAR VERSUS HOPE AND REGRET

One of the oft-touted clichés of investing is that *greed* is the driving force that causes us to get into and stay in investment markets when they are going up, that is, during *bull markets*, and *fear* is the motivation to get out and stay out when markets are declining, that is, during *bear markets*. I'm not sure I fully agree with that any more.

To be sure, when the stock market gives us a 15 percent return, we look for it to give us 20 percent. I guess that's greedy, given that long-term stock market returns are in the 10 to 12 percent range (more on this later). And certainly, the greatest fear of any investor is losing money, so there is a huge temptation to abandon the market when we see trouble ahead. But I think we have become much more sophisticated than that over the past few years. I believe we have moved beyond the simple fear and greed explanation.

For example, despite the fact that most individual investors in today's stock market have been at it for only a few years (and many have never experienced a prolonged market downturn), we seem to have quickly come to understand how the game is played. Market dips don't cause the panic they once did — in fact, more and more people see them as buying opportunities. And when the market gets dangerously high, investors increasingly have a tendency to back off slightly, temper their expectations and psychologically prepare themselves for the eventual and inevitable market pullback.

So in place of greed and fear, I'd substitute *hope* and *regret* with the latter emotion, *regret* being the most powerful. As noted, our expectations for good rates of return increase as the market rises. It doesn't matter whether we are talking about real estate, stock markets, interest rate–sensitive investments such as the bond or mortgage markets or something as esoteric as baseball card collecting. When returns get "above normal" we continue to *hope* they'll go even higher. That's human nature — not greed.

When markets begin to lose steam and decline, it isn't *fear* that tugs at our hearts, it is the *regret* we know we'll feel if we lose money, particularly if it is money we have already spent, literally or figuratively. We'll talk some more about this later, but research studies have shown that most people put the value of a dollar "lost" at least twice as high as the value of a dollar "gained." In other words, I'd have to earn two dollars to overcome my regret at losing one dollar!

Having regret isn't the same as being disappointed. For example, we have learned that investment styles fall in and out of favour and, as a consequence, there is no one strategy that will perform successfully in all market conditions. Knowing that we are sometimes going to be out of sync with the markets and staying the course with our strategy is difficult but perhaps not as ego-bruising as realizing that, in spite of the best planned strategy in the world, we are still going to make mistakes. As long as those mistakes aren't too catastrophic, we'll be disappointed but perhaps not regretful. If we had hoped to earn 20 percent from an investment and only make 10 percent, we might be disappointed; if we *lose* 10 percent when we expected to make 20 percent, we will probably feel regret. At those times, it is important to remember that the very best investment managers in the world will admit that they are right only slightly more often than they are wrong. At the end of the day, the incremental difference of being right more frequently pays huge dividends — but even the pros have to be willing to be wrong sometimes. What separates the long-term achievers from the lesser lights is that they accept their mistakes, analyze them, learn from them and move on. Some investors, particularly those who are new to the game, often believe they have to "marry" their investments. Even though I insist that you keep a long-term perspective, you don't have to take a vow to hold all your investments "for better or worse" or "in sickness and in health." There is another old investment adage that goes "Remember, the stock (or mutual fund, bond, etc.) doesn't know you own it." If you have made a mistake, don't worry about it. The security won't take your error personally. Neither should you.

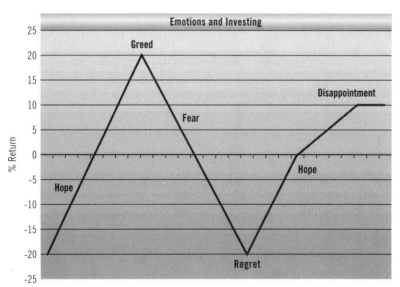

DEVELOPING YOUR INDIVIDUAL APPROACH

Given these facts, what is the most important thing we have to do as investors? Isn't it to develop a market approach that recognizes how we behave as investors *on an individual basis*, and then stick to it? How we personally respond to investment opportunities or crises has a significant bearing on how we should structure our portfolios. This is not to suggest that successful investing means managing a series of calamities or pouncing with split-second timing and precision on unexpected opportunities. Quite the contrary; the strategies I am going to propose are designed to eliminate the need for hasty decision-making. In the ebb and flow of the investment world, those who are most successful maintain their approach throughout full market cycles. They don't let the market's gyrations dictate their approach.

One of the most revealing aspects of our "investor psychology" is the extent to which we are predictable. For many, the sheer complexity — the length and breadth of the investment decision-making process — is overwhelming. Perhaps that is why, to a surprisingly large extent, we rely on other people for advice, even if the closest we've ever come to witnessing the money management skill of that individual was watching how well he or she handled the gratuity when we were last out to dinner. So golf courses, health clubs, beauty salons, cocktail parties and even public transit become our classrooms for learning investment strategies.

We also like to invest in things we can see or touch and, if possible, show off to our friends. We'll park that shiny new (rapidly depreciating) automobile in the driveway for all the neighbours to see. But will we call our friends to tell them one of our mutual funds just went up 10 cents? As the well-known U.S. investment commentator Michael Lipper says, "All investors need 'bragging rights.'"

And because we are natural procrastinators when it comes to investment decisions, we often choose the easy way out: parking our money in places we perceive to be "safe" with the occasional (usually painful) foray into something more exotic that came to us over the tinkle of ice cubes at the company Christmas party or from our spouse's second cousin who is now "in the business" of whatever.

KEEPING THE LONG TERM IN VIEW

As we progress through our investing lives, there will be all kinds of pressure on us to forsake our long-term perspective. Much of it comes from the constant bombardment of information — in newspapers, magazines, radio, television and even mail drops through the door! Would you believe that *Playboy* magazine (so I've been told!) is now publishing its own ranking of mutual funds? Instant and in all its graphic detail, we now hear more about the goings-on in our investment world in a single day than our parents did in an entire year. While things may sound sensational at the time, seldom is anything that makes the evening news going to change the long-term trend of the markets immediately.

The media can become quite overexcited and misguided — for example, the October 16, 1999, edition of a national newspaper carried the headlines "'Gates of Hell' opened as Dow tumbles." The text continued in the same melodramatic fashion, using words and phrases such as "plummeted," "fear flooded the market," "worst week in 10 years," and "investors picked over the wreckage."

The fact is that once a stock market cycle is under way, in either direction, it is not easily or instantly reversed. In this instance, the Dow not only quickly regained its one-day losses but continued its upward trend to finish the year at a new record high that put it up more than 25 percent for the calendar year and 15 percent from the day the "gates of hell" opened. As individual investors, however, when we couple this cacophony with a dearth of time to focus on things like choosing investments, it is no wonder we allow ourselves to be pushed further down the path of least resistance. Because we lack the clearness of mind, the opportunity or the capability to make timely decisions, we opt for simple, low-risk investments. We do this in spite of the fact that we understand higher returns are possible with only small increases in "risk" and that, as rational investors, we should seek to balance risk and reward more judiciously.

Obviously every investor does not react in the ways I have described, but enough do to say there is some commonality. Regardless, however, of our own investment personality, there are certain truths that affect us all. The most important one for us to accept is the inviolate investment axiom that *low-risk investments yield only low rates of return and higher returns are achieved only by moving to a higher level of risk*. What's more, both risk and reward are time-dependent. As time progresses, low-yielding investments become riskier, because of inflation. On the other hand, the returns associated with higher-risk investments become more stable and predictable over time, thereby reducing the level of risk. I'll make this clear with some specific examples later.

Most important, we have to remember that when we buy a stock or an equity mutual fund or a bond or a mortgage fund or even a piece of real estate, we are buying a share in an active, living, breathing business. By definition, then, we are in this for the long term because no successful business focuses solely on the immediate future. Nor can it be evaluated solely on what happened to it in the recent past. We can look back five years or more at the performance of a company's stock or even a mutual fund, for example, and measure its success during that period. But that has little to do with what will happen to it over the next five years. All we can hope for is to be able to make informed investment choices and then let the power of the markets work *for* us rather than in opposition to our objectives. If we really want to let the power of the market shine through, however, it is imperative that our investment time horizon be an extended one. *Investors* think long term — *speculators* think short term.

Before we move on, let me highlight the two key words that will form the foundation for much of this book: *risk* and *reward*. For this is what investing is all about — the tradeoff between the opportunity to earn higher returns and the consequences of trying to do so. We will get to the reward part soon enough. In the next chapter, though, let's delve a little more deeply into that phenomenon called risk.

Summary

- If we want to be successful as investors, we have to understand what motivates us as well as how the emotions of others move investment markets.
- Hope and regret drive markets — not fear and greed.
- Because we lack the clearness of mind, the opportunity or the capability to make timely decisions, we opt for simple, low-risk investments.
- There is an inviolate investment axiom that low-risk investments yield only low rates of return and higher returns are achieved only by moving to a higher level of risk.
- Both risk and reward are time-dependent. As time progresses, inflation makes low-yielding investments riskier while higher-risk investments become more stable and predictable over time.
- When we make an investment, we buy a piece of a business. By definition, then, our time horizon must be long term.

2 Risk Is STILL a Four Letter Word

People would rather be promised a (presumably) win-
ning lottery ticket next week than an opportunity to
get rich slowly.
— WARREN BUFFETT, CHAIRMAN, BERKSHIRE HATHAWAY INC.

The most popular investor workshop I conduct is called "How to Get a Piece of the Action . . . with Peace of Mind." That title wasn't chosen just for its play on words. It evolved from discussions with thousands of investors across the country.

As I listened to them describe their learning experiences, one thing stood out above all else — most of the investment advice that people had received in the past dealt with only half of their concerns. I think we all know by now that investing is a tradeoff between risk and reward. Unfortunately, the majority of investment strategies or tactics recommended almost always focused on the reward side of equation. There were all kinds of ideas for maximizing returns. But what so many people told me was that, as investors, they were as interested in managing the risk side of the equation as the reward side. They said, "There is no point in trying to generate superior returns if the strategy I have to use to do so keeps me awake at night!"

So let's talk a bit about managing risk. Before we do so, however, we should define it, because risk means different things to different people.

For a number of years, I hosted a radio show in Vancouver called "Money Matters." It was one of those typical financial advice shows where investment managers, stockbrokers, financial planners, insurance agents, lawyers, accountants, financial writers and authors would appear as guests. We'd talk about the things they knew best, and then we would open the telephone lines for our listeners to call in with their questions and comments. Want to know the most frequently asked question?

"What can I invest in over the next 12 months that will give me the highest rate of return without much risk?"

As a good host, naturally, I was always prepared with the answer.

"It all depends!"

To which, of course, the caller would respond with the obvious question.

"On what?"

From that point on, we could begin a series of questions. The easiest ones for people to answer were the "hard" facts such as:

- How old are you?
- What is your investment objective? (retirement, children's education, home purchase, business expansion, etc.)
- What percentage of your total investment assets does the current investment represent?

+ What is your tax situation?

. . . and so on.

More difficult were the "soft" fact questions like:

+ How would you describe your risk tolerance? (low, moderate, high)
+ Are you sure that's the way you really feel?
+ How do you behave as an investor when things go wrong?
+ Will other people affected by your investment decisions think, feel and behave the same way? (family, business associates, etc.)

Such an easy and natural divergence into these two broad areas of discussion demonstrated an obvious reality: investment risk has two dimensions — an unprejudiced, measurable assessment of my personal situation and that deep-down gut feeling that arises from my past experiences as an investor. We'll deal with both.

In *Risk Is a Four Letter Word*, I defined risk as the *potential for loss*. The obvious next question is *loss of what?*

There are a number of technical interpretations of risk (systematic, non-systematic, default, etc.). Personally, though, I don't think we need to be that complicated. For most of us, investment risk can be summed up in two questions:

1. What is the possibility of losing my money?
2. Assuming I don't lose it, will I have enough money at the time I want or need it?

And the greater risk is the first one. As the cowboy philosopher Will Rogers observed so many years ago, "People are as interested in the return *of* their money as the return *on* their money." The biggest fear we all have as investors is losing money.

And there's the dilemma — we know that risk and reward go hand in hand. If we want reward, we must accept some risk. But how much? As noted in the radio show vignette, it depends on a number of things. For example, the amount of money we have or earn is often an influence. Higher-income individuals are generally more risk-tolerant as are those with substantial assets. It is certainly not the case in every instance but, overall, people who have more assets or the ability to replace lost value through income show a greater willingness to take on risk.

Family circumstances also play a role. If our house is paid for and the children's education looked after, we are frequently more confident in taking risk than if we are raising a young family and bearing the weight of a large mortgage.

Our own past experience as investors and the dinner table lessons from our parents are also pretty powerful influences on the way we think about risk.

With these thoughts in mind, let's go back to our two questions and examine each in regard to the specific risk they describe.

| Question 1 | What is the possibility of losing my money? |

In slightly more technical language, we could label this as *loss of capital risk*. In *Risk Is a Four Letter Word*, I wrote about the importance of winning by not losing because the rate of return required to make up for money we have lost is much greater than most of us realize. For example, if I start with $100 and lose 50 percent of it, I would have to earn 100 percent on the remaining $50 just to get back to where I was at the beginning. This chart from *Risk Is a Four Letter Word* shows the rates of return required to overcome various declines. The period is five years, and there are two scenarios — a 10 percent target rate of return and a 15 percent target rate of return.

Annual Gain Needed Next 4 Years to Meet Target

First-Year Loss	10% Target	15% Target
10%	16%	22%
15%	17%	24%
20%	19%	26%
25%	21%	28%
30%	23%	30%
40%	28%	35%
50%	34%	41%

Notice how the spread between the amount of the loss and the required gain over the next four years widens as the magnitude of the loss is increased. In the 10-percent target scenario, for example, with a 10 percent first-year loss, the increased return required is 60 percent higher than the original target (16 percent versus 10 percent); at a 25 percent loss, however, it is more than twice as high (21 percent versus 10 percent). Large losses are, obviously, much more difficult to overcome than smaller ones.

Not only that, but we should also consider the type of investments we'd have to look for to continue to meet our objective. For example, even a 10 percent loss in the first year of a five-year program would have us wanting to earn 16 percent average over the remaining four years to get back on track. How much risk would there be in a portfolio shooting for 16 percent compared to one targeted for 10 percent? Clearly, a lot more.

So we want to avoid or at least reduce the chance of loss of capital. The question is "How?"

The traditional approach to avoiding loss of capital has been to put our money in safe or so-called guaranteed (the return is guaranteed but the purchasing power is not) investments such as Canada Savings Bonds, Guaranteed Investment Certificates, Treasury Bills or the bank. As long as interest rates did not fluctuate too much, these types of investments were fairly comforting, from a risk point of view at least. But let's take a closer look at what has happened to interest rates. In the graph that follows, I have used the returns over a 49-year period (1951–1999) for Treasury Bills and bonds issued by the Government of Canada to illustrate interest rate trends. Don't worry too much about the absolute numbers: first look at the left half of the graph, which covers the period of the 1950s and 1960s. There we see that, although interest rates did fluctuate, they did so in a fairly predictable manner and within a moderate range of, say, 10 to 15 percent. In that environment, we could have some confidence that we would earn reasonable but modest returns with only moderate risk to our capital.

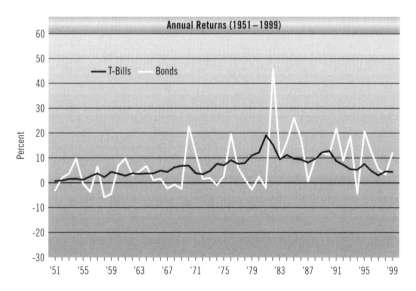

Now look at the right half of the graph, showing the 1970s through the 1990s, and note the difference. From the early 1970s on, the range of return (up *and* down) is doubled. Volatility or uncertainty of return has become a real fact of life for even the most conservative investors.

Furthermore, in a world where interest rates could (and did) change dramatically and swiftly, there was suddenly a much greater risk of capital loss. This turned out to be a surprise for many investors who didn't understand "interest rate risk." In those years, I was overwhelmed by the number of people who didn't appreciate the relationship between interest rate changes and the market value of investments such as bonds and mortgages.

In early 1994, my good friend Dan Richards, president of Marketing Solutions, one of Canada's leaders in investment research, coined the term "GIC refugees." This described the thousands of heretofore conservative investors who fled from their traditional "safe" havens of bank and trust company term deposits and GICs (Guaranteed Investment Certificates) for the higher returns that had been posted by bond and mortgage mutual funds. What prompted them to do so was that interest rates, for example on their GICs, had fallen from 12 percent when they bought them in the late 1980s to 6 percent when they went to renew them five years later. That same interest rate plummet, however, had the opposite effect on bond and mortgage mutual funds. Because these funds were made up of longer-term fixed income investments, they were able to continue to earn higher yields for a few more years. That caused their market value to rise, which made the declining term deposit interest rates pale in comparison. Many bond mutual funds were able to report 20 percent or greater annual returns. So the shift was on.

The trouble was that the bonds and mortgages in those mutual funds gradually matured as well, and the returns fell into a more normal range. However, they were still affected every day by interest rate changes — something GIC and term deposit investors weren't used to, hence their surprise. So what were the alternatives? Well, how about the stock market?

Let's look at the stock market by superimposing its returns on the same graph we used earlier. I have used the Toronto Stock

Exchange (TSE) to represent stock price changes.

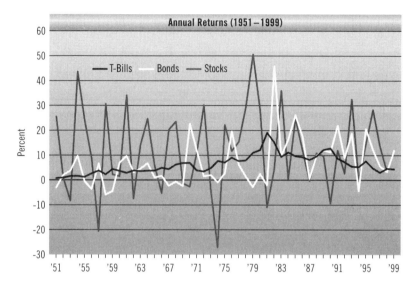

No surprises here — stock markets have always been volatile! And what's more, there is the very real *probability* — notice I didn't say *possibility* — that we will suffer a capital loss sometime during our stock market investing.

So it would appear that *all* investments fluctuate in value or relative rate of return. It doesn't seem to matter whether we are talking about stocks, bonds, real estate, artwork, the family jewels or Grandpa's farm. There are times when each appears to be a better or worse investment than the others. The potential for capital loss is common to them all, with some being riskier in that respect than others. Let's move on to the second question in our definition of risk.

Question 2	Assuming I don't lose it, will I have enough money at the time I want or need it?

This is actually a two-part question because it requires that we look at the accumulation of wealth from a couple of perspectives. First would be an expectation for the performance of my portfolio. In other words, "Will my investments generate a sufficient rate of return between now and the day I need the money to meet my objectives?" This has to be quickly followed by "What impact will *inflation* have on my results?" I want to address this one first because it is the one we seem to have forgotten in recent years.

In reality, I guess we shouldn't be too surprised that we haven't thought too much about inflation in the past few years, given our recent experience. From its peak in 1982 at over 12 percent, inflation has been generally declining. As I am writing this, the official rate of inflation in Canada is around 2 percent.

My worry is that, given this recent experience, people will do their long-range investment planning using assumptions about inflation that are far too low. We regularly hear news reports about the Bank of Canada or the U.S. Federal Reserve Board looking at prices, production and employment statistics to see if inflation is creeping back into our economic lives. They are concerned about it. I think we should be too. Let's look at what has happened to inflation over the past 50 years or so, note where we are today and then try to guess what will happen in the years to come.

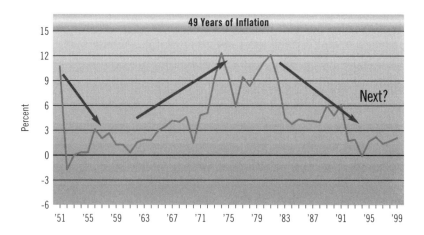

Obviously, today we are on the low end of the inflationary cycle. That is why so many of us have pushed inflation to the back of our minds as a concern. Yet every day, I seem to encounter a price increase in something I buy or use that certainly adds up to more than a marginal rise. Sometimes the increases aren't even that obvious. Here's an example.

A few years ago I moved from Toronto to beautiful British Columbia (sorry, Toronto, — it's not that I don't love you — after all I was born there. There's just something about the mountains, the sea and golf in December!). Anyway, one of the things you usually do when you move into a new house is to paint some of the walls to match your furniture and reflect your style. It had been about five years since I'd last gone through that exercise, so it had been about five years since I'd bought paint. I discovered something — a bucket of good-quality house paint cost about the same then as it did five years previously — about $24.95.

But what had happened in that time to the size of the bucket? It doesn't seem all that long ago that you bought paint by the gallon. Then the country went metric and the size of the paint can slipped to four litres (slightly less than 9/10 of an Imperial gallon). Today, paint comes in 3.78-litre tins (one U.S. gallon) — or about 83 percent of our old gallon. I'm in favour of metrication but that's a 17 percent decrease in size or, alternatively, a 17 percent increase in price over five years. The official rate of inflation during that same five-year period was only 11 percent! It seems to me that the basket of goods and services I use must be very different from the one used to measure inflation. It's called the CPI — Consumer Price Index. I call it my PPI — my Personal Purchasing Index — and my personal rate of inflation appears to be much higher than the CPI!

Here's a very simple example to illustrate the impact of inflation using a 6 percent average increase in the cost of living and an 8 percent investment return.

Year	Capital @ 6% Inflation	Income @ 8% Return
Now	$500,000	$40,000
12 Years	$250,000	$20,000
24 Years	$125,000	$10,000
36 Years	$ 62,500	$ 5,000

Let's look at the middle column first. Note that if we start with $500,000 of capital and average 6 percent inflation, it takes only about 12 years for the value of our wealth, *in today's dollars,* to decline by 50 percent. In other words, if you took half a million dollars and buried it in your garden, then went back and dug it up 12 years later, assuming we averaged 6 percent inflation during that time, your stash would be worth only half as much *in current dollars* as when you buried it. And every 12 years thereafter, its value would likewise be cut in half. So here is the first negative impact of inflation — it destroys wealth.

But if we think about it, accumulating a pool of capital, that is, building wealth, is for most of us only an intermediate step. The real reason we invest is to provide income at some point in our lives. Ultimately, we all want to replace our *working* income with *investment* income. The only difference among us is *when* we want to begin receiving that income. Some people want it right away because they are already retired. Others won't need it for 10, 20 or 30 years. So, assuming that generating income from your investment is your ultimate goal, let's look at what a 6 percent rate of inflation does to investment income over time. That's the third column.

In this example, an 8 percent return on a half million dollars invested would yield $40,000 annually. But at that same 6 percent inflation rate, the purchasing power of that income in 12 years would buy only half as much as it would today *even though we earned a rate of return in excess of the rate of inflation.* By the time you reach 84 (which is about normal life expectancy these days for someone retiring at age 60), the purchasing power would be cut in half once more. If you were fortunate enough to live to age 96, you would be trying to get by on one-eighth of the purchasing power with which you had retired. Inflation is a very serious problem and although its severity fluctuates, it never disappears entirely. It always cycles back from low to high. In fact, in the long run, loss of purchasing power is the greatest investment risk we face because so many of us underestimate its impact.

A primary reason we do that is because most of us are too short-sighted when it comes to calculating the number of years during which investment income is going to be important to us. When we were doing the research for my original book *Risk Is a Four Letter Word*, we asked a sampling of Canadian investors for their opinions on the minimum period for which they should consider investing. The most frequently cited time was five years. Although almost everyone agreed that investing was a long-term proposition, when it came right down to it most people didn't plan much beyond the next five years.

This mistake becomes particularly acute the closer we are to retirement because then we tend to equate investment time with the difference between our current age and our desired retirement age. So if you're 56 and plan to retire at age 60, you'll likely do your investment planning for a four-year period. And chances are that if we are in the right place in the cycle, inflation won't be a concern. If we have just come through a period of three or four years of relatively low increases in the cost of living (as we saw in 1995 to 1999), you may well have failed to take inflation into account adequately in your retirement income calculations.

The awful truth is that inflation continues well beyond retirement. And with demographic changes, it won't be too long before a large number of people are spending as many years in retirement as they did working. Let me illustrate with this statistic.

In the 1960s, the average retirement age in Canada was traditionally 65. And the average life expectancy for someone who retired at age 65 back then was approximately eight years — to age 73. Many readers will know of relatives or friends who retired about that time at that age and lived approximately seven or eight years beyond retirement. Today, the story is very different. The average retirement age is now about 60 and average life expectancy for someone retiring at age 60 is approximately 80 years for men and 84 years for women. That's an average of up to 24 years spent in retirement — three times as long as a single generation ago. How many of us believe that if we are retired for 20 or 25 years, prices will never go up?

Let me add more strength to the argument by reproducing some excerpts here from the most recent life expectancy tables used by the Canadian life insurance industry. You might be surprised at how long most of us are going to be around — and the tables make no allowance for any medical or other technological breakthroughs that may extend life spans even further. This is also a sneaky way for me to make a point about the longevity of non-smokers versus smokers!

Years to Live

Current Age	NON-SMOKER		SMOKER	
	Male	Female	Male	Female
45	32.3	36.1	28.0	33.7
50	28.0	31.7	24.2	29.7
55	24.0	27.6	20.9	26.0
60	20.5	23.7	18.0	22.6
65	17.4	20.1	15.5	19.3
70	14.8	16.6	13.5	15.9
75	9.0	10.9	7.8	10.3
80	6.6	8.0	6.3	8.1
85	5.0	6.0	4.7	5.8
90	3.4	4.0	3.3	3.9

A few words on this table:

- The obvious — women live longer than men do.
  - On average, a same-age woman will outlive her male companion by at least two to three years.
  - A 60-year-old woman should survive a 65-year-old man by at least six years.
- Non-smokers outlive smokers.
  - And they have more money!
- The numbers at each age represent an *average* life expectancy for 50 percent of the population. In other words, a 60-year-old male non-smoker has a 50 percent chance of living to *at least* age 80 and a half.
- As we age, our life expectancy increases. For example, a 65-year-old female non-smoker is expected to survive until at least age 85 while a 70-year-old female non-smoker is expected to live beyond age 86.

These life expectancy tables lead me to think about a further point that we will be addressing in a later chapter but is worth mentioning here. In many investment scenarios, when we look at the time horizon, we are frequently talking about a period that extends beyond our own time on earth. In other words, your *investing* time horizon may be greater than your *living* time horizon. I am referring, of course, to the fact that some people intend to leave to their heirs at least part of the assets they have accumulated. Therefore, even though you may be well into your retirement years, your portfolio may have to live longer than you do. Consequently, it should, at least in part, be structured for long-term growth regardless of your age. I bring this up now because I have encountered too many investors who have been told things like "When you retire, get rid of all those risky assets. Sell those stocks and buy Canada Savings Bonds." That might be prudent if (a) you had sufficient capital to generate adequate income from the bonds, including an allowance for inflation, (b) you knew exactly when you were going to die and (c) you had no desire to leave anything to the next generation. If those conditions do not exist for you, think carefully about your time horizon when setting your investment objectives.

MANAGING THE RISK OF LOSS OF PURCHASING POWER

So how do we deal with the risk of inflation or loss of purchasing power? Well, the first thing is to incorporate it into our calculation for our long-range retirement needs. I offer the following as a rough guide, based on where we are in the inflation cycle today.

Current Age	Annual Inflation Allowance
80	0%
70	1%
60	2%
50	3%
40	4%
30	5%

Once we have planned for inflation, there is only one reliable way that I know to ensure we can actually beat it. That is to invest in something which generates a rate of return *significantly* greater than the rate of inflation so that the *net* result is sufficient for our assets to have *real* growth in value.

And what types of investments are most likely to do that? Historically, equity investments such as stocks have provided the highest average returns. In fact, they are the only assets that have done a consistently good job of beating inflation. Below is essentially the same chart we looked at earlier, except that I have stretched out the lines to show the *cumulative* results of investing in cash, debt or equities compared to overall increases in the cost of living.

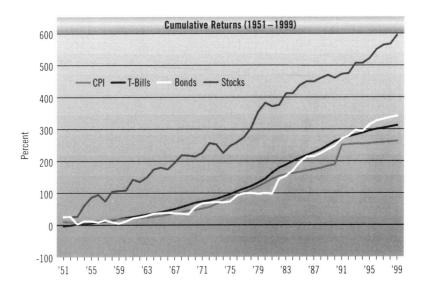

We will cover this topic more extensively in the next couple of chapters, but the conclusion we will come to is that *the risk of loss of purchasing power is higher for investors in cash and debt type assets such as GICs and bonds than it is for equity investors, simply because equities give us higher returns in the long run.* It would appear, then, that to minimize the risk of loss of purchasing power, we have to invest in equity type assets such as stocks. But that means what? It means accepting the other risk — short-term loss of capital. What a dilemma!

The question for all of us is "Which one is the greater risk?" There is no clear answer. If you are the sort of investor who wakes up in the morning, turns on the radio and, upon hearing that the stock market dropped 200 points the day before, dives back under the pillow, then *the risk of loss of capital* is probably your key concern. On the other hand, if you look out over the next 20 or 30 years and think you are going to rely on investment income to supplement your company pension (if you're entitled to one) or government benefits (if they are still around and not "clawed back" by the tax system) and you see a declining standard of living, you'd better be concerned about *loss of purchasing power*. But realize that if you want to stay ahead of inflation, you must be able to deal with the risk of being in the market. And that requires you to assess your attitude toward bearing market risk. Are you emotionally prepared for fluctuating portfolio values? If you're not certain, you might find solace in the knowledge that over time, stock markets have a distinctly bullish (or positive) bias. The "up" phases tend to last longer than the "down" phases and the percentage changes upward are, on average, greater than the declines. The chart below illustrates this fact.

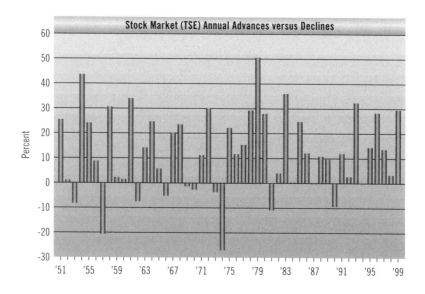

Clearly, though, if you are going to invest in anything more aggressive than bank accounts and Canada Savings Bonds, you have to accept the likelihood of experiencing a loss of capital somewhere along the way. The key to your success, however, will be to limit those losses to a range that does not threaten the prospect of attaining your long-term goals. So if you can't avoid occasional losses, how do you at least reduce their negative impact? The answer lies in understanding that the **total risk** of investing is actually a combination of the risk associated with the specific securities we choose to put in our portfolios — call that *business* risk — and the risk of simply being in fluctuating markets — call that (not surprisingly) *market* risk. That's what the next chapter is all about. Before we go there, however, I feel compelled to visit the emotional side of investing one more time.

BUY LOW — SELL HIGH

In my travels across the country, when I ask people what is the single most important tenet of successful investing, voices will ring out in unison "Buy low and sell high." Intellectually that makes sense — emotionally it does not.

When does the opportunity to buy low appear? When prices have fallen because there are more sellers than buyers. We ask ourselves, "Why should I buy what no one else seems to want?" So buying low means being at odds with the rest of the world, and the majority of us aren't comfortable with that state of affairs.

Eventually, however, as described earlier, prices begin their rebound and we start to wonder, "Everyone else appears to be buying; shouldn't I get in on the game?" If prices continue to increase even further, we start believing that the climb will never end. So selling high is also counter to the emotional pull of rising prices.

Another popular adage in the investment business says, "A tree doesn't grow to the sky." Just as they inevitably went up, prices falter at the top of the cycle and the rush to the exit begins. "Do I want to be the last one holding on to this?" becomes the question of the day. It is easy to see, then, that being a *contrarian* — doing the opposite of what everyone else is doing — means managing our emotions when what's logical becomes illogical and vice versa. In an investment context, as Sir John Templeton is so often quoted as saying, this means "to buy when everyone else is mired in pessimism and to sell when they are at the height of their optimism."

THE MADNESS OF CROWDS

Let's not be too hard on ourselves. The challenge of avoiding the crowd mentality has been around for a long time. From our beginnings on Earth, we have always gathered together in groups, particularly when threatened by beast, famine or the stock market! In fact, a number of wonderful books were written on this subject many years ago, including *Extraordinary Popular Delusions and the Madness of Crowds* in 1841 by Charles MacKay and *The Crowd* written a century ago by Dr. Gustav LeBon. In this latter work, Dr. LeBon observed that our ability to reason deteriorates as we join others in a common belief. We often become impulsive and prone to exaggeration and irresponsible thinking. Furthermore, he believed that the larger the crowd, the more irrational we become. With millions of relatively inexperienced investors now playing the market directly or through mutual funds, the "madness of crowds" has been in evidence all too frequently in the past few years and will doubtless continue.

I am reminded of a young woman I dated while in high school. She was Miss Demure, Prim and Proper on campus. Then one evening we went to a Rolling Stones concert. Wow! That hysterical demon, dancing on her chair, screaming as loudly as any of the other 20,000 people there was not the Brenda I knew. People will do things "in concert" with others that they would never do if they were not part of the crowd.

Here is a further example of this psychological phenomenon. It occurred in 1987 as the stock market peaked and then crashed on the infamous Black Monday, October 19. At that time, I was the marketing vice-president for a fast-growing mutual fund company. As the markets continued the runup toward their peak in August of that year, our best performing funds, not surprisingly, were the most speculative ones — exclusively invested in natural resource stocks. Some of them had gained up to 60 percent in the previous six months! On a daily basis, our client service department was inundated with an ever-increasing number of orders to switch from our more conservative funds to these more aggressive ones. Investors (and some investment advisers) fell into the trap of thinking that since the more aggressive funds in their portfolios were substantially outperforming the others, they ought to have *all* of their money in them. Human nature (greed?) was taking hold. Well, you can guess what happened, can't you? When the market corrected sharply, these same speculative funds were hit the hardest. Those clients who jumped on the bandwagon at the height of the excitement suffered major losses.

How much better off they would ultimately have been if they had remembered why they originally put together a diversified portfolio of funds — to reduce risk and improve the chances of meeting their long-term objectives. If they had stopped for a moment to realize that when markets were advancing so rapidly, they should have *expected* their more aggressive funds to be the best performers and that shifting everything into them substantially increased the risk. I know that if I'd had the opportunity to talk to each investor individually, they would have agreed with me intellectually. But the magnetic pull of emotions sent them chasing the best short-term performers. The strength of that force cannot be overstated. Successful investors have to guard against their own emotions and stick with their long-term plans.

You might be wondering why I am spending so much time on this. First of all, this is a book about managing *risk* as well as *reward,* so I think it is appropriate to cover both aspects thoroughly.

Perhaps more important, however, it is the market conditions of the past few years that prompt me to really emphasize the psychology of investing.

By the time you read this, I don't know how investment markets will be behaving. What I do know, as I am writing this, is that we have experienced the longest bull market run in history over the past number of years. Precisely when it started (and when it did or will end) is a matter for academic debate. Some would argue that it has been going on for more than 20 years! Regardless, the stock market has gone higher than any of us could ever have envisioned had you asked us last year or 10 years ago for our opinion.

During that time, we have fallen in and out of love with most sectors, from precious metals and natural resources to the Pacific Rim; on the fixed income investment side, we flocked to high-yield or "junk bonds." And, as noted earlier, today, we are seeing a similar trend in technology stocks, particularly anything to do with the Internet. Each of these favourites, in turn, has risen to heights once thought impossible. My concern, however, is that we not confuse a good concept with good investment value.

Many clever, innovative products and investment opportunities have been presented to us over time, yet few appear to have great sustainability. At one time, for example, you could have invested in over 200 publicly traded automobile company stocks. Today, only a handful remains in business. How about that essential invention, the computer? Recall names like Commodore, Wang, Atari and Digital. Where are they now? And who is this upstart, college dropout Bill Gates, anyway? Ten years ago, I'd never heard of him or his company called Microsoft.

One thing we do know is that in the world of investing, tomorrow is unlikely to look like today, but that doesn't mean we can't learn some lessons from what is happening around us currently. John Kenneth Galbraith is an astute observer of human nature.

He wrote an insightful book titled *A Short History of Financial Euphoria*. In it he identified four beliefs investors might have that could be warning signals that we are getting close to what Alan Greenspan, chairman of the U.S. Federal Reserve Board, called "irrational exuberance." I paraphrase those beliefs here:

1. The reward will outweigh the risk.
2. This time it will be different.
3. Any setbacks will be only temporary.
4. Anyone who disagrees with the above is stupid.

The truth is that neither you nor I nor anyone else has a monopoly on uncertainty when it comes to investing. It should go without saying that if we engage the services of a professional adviser, we expect a certain level of knowledge and experience from him or her. But we have the most important role to play. Our job is to wear a coat of healthy scepticism derived from our personal experience, education and intuition. Even neophyte investors know better how they are likely to think, feel and behave than anyone else could hope to. That understanding is as essential to investment success as a comprehensive, technical appreciation of what causes markets to move up and down.

Summary

* There is no point in trying to generate superior returns if the strategy you have to use to do so keeps you awake at night!
* Investment risk has two dimensions – an unprejudiced, measurable assessment of our personal situation and that deep-down gut feeling that arises from our past experiences as investors.
* Investment risk can be summed up in two questions:

1. What is the possibility of losing my money?
2. Assuming I don't lose it, will I have enough money at the time I want or need it?

* In the long run, loss of purchasing power is the greatest investment risk we face because so many of us underestimate its impact.
* "Buy low and sell high." Intellectually that makes sense — emotionally it does not.
* Don't confuse a good concept with good investment value.

3

To Market . . .
to Market . . .

Two things cause a stock to move — the expected and the unexpected.
— Gary Helms, in *Financial Analysts Journal*, January 1978

Here is some really good news. We can achieve above-average investment results simply by doing a few things right and avoiding serious mistakes. Want some more good news? It isn't all that difficult. We don't need the expertise of a professional money manager — just a fundamental understanding of the way investment markets work, an appreciation of the tradeoff between risk and reward and a sense of how emotions come into play. So far in this book, we have touched on the latter two of these and we will come back to them again. Right now, though, I'd like to focus on how markets function, that is, what causes values and returns to fluctuate.

To begin, let's look at the concept of *total risk*. In the previous chapter, I noted that total investment risk was a combination of *business risk* and *market risk*.

BUSINESS RISK

Simply put, *business risk* (also called *unique* risk by some and *non-systematic* risk by the real technocrats) is the hazard of investing in a particular business. If I were considering, for example, adding shares of Ford Motor Company to my portfolio, I would first want to gain some confidence by knowing the answers to such questions as:

* Has the company been profitable over the past few years?
* Are those profits rising, falling or the same as in the past?
* What is their history of paying dividends to shareholders?
* Is the stock fairly priced relative to the company's profits?
* Have they kept up with product development?
* Do consumers like their products?
* Are their labour relations good?
* Is management stable and competent?
* How do they rank with their competitors?

In real life, of course, I may choose not to do the evaluation myself — that's what stockbrokers and investment analysts are for. But it would at least be a good idea for me to know the questions that should be asked. If Ford scores well on these criteria, I may decide to buy some of their stock because I believe they are well positioned to grow along with the automotive industry. In other words, owning a piece of Ford would mean I own a piece of a good *business*.

Managing Business Risk

Buying shares in a good company, however, does not automatically guarantee investment success. We all know that even the best-run companies, from time to time, suffer setbacks. That's why our parents taught us to not "put all our eggs in one basket." So in an effort to heed their advice (and because it intuitively makes sense to us), we *diversify* by buying shares in more than one company. Thus, we might add some bank stocks, oil companies, retailers, manufacturers and service firms to our portfolio to spread the risk around.

And it works — to a point. We might expect that each time we added a new stock to our portfolio, we would reduce the risk through increased diversification. That is true, but the impact of each additional stock is normally less than the one before. Let's take a simple example. Assuming that our portfolio is divided more or less equally among our chosen securities, it's easy to see that increasing the number of stocks in our portfolio from two to three has a greater impact on risk reduction than increasing the number from 49 to 50. In the first instance, the new stock's performance will represent one-third (33 1/3 percent) of the portfolio's total performance, whereas in the second case, the additional stock's contribution represents only one-fiftieth (2 percent) of the overall result. This is an oversimplification, but I think it makes the point.

It has been statistically shown that a portfolio made up of 40 to 50 different stocks has probably gone about as far as it can to reduce *business* risk. Adding more companies beyond that may increase return if the additional stocks perform well — but they don't contribute much to further reduce risk. It should be no surprise, then, to learn that almost all equity (stock) mutual funds own shares in at least 40 to 50 different companies — to wring the *business* risk out of the portfolio.

If we were building our own portfolio using individual securities, few of us would have that many companies represented. It is more likely to be in the 10 to 12 range at most, so don't be concerned that you don't own 40 to 50 stocks. Remember that professional portfolio managers are held to a much higher performance standard than any of us are likely to impose on ourselves. In their highly public, closely scrutinized world, a small difference in performance can be important, so they seek every advantage. In *Risk Is a Four Letter Word* I often repeated the maxim *"It is better to be approximately right than precisely wrong."* It applies here too.

MARKET RISK

So is that all there is to it — build a portfolio of quality stocks and then rest comfortably in the knowledge that our investments will increase in value? Of course not! While diversification will reduce *business* risk, there isn't much consolation in owning a broadly diversified portfolio of stocks if the entire stock market is on its way down. When the stock market falls, as it inevitably does from time to time, chances are that even the best chosen stocks will go along for the ride.

Market risk (*systematic* risk to those who are really interested) will always exist because there are so many broad-based influences on our economic world. We have to cope with interest rate fluctuations, global conditions, currency valuations, inflation, recessions, political stability and, of course, as noted previously, investor confidence. While investments such as mutual funds may be ideal for substantially mitigating the risk of holding individual stocks and bonds, *market* risk still remains.

Managing Market Risk

So we have accepted the notion that there is underlying wisdom in spreading the risk by building a diversified portfolio of stocks — for example, to deal with *business* risk. Our next question is "Can a portfolio also be diversified to deal with *market* risk?" Good news again — the answer is "Yes." Just as it makes sense to diversify *within* an asset class such as stocks by owning a number of them, it is equally appropriate to diversify *among* various asset classes. We know that individual stocks do not all fluctuate in value in perfect tandem; neither do stock, bond and cash asset classes. Again, we called upon the researchers and they have indicated that *a portfolio of five or six different asset classes is probably optimal for reducing* market *risk to its minimum.*

Is it hard to build a portfolio balanced among five or six asset classes? Not really. We can start with the three most basic ones — cash, debt and equity — and further diversify within them in many different ways. I am not at all suggesting that your portfolio should look like this, but here is an example of just how possible it is to diversify across asset classes.

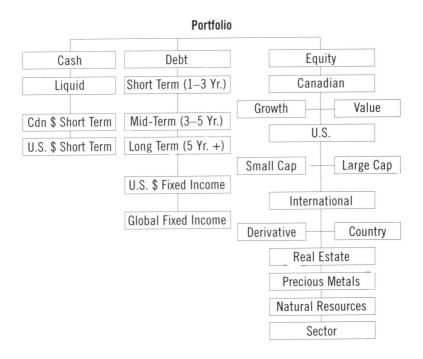

Portfolio

Cash assets offer the least risk to capital and, therefore, provide the lowest returns.

Debt assets normally offer lower returns than equity but greater returns than cash. Capital value can fluctuate as interest rates change and most debt-type assets provide steady income in the form of interest, mortgage payments, etc.

Equity assets exhibit the greatest short-term risk to capital but have demonstrated over time that they provide the highest long-range returns.

How to implement an intelligent approach to allocating your assets among these three basic asset classes and their subsidiary asset classes is something we will spend a considerable time on later in this book.

TOTAL RETURN

Now that we have talked a little about managing *business* and *market* risk, how about the "reward" part?

In most instances, when we talk about investment returns, we are usually thinking of *total return* even though we seldom express it that way. In reality, however, investment returns can be generated in a number of ways, depending on the asset or security in question so the concept of *total* return is an important one.

CASH ASSETS

Cash assets such as bank accounts and money market mutual funds earn interest. We all know how that works — periodically our account is credited with some percentage of the original investment. Depending on the account, interest can be added on a daily, monthly, quarterly or annual basis.

DEBT ASSETS

Debt assets such as bonds and mortgages also earn interest in the same way that cash assets do. But these investments also earn capital gains (or conversely, have capital losses) if interest rates change. We talked about this in the previous chapter with my reference to "GIC refugees." What these people have not understood, regrettably, is the relationship between interest rates and the value of fixed income investments such as bonds and mortgages. So here's the simple rule: *they move in opposite directions*. As interest rates rise, the market value of fixed income securities falls, and as interest rates fall their market value rises.

Why? It is not too difficult to understand. If I own a bond that offers a 10 percent interest coupon, and interest rates suddenly decline to 5 percent, wouldn't that make my 10 percent bond immediately more valuable? Of course it would! Anyone looking to purchase a bond would be willing to pay more for my "old" bond that offers a 10 percent return than for a "new" one offering only 5 percent. So the current market value of my bond increases.

Of course, the reverse occurs if interest rates rise. My 10 percent bond becomes worth less if interest rates rise, say, to 15 percent.

The next question is "Just how much will my bond increase or decrease in market value when interest rates change?" That depends on two factors. One is the "spread" between the rate my security is offering and the current rate. The other factor is the length of time until my security matures. Obviously, a longer time to maturity works in my favour if interest rates decline. If my bond offers 10 percent for the next *five* years and interest rates fall below that level, it will be worth more than one offering 10 percent that matures in only *one* year. Again, the converse would be true in periods of rising interest rates.

The actual calculation of the value of any fixed income security is reflected in what is called the *yield*, which is a combination of the rate of interest and the time to maturity. And the yield will almost always be different from the annual interest rate credited to the bond. It is the "yield to maturity" then that determines market value. Again, this is an oversimplification because there can be other factors, including investor psychology and supply and demand, that influence the market price of fixed income securities. This explanation is sufficient, however, to make the distinction between cash and debt assets. Furthermore, we could do some number crunching to show the actual calculation of yield based on current interest rates and time to maturity — but why bother? That's what computers are for! However, as an example, here are some real-life bond values at the time of writing to illustrate what we have just been talking about.

Issuer	Maturity Date	Coupon Rate	Yield	Market Value (per $100)
Government of Canada	Dec. 1/01	5.25%	5.42%	$ 99.63
Government of Canada	Dec. 1/01	9.75%	5.58%	$108.55
Government of Canada	June 1/21	9.75%	5.92%	$146.39
BC Tel	June 19/21	10.65%	7.10%	$139.00

There are a number of lessons in the above list.

Look at the first two Government of Canada issues. Both mature on the same day but one offers a 9.75 percent coupon while the other one is set at only 5.25 percent — yet the yield is approximately the same — around 5.50 percent. The difference, of course, is reflected in the market value. I'd have to pay more than the face value of the second one ($108.55 versus $99.63 per $100) to be entitled to receive the 9.75 percent rate of interest. In this example, interest rates must presently be lower than 9.75 percent.

Now compare the second Government of Canada bond to the third one shown. Both have a 9.75 percent coupon but the maturity dates are 20 years apart! The yield on the longer-term bond is better because the risk is greater in guessing where interest rates will be so far down the road. The real difference, however, is reflected in the price ($146.39 versus $108.55) (a 9.75 percent interest rate guaranteed for an additional 20 years is worth something!

Finally, note the differences between the third Government of Canada bond and the one issued by BC Tel. Both mature at about the same time (June 2021). The coupon rate and the yield of the BC Tel bond are better for the investor yet the market price is lower! How come? This is direct recognition of the relative *credit risk* of the two securities. Investors feel more confident in the ability of the Government of Canada to honour its long-term debt obligations than they do in the telephone company of British Columbia. That is not to suggest that the BC Tel bond is not a secure investment. It's just that in the minds of the financial community, there is some risk of default that is not present in the securities backed by our federal government.

Although many readers will understand this concept well, too many investors did not appreciate this relationship as they allowed themselves to be enticed out of their GICs into bond and mortgage funds based on higher returns from these investments *in the previous year*! I think it is of value to make this point dramatically.

One additional characteristic of interest rates worth noting is that, in most cases, long-term interest rates are higher than short-term rates. This is because, in a world of fluctuating interest rates, the longer an investor ties his or her money up, the greater the risk that rates will someday exceed those being offered at the time of the original investment. So investors demand greater reward for the increased risk. It is the same principle under which banks typically charge higher rates for a five-year mortgage than for a one-year term. They want to protect themselves somewhat against the possibility of having money tied up in long-term mortgages if rates go higher.

Periodically, however, short-term interest rates exceed long-term ones. This usually occurs as a result of government fiscal or monetary policy, when it is trying to slow down an inflationary economy by raising interest rates or to protect the value of the Canadian dollar by offering higher rates on government securities to attract foreign investors. When short-term returns exceed long-term rates, we have what is called an inverted yield curve. It normally lasts only a few months but occasionally can be longer. Eventually, however, the situation rights itself and we return to a more traditional relationship.

EQUITY ASSETS

We have spent a lot of time illustrating how the total return of debt-type assets includes both interest and capital gains or losses. Equity-type assets, such as stocks, also derive their total return from two sources — dividends and capital gains or losses. Real estate normally earns rental income as well as capital gains (or losses). In either example, the latter type of return is straightforward — the difference between what you paid for an asset when you bought it and what you receive for it when you sell it is a capital gain or loss.

Consider for a moment a non-financial asset such as a piece of artwork. If you have ever attended an art auction, you know that the current market price of, say, a painting, is directly related to demand. If the artist is famous and his or her works are in limited supply or the artist's style appeals to a large number of people, the price will be bid up. When we consider more popular equity investments such as stocks, there is some similarity as supply and demand come into play there too. However, there is also a more fundamental underpinning to their valuation, and we should at least be familiar with the terminology.

Stated simply, the price of a common stock is related to the profitability of the firm issuing the shares, that is, its *corporate earnings*. The terminology here is "earnings per share" or EPS, which is calculated by dividing the firm's net annual profits by the number of shares issued to shareholders. Assuming the number of shares is relatively constant, as earnings rise, we would expect the stock price to do so as well.

The second important calculation is called the "price-to-earnings ratio" or P/E ratio. We get this number by dividing the market price of the shares by the earnings per share.

Let's follow an example through. ABC Corp. has 1 million shares outstanding. At the end of the year, it is determined that the company made a net profit of $500,000. That would equal an EPS of $0.50 ($500,000 ÷ 1,000,000 shares). The share price in the market then should be some multiple of that 50¢ per share earnings. Just what that multiple will be depends on a host of other factors. Suppose you talk to a stockbroker about ABC Corp. and he says, "The stock is trading at 12 times earnings." That would mean the market price was $6 per share (12 x $0.50).

Does that also mean the stock of ABC Corp. is *worth* $6? Regrettably, no, that would be too easy. In a perfect world, what the investment analysts call an "efficient market" would prevail where security prices accurately reflected their underlying value. In our not-so-perfect world, however, things don't work out quite that way.

As important as EPS is, the actual price of the stock on any given day reflects other influences — not the least of which is our old friend, investor psychology. If people are rushing into the stock market, buying anything in sight, prices will naturally rise as the demand increases. The price of ABC Corp., for example, may be bid up to $8, $10, $12 or even higher. The company's profitability may not have changed, so the EPS would be the same. However, as the market price escalated, the P/E ratio would rise, in this example, to $8 ÷ $0.50 = 16x; $10 ÷ $0.50 = 20x; or $12 ÷ $0.50 = 24x. Nothing else has changed except that investors feel the stock market is going to continue to go up and all stock prices will rise along with it.

Eventually, reality takes hold. Clearly, the higher the P/E ratio is, the longer it will take an investor to recover his or her money through earnings. Assuming earnings remain constant at $0.50 per share, it would theoretically take me 12 years to get my money back at a $6 share price; 16 years at $8 and so on. Again that is in a hypothetical world. In real life what happens is that the price-to-earnings ratio can eventually get so high that there is little or no chance of recovering the purchase cost through earnings. Investors begin to realize this, decide they cannot profit further from earnings but can likely gain by selling at a price higher than their original purchase cost, so they begin to sell. As the selling momentum increases, we have a stock market "correction." As an example of how far out of hand this can get, just before the crash of the Japanese stock market in 1992, the P/E ratio on some stocks was more than 100 times!

For more recent evidence of the phenomenon, we don't have to look any farther than the current love affair with technology stocks, in particular, those associated with the Internet — the so-called *dot.com* stocks. Some of them are selling at 80 to 100 times their issue price and the companies have yet to show *any* profits! Forewarned is forearmed.

Of course, once more the opposite can occur when investor sentiment is driving people out of the market. Stock prices will fall until the P/E ratios get so low that the stocks become "real bargains" and smart investors begin to buy again. That halts the slide in prices and the market begins to rebound or move up once more.

As mentioned earlier, the other contribution to total return of an equity investment might be in the form of *dividends*, some part of their annual profitability that many publicly traded stock companies pay out to shareholders. Very few firms distribute 100 percent of their annual earnings, preferring to keep some back for future expansion or to carry them through the not-so-good times. These "retained earnings," however, are reflected in the underlying share value.

For your interest, here is a sampling of the type of information found in the daily newspapers about stocks.

52W High	52W Low	Stock	Ticker	Div	Yield %	P/E	Vol. 00s	High	Low	Close	Net Chg.
32.75	26.75	BC Gas	BCG	1.18	4.3	14.7	120	27.85	27.45	27.75	+0.05
62.00	20.10	Teleglobe	TGO	0.34	1.0	40.5	7040	34.10	32.65	33.70	+0.95

Obviously there is a lot more to a stock story than is revealed here. However, we can learn a number of things from these limited data. Looking at the first listing for BC Gas, for example, we note that:

* The stock has traded as high as $32.75 in the past year (52 weeks).
* Its 52-week low price was $26.75.
* It is identified on the stock exchange where it trades (TSE) by the symbol BCG.
* Last year's dividend payout was $1.18 per share.
* The dividend yield for the past year was 4.3 percent.
* The P/E ratio is 14.7 times earnings.
* 12,000 shares traded that day.
* The highest trade in the past day took place at $27.85.
* The lowest trade in the past day took place at $27.45.
* At the end of the last trading day, the closing price was $27.75.
* The closing price of $27.75 was a gain of $0.05 over the previous day's closing price.

Quickly comparing BC Gas to Teleglobe, we can see that:

- Teleglobe has declined substantially from its 52-week high.
- Dividend yield is lower.
- The P/E ratio is much higher.
- Large volumes of shares are traded daily.

The topic of fundamental security analysis is beyond the scope of this book, and I do not want to suggest that our investments need to be monitored closely or actively traded whenever we see something about them change. Indeed, that would be the direct opposite to my philosophy of *choosing wisely and letting the market work for us.* However, I believe it is worthwhile for all investors to have some "feel" for their holdings. A periodic check will give you confidence that things aren't happening around you without your knowledge. When someone declares that an individual stock or the market as a whole is "over-priced" or "undervalued," you'll have some idea of what they mean and why. Such knowledge will make you less prone to irrational thinking and impulsive action.

Returning to the concept of total return, it is important to consider both dividend income and capital appreciation possibilities when evaluating equity investments such as stocks. Professional money managers look at these factors in addition to assessing the reasonableness of the P/E ratio, among many other things. To provide a frame of reference, however, and considering for moment just the three basic asset classes, here is an approximate breakdown of the average *total returns* over the past 20 years in Canada.

Asset	Interest	Dividends	Capital Gains	Total
Cash	4%	0%	0%	4%
Debt	5%	0%	3%	8%
Equity	0%	3%	9%	12%

THE NATURAL ORDER

So far I have referred to the three basic asset categories in a rather informal fashion: cash — the least risky with the lowest returns; debt — moderately risky with moderate returns; and equities — the riskiest but offering the greatest payoff. This is the natural order. It has to work out this way, even though it may occasionally get out of whack. There will be times when bonds will outperform stocks and vice versa, but over the long term the natural order will prevail. Why? Perhaps this simple example will illustrate the answer best.

Let's suppose that at the end of a month you found yourself with $100 left over. The pantry has been re-filled, the bills paid, the new sweater purchased and enough restaurants visited. So you decide to "save" the extra $100. A good financial planner, by the way, would insist you save the hundred bucks first — otherwise there is seldom anything "left" at the end of the month. That is sound advice. However, for our purposes, let's just say you elect to put the money into your savings account at the bank.

The bank is going to pay you interest on your money because, in effect, you are lending it to them. The rate of interest won't be very high on the savings account because the bank doesn't know how long you intend to leave your money there, so they have some restrictions on what they can do with it. But let's say they pay you 2 percent interest. What, then, does the bank do with your money?

One choice might be to lend it to someone else, perhaps a business owner. Let's suppose they do that and they charge 8 percent interest to borrow the money. What do business owners do with borrowed funds? They usually invest them in their own businesses. Why? Because they feel confident they can generate a return in excess of what it cost them to borrow the money. Otherwise, as good businesspeople, they wouldn't do it.

So there is the natural order. You lend the bank your money for 2 percent; the bank lends the money to a business owner at 8 percent; he or she invests it to earn, say, 12 percent. The return obviously increases as the risk does. There's little chance that the bank won't have your $100 when you go to claim it so the interest they pay you has little or no allowance for risk. There's some chance, however, that the business owner will default on the loan, so bankers demand a premium in the form of higher interest charges to compensate them for that possibility. From the perspective of business owners, if they're going to invest in their own firm, with all the risks that assumes, they have to expect a higher reward than if they had simply left their money in the bank or even loaned it to someone else.

As investors, we have the opportunity to place our money in any of the three basic asset categories. We can leave it in cash, that is, put it in the bank. That would, in this example, earn us 2 percent. We could lend it directly to someone through a loan or mortgage or to the government by purchasing a bond. We would hope to earn about 8 percent in that case. Alternatively, we could invest directly in a business enterprise by purchasing shares of that firm in the stock market. In this example, like the business owner, we would want to earn about 12 percent for doing that. The choice becomes the level of risk we are willing to assume based on the rate of return we expect to receive.

Basic Asset Classes — Risks and Advantages

Asset Class	Risk	Advantage
Cash	Long-run inflation	Liquidity
Debt	Mid-term volatility/long-run inflation	Fixed maturity value
Equity	Short-term volatility	Inflation hedge

RATES OF RETURN

In the next chapter, we'll take the final step in preparing ourselves psychologically to invest. That requires that we develop some realistic expectations about the kind of returns we are likely to achieve by choosing among the three basic asset classes. To simplify the process, I'm going to pick just one specific investment from each class and use it as a representative for the entire class. This will not give us 100 percent accuracy, but it will assist us in developing the notion of asset allocation reasonably well. You can substitute your own investment preferences for the ones I have chosen. It is the *concept* that is important at this stage.

As the saying goes, "History has a way of repeating itself," so we'll begin with a review of how these asset classes have performed in the past. We will then project the current trends into the future. The most likely candidates for examples are those for which we can obtain the most data — this will aid our accuracy. With that in mind, I have chosen the following:

Asset Class	Investment
Cash	Treasury Bills
Debt	Bonds
Equity	Stocks

More specifically, we'll use Government of Canada 91-Day Treasury Bills for the cash component; Government of Canada Bonds with maturities in excess of ten years to represent the debt portion; and the Toronto Stock Exchange (TSE) Index for stock price change calculations. The Consumer Price Index (CPI) will reflect changes in the cost of living. Don't be alarmed — we aren't going to spend too much time crunching numbers. Again, it is the concept that matters most.

Summary

* *Total investment risk* is a combination of *business risk* and *market risk*.
* *Business risk* is the hazard of investing in a particular business.
* To reduce *business risk* we diversify by buying shares in more than one company.
* *Market* risk will always exist because there are so many broad-based influences on our economic world. We have to cope with interest rate fluctuations, global conditions, currency valuations, inflation, recessions, political stability and, as noted previously, investor confidence.
* A portfolio of five or six different asset classes is probably optimal for reducing *market risk* to its minimum.
* *Cash* assets offer the least risk to capital and therefore provide the lowest returns.
* *Debt* assets normally offer lower returns than equity but greater returns than cash.
* *Equity* assets exhibit the greatest short-term risk to capital but have demonstrated over time that they provide the highest long-range returns.

4 Do You Believe in Magic?

The best way to suppose what may come is to remember what is past.
— George Savile, Marquess of Halifax (1633–1695)

When the first edition of *Risk Is a Four Letter Word* was published in 1991, it had an obvious bias. The message was loud and clear that *over time stocks would outperform debt and cash assets as well as provide the only real hedge against inflation.* That has not changed. What has altered, and rather dramatically, is the attitude of investors toward stock market participation. A decade or so ago, despite the many compelling arguments in favour of equity ownership, the majority of investors weren't all that interested. Due to perceived riskiness, stocks were something one owned only in limited quantity for "fun" or as a small part of a saner, more balanced portfolio. But that is not the case today — stocks are no longer seen as the untamed and unpredictable adventure they once were. Getting people to build a portfolio with a significant equity component does not require a hard sell now. In fact, the opposite is true (and equally frightening) — too many people now see the stock market as a sure path to double-digit returns. The historical annual compound returns of 10 to 12 percent of the past 50 years have begun to look paltry compared to the 20 percent or more yearly gains of the recent bull market runup. The result has been, as mentioned previously, a dramatic shift of household and retirement assets from bank accounts, term deposits and other conservative investments into the stock market. Not to be outdone or wanting to miss an opportunity, the Canadian government has announced that it is going to start investing some of the assets of the Canada Pension Plan in the stock market — to achieve higher returns!

The real evidence of this phenomenon, though, can be seen in the mutual fund industry. Here, there has been an explosion of atomic proportions, fuelled by the unending onslaught of new product offerings, intensified media coverage and the scramble by just about every institution in the financial services industry to offer mutual funds to their customers. There is even at least one grocery chain now in the business!

Regrettably, the hype has also attracted a stampede of neophyte investors who, in many cases, haven't the time, interest or ability to sort through the maze or determine if, in fact, they should invest in funds at all. It is estimated that at least half of the purchasers of mutual funds in the past two years have been first-time buyers. Couple that fact with the proliferation of do-it-yourself books and on-line trading facilities and we have a market in which some folks are certain to suffer the consequences of misguided and inappropriate investments.

Obviously, when any market is rising, investor expectations rise along with it. We have seen that experience with gold, real estate, stocks, bonds, fad-of-the-year Christmas toys and tulip bulbs, to name a few. What I am concerned about, however, is that amidst all the excitement, unrealistic expectations about investment returns could easily cause some investors to fall short of their financial objectives. Increasingly, financial advisers are telling me that the biggest challenge they face is getting their clients to make long-range plans based on rates of return that are achievable. In fact, they say that *most investors have portfolios that are too small to meet all their objectives, given realistic expectations for return.* Yet because we continue to recall 20 percent bond yields and the 30 percent or more mutual funds have earned from time to time, somehow all things seem possible. In this chapter and the next, I am going to let the economist in me out to play with a few charts and graphs to demonstrate the truth about investment returns. Then we can confidently approach the task of setting achievable goals for our portfolios.

REALISTIC EXPECTATIONS — REALISTIC RETURNS

The feedback from readers of *Risk Is a Four Letter Word* is that the data that follow have been among the most revealing and important they have seen on the relationship between returns of various asset classes of investment and the importance of time. I hope that you will find the same thing. Let's begin by re-examining a little more specifically the graphs we presented earlier.

The first one (see the top of page 54) shows the actual results on a year-by-year basis for Treasury Bills, Government of Canada bonds and the CPI for the period 1951 to 1999. What do we see? Well, first of all, each line fluctuates — some more than others. We knew that was going to happen. The T-Bill line and the CPI line tend to pretty much parallel one another while the bond results are more varied; again, more or less as anticipated, given our previous

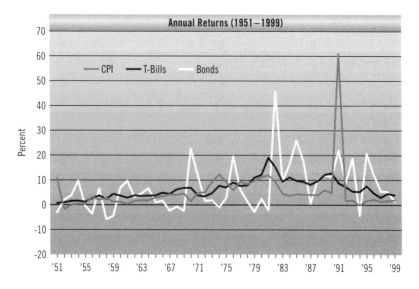

discussion about cash and debt instruments. The important thing to note, however, is the range within which these three lines fluctuate.

As was pointed out before, interest rate fluctuations have become wider over the past few years. There are also several periods when the inflation line is higher than the bond and T-Bill lines.

That takes care of two of the three asset classes. In the next graph, at the top of page 55, let's add the third asset class: stocks.

Look at the difference! See how erratic the stock results have been and how much wider the range is. Given that kind of volatility, why would anyone invest in the stock market? The answer can be found in the second graph on page 55.

If we "stretch out" the lines by adding all the positive results together and subtracting the negative ones, we're left with the cumulative trend lines indicated. The significance is apparent from the dollar figures shown. Recall the $100 we put in the bank a few pages ago? If we had invested that $100 in T-Bills in 1951 and reinvested all interest earned, we would have accumulated about $2,000 by the end of 1999. Similarly, $100 used to buy a bond would have grown slightly more, to almost $2,300. But investing

Do You Believe in Magic?

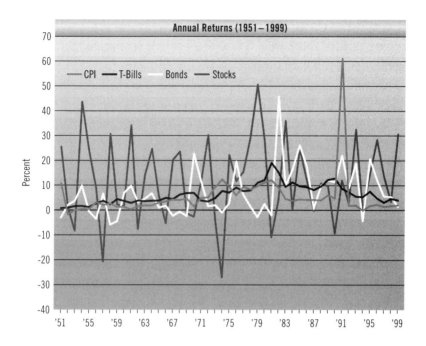

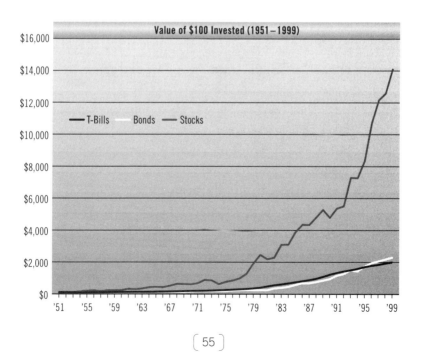

that $100 in the stock market would have us owning a portfolio worth slightly more than $16,000 — that's seven or eight times better than the alternatives!

So why wouldn't we put all of our money in the stock market? Take a look back at the top graph on page 55. In the 49-year period between 1951 and 1999, there have been at least 11 significant market declines. How many of us would have been strong enough to hold on through those downturns? If the stock market had been our only investment choice, we could either be very rich or very poor, depending on when we started and stopped. Because in that same 49-year span, the stock market has also gone up substantially at least 17 times!

Here's some information that might provide additional perspective. Buried in the data used to develop the graphs we just examined are some statistics I've left out for fear of boring you. Bear with me as I share some of the details that are not immediately evident from the "pictures" but are worth knowing.

If we look at stock market cycles — through bear and bull markets — over the past 49 years, we see that:

- On a monthly basis, the stock market was up about 70 percent of the time.
- The average bull market gain was about four times greater than the average bear market loss.
- Bull markets lasted almost three times as long as bear markets.
- Even within bear market conditions, on a monthly basis, the market was up one-third of the time.
- During bull markets, 60 percent of the gain came in 20 percent of the time period involved.

From this information we can see that although stocks generate superior returns, the gains come in periodic bursts rather than in a consistent and predictable manner. The uncertainty as to when returns will be positive is the reason many investors have perceived stocks as risky. It also explains why some people are willing to accept the lower returns of T-Bills and bonds. They want to have more confidence in the outcome of their investment strategy, in the short term, at least.

Unfortunately, as we discussed previously, this concern over short-term volatility of stock returns often masks the real danger to meeting our long-term objectives. That risk is further exacerbated by the practice of most investors in thinking of their returns in *nominal* terms only, that is, *before inflation*. On a *real return* (or inflation-adjusted) basis, the numbers might surprise you. For example, during 1979 and 1980, when inflation reached its modern-day peak of 11 to 12 percent, Treasury Bills were also making new historical highs — yet returning only about 1 percent more than the rate of inflation! Investors were rejoicing at the unusually high returns of these government-backed securities while their *real*

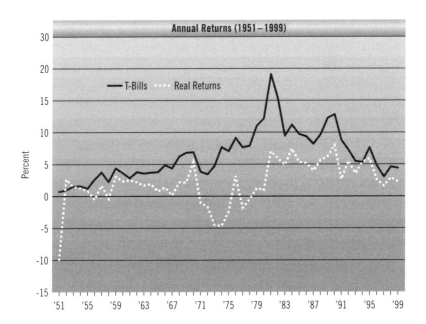

returns weren't even enough to pay the taxes on the interest they were earning! Many people long for those "good old days" of double-digit T-Bill returns, forgetting that we are normally better off in a lower interest–rate environment.

It would be interesting to see how investors would view these so-called safe investments if returns were reported to them on an after-inflation basis. Note from the graph on page 57 how much narrower the spread is between the nominal and the real returns when interest rates were low — for example, during the 1950s, 1960s and again in the 1990s — than it was during the high interest rate years of the 1970s and 1980s.

RANGE OF RESULTS

Now it's time to bring out some of the "big guns" to prove what I have been saying about the relative attractiveness of T-Bills, bonds and stocks as investment alternatives. The following table looks intimidating simply because of the amount of data it presents. If you don't want to bother with it, skip to the shorter summary titled "Time Horizon — the Key." It has most of the good stuff in it, anyway.

Investment Results — Various Time Horizons (1951–1999)

49 One-Year Time Horizons

	Stocks	Bonds	T-Bills	CPI
Highest Annual % Return	50.6%	45.8%	19.0%	12.3%
Lowest Annual % Return	−27.0%	−5.8%	0.5%	−1.7%
No. Periods with Negative Return	12	13	N/A	2
No. Periods Outpacing Inflation	35	28	39	N/A
No. Periods with Best Return	23/49	15/49	11/49	N/A
% Time Best Asset Class	47%	31%	22%	N/A

45 Five-Year Time Horizons

	Stocks	Bonds	T-Bills	CPI
Highest Annual % Return	27.0%	23.2%	13.4%	10.2%
Lowest Annual % Return	1.6%	−1.5%	1.2%	0.4%
No. Periods with Negative Return	0	3	0	0
No. Periods Outpacing Inflation	40	31	38	N/A
No. Periods with Best Return	31/45	13/45	1/45	N/A
% Time Best Asset Class	69%	29%	2%	N/A

40 10-Year Time Horizons

	Stocks	Bonds	T-Bills	CPI
Highest Annual % Return	19.0%	17.2%	11.7%	9.7%
Lowest Annual % Return	5.1%	1.2%	2.3%	1.0%
No. Periods with Negative Return	0	0	0	0
No. Periods Outpacing Inflation	39	28	33	N/A
No. Periods with Best Return	29/40	10/40	1/40	N/A
% Time Best Asset Class	73%	25%	2%	N/A

25 25-Year Time Horizons

	Stocks	Bonds	T-Bills	CPI
Highest Annual % Return	14.2%	10.9%	9.1%	6.5%
Lowest Annual % Return	9.3%	2.9%	3.9%	3.3%
No. Periods with Negative Return	0	0	0	0
No. Periods Outpacing Inflation	25	19	25	N/A
No. Periods with Best Return	25/25	0/25	0/25	N/A
% Time Best Asset Class	100%	0%	0%	N/A

Here are the summary numbers that I find so convincing:

Stocks and the Importance of Time (1951–1999)

Stock Results	Time Horizon			
	1 Yr. (49)	5 Yrs. (45)	10 Yrs. (40)	25 Yrs. (25)
Highest Annual % Return	50.6%	27.0%	19.0%	14.2%
Lowest Annual % Return	−27.0%	1.6%	5.1%	9.3%
No. Periods with Negative Returns	12	0	0	0
No. Periods Outpacing Inflation	35	40	39	25
No. Periods with Best Return	23	31	29	25
% Time Best Asset Class	47%	69%	73%	100%

TIME HORIZON — THE KEY

The value in these statistics is their ability to point out the importance of time horizon when considering stock investments. In the 49 years between 1951 and 1999, there were, obviously, 49 one-year investment periods. Under the first column, then, are the results assuming investments were held for one year only. We see that the highest annual return in the 49-year period was 50.6 percent and the lowest in any one year was −27.0 percent. That's quite a range!

Looking farther down that same column, stocks had negative returns 12 out of the 49 years. On a more optimistic note, a stock portfolio would have beaten inflation 35 of the 49 one-year periods. Finally, stocks provided the best returns (compared to T-Bills and bonds) 47 percent of time — that is, 23 out of 49 years.

Now let's stop right here. Suppose you were to say to me, "Okay, George, I believe you when you say that stocks will give me better performance than cash or bonds so I am willing to give them a go. If I invest in the stock market for the next 12 months, what should I expect?"

My response would be immediate. I'd say to you, "Based on

my research, which goes back almost 50 years, I can confidently predict that if you invest in the stock market over a 12-month period, you will get a return somewhere between +50 percent and −27 percent!"

Furthermore, I'd add, "You'll have about a one in four chance of losing money *and* a 53 percent probability of being in the wrong asset class! How does that fit with your investment comfort zone?"

Chances are you'd say, "It doesn't!" but that is exactly what the one-year investing experience for the TSE has been from 1951 to 1999.

Surprisingly, some investors would say, "Yes, I can deal with that." And what would cause them to respond that way? It would probably be because they were thinking to themselves, "If I *lose* money one out of every four years, that means I *make* money three out of four and if, when I make money, I make lots of it — that's worth the risk!" For their individual risk tolerance, that might be quite acceptable. The majority of investors, however, would not feel very comfortable with that prospect.

The good news, though, is that I also know from meeting so many people across the country that the message about successful investing requiring a long-term approach has gotten through. In fact, most investors, when asked, will now say that an appropriate time horizon is at least five years. (We don't always *act* that way but at least we are *thinking* correctly.)

So let's expand the time horizon to five years. In the period between 1951 and 1999, there were 45 opportunities to invest for five years (1951–1955, 1952–1956, . . . 1995–1999). What happens when we extend our holdings to five years?

As indicated in the second column, the highest average annual return over five years dropped to 27 percent while the lowest climbed substantially from the one-year number of −27 percent to 1.6 percent. So whereas the range of results over one-year periods was almost 80 percent (−27 percent up to +50.6 percent), when we stretch our holding to five years that range narrows by about two-thirds to approximately 25 percent (1.6 percent to 27 percent).

Examining the rest of the column shows us that we would have had positive returns in all of the five-year periods and would have beaten inflation 40 out of 45 times. Stocks outperformed T-Bills and bonds more than two out of three times.

So now, if you came to me with the same question, only this time with an extended time horizon, I could reasonably say to you, "If you invest in the stock market over a five-year period, I am highly confident that you will get a return somewhere between 1 percent and 27 percent. Furthermore, your chances of losing money are slim and more than two-thirds of the time, you will be in the right asset class. How does that fit with your comfort zone?"

Chances are a lot of us would feel much better about that scenario than the first one. I won't summarize the other columns for 10-year and 25-year holding periods. You can do that yourself. The message is clear from the graph that follows — as the time horizon is expanded, stocks become increasingly better investments: the volatility declines and the range of returns becomes more predictable. And if you are like me, the more predictable returns are, the better you'll feel about the investment.

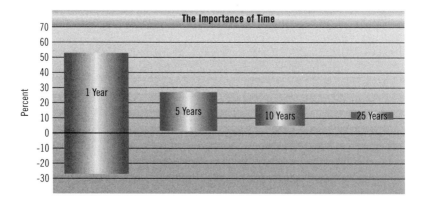

Clearly, stocks are also the best for keeping up with increases in the cost of living. This is why I am adamant that people who are retiring in good health at age 60 or 65 should not suddenly dispose of all their equity investments. We'll revisit this in more detail later.

We now have irrefutable proof that over the long term, stocks outperform bonds and T-Bills. The all-important element in any of these arguments, though, is time. Time has been called the "Archimedes lever of investing" because it turns what, at first glance, appear to be shaky investments into great ones and vice versa. Stocks look risky in the short run but eventually prove to do the best job of meeting long-term objectives, while more conservative choices seem safer in the short term but ultimately put us at the greatest risk of falling short of our goals.

So here is another key bit of information in our quest to find peace of mind in our investing endeavours. We now know that "time diversification" reduces investment risk in the same way that asset class diversification does. Combine the two and we have a very powerful tool to combat investment risk overall. That's where we are going in the next chapter.

Summary

- Too many people now see the stock market as a sure path to double-digit returns.
- Most investors have portfolios that are too small to meet all their objectives, given realistic expectations for return.
- Over the past 49 years, we see that:
  - On a monthly basis, the stock market was up about 70 percent of the time.
  - The average bull market gain was about four times greater than the average bear market loss.

- Bull markets lasted almost three times as long as bear markets.
- Even within bear market conditions, on a monthly basis, the market was up one-third of the time.
- During bull markets, 60 percent of the gain came in 20 percent of the duration.
- Many people long for those "good old days" of double-digit T-Bill returns, forgetting that we are normally better off in a lower interest rate environment.
- Time has been called the Archimedes lever of investing because it turns what, at first glance, appear to be shaky investments into great ones and vice versa.
- Time diversification reduces investment risk in the same way that asset class diversification does. Combine the two and we have a very powerful tool to combat investment risk overall.

5

Realistic Expectations

It is often easier to tell what will happen to the price of a stock than how much time will elapse before it happens.

— PHILIP FISHER, *COMMON STOCKS AND UNCOMMON PROFITS*

Before we go too much further, let's summarize the key points from the previous chapter:

1. In the long run, stocks yield higher returns than bonds, which in turn are better than cash assets.
2. In the short run, stock returns are more volatile than those demonstrated by bonds, which in turn are greater than those produced by holding cash investments.

3. Volatility of return for all asset classes decreases over time and returns become more predictable.

Now it's time to put some meat on the bones, so to speak, by being more specific with the data derived from the graphs we looked at earlier. So here is some vital information:

- The average annual return of common stocks listed on the TSE over the past 49 years has been approximately 12 percent.
- The average annual return of long-term Government of Canada bonds over the past 49 years has been approximately 7 percent.
- The average annual return of Government of Canada Treasury Bills over the past 49 years has been approximately 6 percent.

With this information about long-term returns for each asset class (equity, debt and cash) in hand, we should be able to boldly go forth and plan our investment strategy . . . or should we? Is there anything else we'd like to know? Do these rates of return match the ones you have earned in the past? Chances are they do not.

The truth is that, regardless of the time period under review, unless you invested your money at the precise start and took it out at the exact end of the period, your individual experience is liable to be very different from the long-term averages. It's for that same reason that so many people ask themselves, "How come the mutual funds in my portfolio never seem to match performance shown for them in the newspaper?"

Certainly, it is possible to add up all the annual returns from any investment and calculate the average over a period of time. And that average will be valuable to you in choosing what type of assets to include in your portfolio. But it doesn't help much to know that stocks have provided a 12-percent average annual return when you are caught in the middle of one of those horrific years when the market is taking wealth away from you rather than creating it.

What you need to know, of course, is the possible *range* of returns *before you invest*. Then you can decide the extent to which you want to play the game, if at all. As you saw in the previous chapter, stocks had an annual range of returns almost 80 percent wide! Here are the actual numbers:

Range of Annual Returns (1951–1999)

	High	Low	Average
Treasury Bills	19.0%	0.5%	6.2%
Bonds	45.8%	−5.8%	7.1%
Stocks	50.6%	−27.0%	11.8%
Inflation	12.3%	−1.7%	4.2%

"Well, having a range of returns is nice," you say, "but that still doesn't give me the degree of comfort I'm looking for. Besides, I know that annual returns aren't normally that varied — there were some unusual years in there." And that is true. In fact, the *normal* range of returns can be calculated, and that calculation becomes a much more useful piece of information. The statisticians call it "standard deviation," and in *Risk Is a Four Letter Word* I referred to it as the "fluctuation factor." Let me try to explain with a familiar example.

Imagine for a moment that your long-lost cousin was coming to visit you from another country for the very first time. The trip was planned months in advance and there were lots of e-mail messages flying back and forth in preparation for a July arrival. In one of those communications, your cousin asked what the weather was likely to be. How would you respond?

One way would be to say, "Oh, it'll be fine — nice and warm." But would that give your cousin the information really needed to ensure that the proper clothes are packed? "Nice and warm" would have a different meaning to someone from northern Finland than someone visiting from the Caribbean. How much better would it be if you checked with the weather office and were able to offer the following?

* Average temperature for July is 21 degrees Celsius.
* Normal high temperature for July is 25 degrees Celsius.
* Normal low temperature for July is 17 degrees Celsius.

Obviously, this information would be more useful to your cousin than "nice and warm." But how confident would you be that those temperatures would be between 17 and 25 degrees when your cousin visits? Is the temperature *always* between 17 and 25 degrees Celsius in July? Of course not; some years it would be much warmer or cooler. What the weather office would have given you, however, was their expected range of temperatures *based on a review of historical data.* They look back on years of meteorological records and determine that, in most years, July temperatures were in the 17 to 25 degree range. In fact, they'd find that they were correct in their forecast of *expected* temperatures about two out of every three years. In the other year, temperatures would fall below 17 degrees or rise above 25 degrees.

Being confident in predictions two-thirds of the time is a common statistical measure. It is used in a wide variety of instances to estimate everything from the average height and weight of a group of people to political polls, school examination results, weather forecasting and expected returns on investment. Statistically speaking, the terminology is *standard deviation*, and it measures how far away from the average the results are likely to fall. That average, by the way (21 degrees, in our temperature example), is called the *geometric mean.* If statistics was one of those school courses you managed to avoid, congratulations, and don't worry about this stuff too much. I only bring it up because the terminology is beginning to appear in various investment publications, such as the newspaper mutual fund tables.

In the investment world, standard deviation has been used as a synonym for *risk* because it measures how far *above* or *below* the long-term average returns are expected to fall. Investments with high standard deviation are considered riskier than those with low standard deviation. That is not entirely accurate either because, as noted, standard deviation measures fluctuation both *up* and *down* and many people argue that upside volatility (that is, positive return) isn't *risky* — only the downside. Consequently, there is growing interest in measuring the downside risk of an investment. To date, however, there isn't universal agreement on the use of an appropriate statistical tool to calculate such a risk.

We'll leave the debate to the academics until a consensus and a better way of assessing risk emerges. What is clear is that standard deviation is one of several useful ways to evaluate investments. If I am choosing between two mutual funds that have the same long-term track record but one has a higher standard deviation, I will probably be more comfortable with the fund with the lower standard deviation. All other things being equal, both will give me the same accumulation over time but the experience in the less volatile one will likely be more enjoyable. The ride will be smoother as the fluctuations will be more moderate. For our purposes, here are the relevant numbers for our three major asset classes:

Asset	Average Annual Compound Return	Volatility (65% Confidence)	Volatility (95% Confidence)
T-Bills	6%	±4%	±8%
Bonds	7%	±10%	±20%
Stocks	12%	±16%	±32%

Note from the above that measuring *standard deviation once* gives us approximately a two-out-of-three (65 percent) chance of being accurate while *doubling the range of expected results* (two standard deviations) provides us with the results we are likely to have 95 percent of the time. In other words, stocks, for example, are expected to yield returns between –4 percent (12% – 16%) and 28 percent (12% + 16%), 65 percent of the time and between –20 percent (12% – 32%) and 44 percent (12% + 32%) 95 percent of the time. If you are really interested in this, you'll be pleased to know that *three standard deviations* will bring us to a confidence level of more than 99 percent. That means we expect stocks to almost always yield 12 percent ±48 percent (–36% to +60%) — not much help, is it?

So, as stated, this is some of the information you can use to evaluate the appropriateness of an investment for your personal portfolio. You can say to yourself, for example, "If I increase the number of stocks (or equity mutual funds) in my portfolio, I can improve the *expected* return on that portion from 7 percent to 12 percent. That would be a good thing. But the *expected* volatility would also increase, from ±10 percent to ±16 percent. Am I willing to accept that tradeoff between risk and reward?" If the answer were "Yes," it would seem obvious that you should proceed. If not, maybe you should think about it a little more. In the real world, as we know, things are seldom that straightforward. There are several other factors to consider which we will get to very shortly. But let me give you a little insight into where we are going, along with some more good news. It is possible to both *increase* reward and *decrease* risk, and I am going to show you how to do this in Chapter 8.

TODAY'S EXPECTED RETURNS

When I am speaking at a seminar or conducting a workshop, people will often ask me, "How do I know the future will be like the past when it comes to investment returns?" And the obvious answer is that we don't know. What we can do is get some sense of the *direction* of the markets. This won't tell us where they are going to be next week or next year but as I mentioned earlier, once a trend (up or down) is established, it is not normally easily or spontaneously reversed. So let's look at the actual returns from our three asset classes over periods more recent than 49 years, for while those numbers are useful, few of us tuck our investments away in a drawer for half a century at a time. Trends have developed in these returns in the past few years that we should know about.

Annual Return and Volatility Trends (1951–1999)

	Cash (T-Bills)		Debt (Bonds)		Equity (Stocks)		Inflation (CPI)	
	Return	Volatility	Return	Volatility	Return	Volatility	Return	Volatility
Over Last 49 Years	6%	±4%	7%	±10%	12%	±16%	4%	±4%
Over Last 30 Years	8%	±4%	10%	±11%	12%	±16%	5%	±2%
Over Last 20 Years	9%	±4%	12%	±11%	11%	±13%	4%	±3%
Over Last 10 Years	6%	±3%	11%	± 8%	11%	±13%	3%	±2%
Over Last 5 Years	5%	±2%	10%	±7%	14%	±9%	2%	±1%

What we see from these numbers is that:

- T-Bill returns are getting back to their historical long-range average of 6 percent with decreasing variability.
- Bond returns have been above average and are now declining toward their long-term level with decreasing variability.
- Stocks have consistently provided returns in the 11 percent to 12 percent range until recently when they jumped higher. Volatility in the most recent past has decreased significantly.
- We are at the low end of the inflation cycle.

With these trends in mind, let me boldly set out the following as the *expected* average rates of return I would use today to design a long-term portfolio. We will use these assumptions later on but, for now, bear in mind two important things:

* These are averages only and I expect them to be accurate approximately two-thirds of the time. One-third of the time, the results will be higher or lower.
* These numbers are for *planning purposes only* and are based on my view of the world *today*. If something happens along the way to change my "guesstimate" of expected returns, I will have to change my plan to account for the new assumptions.

Here, then, are my numbers:

Compound Annual Returns and Volatility		
Asset	Return	Volatility
Cash (T-Bills)	4%	± 3%
Debt (Bonds)	8%	± 9%
Equity (Stocks)	12%	±15%
Inflation (CPI)	4%	± 2%

DETERMINING RATES OF RETURN

The average rates of return we have developed so far are useful in comparing the risk and reward tradeoff among various investments or asset classes — higher returns are linked with greater volatility. The next question, then, might be "*Why* does cash give me a 5 percent return?" or "*Why* do bonds, on average, yield 2 to 4 percent more than T-Bills?" or "*Why* has the stock market consistently offered double-digit returns?" We have touched on a number of reasons for the *relative* returns. Now I'd like to zero in on how the actual numbers are derived. For simplicity, let's stick with our hypothetical example of a $100 investment used previously.

The rate of return I should realistically expect to earn on my investment is a function of three components:

1. Riskless real return
2. Inflation factor
3. Risk premium(s)

Corresponding to these components, if I am to invest my $100, I should expect to be rewarded for:

1. The use of my money
2. Decreases in purchasing power while it is being used
3. Any chance that I will lose all or part of it

So let's see how this works. We'll begin by assuming that the *risk* associated with owning Government of Canada Treasury Bills is zero, except for inflation. It is a pretty safe bet that the government won't default on its short-term obligations. So except for inflation, we could consider cash assets (T-Bills, in our example) to be relatively *risk-free*. Looking back at our historical long-term rates of return for T-Bills and subtracting the numbers recorded by the CPI, we find that the *riskless real return* in Canada over the past 49 years has been about 2 percent. So that's where we will start to determine how rates of return are derived — with 2 percent as our base.

Next, we have to add an allowance for inflation. As I am writing this, inflation in Canada has been approximately 2 percent per year for some time so let's use that number. Here, then, is how we'd come up with the expected return for T-Bills:

Example 1

Riskless Real Return	2%
Inflation	2%
Default (T-Bills)	0%
Total Expected Return	**4%**

Now we add in a little for the risk of losing part or all of my money. How would it work out, for example, for bonds? Like this:

Example 2

Riskless Real Return	2%
Inflation	2%
Default or Market Risk	4%
Total Expected Return	**8%**

And the stock market?

Example 3

Riskless Real Return	2%
Inflation	2%
Market Risk	8%
Total Expected Return	**12%**

Finally, how about, say, pork belly futures?

Example 4

Riskless Real Return	2%
Inflation	2%
Market Risk	20%
Total Expected Return	**24%**

Pretty simple, isn't it? If I put my $100 in T-Bills for a year and I expect inflation to be about 2 percent during that interval, I should realistically expect to earn 4 percent on that investment (2 percent riskless real return + 2 percent inflation). So my T-Bill account should be worth $104 by year's end. And I shouldn't invest my hundred bucks in pork belly futures unless I am reasonably confident of having it grow to be worth $124. And so it is with any investment alternative you may choose. The reward has to bear some relationship to the anticipated risk.

As straightforward as this process appears to be, there is a practical limitation on its usefulness. The truth is that regardless of how carefully we make these calculations, using reams of statistical data, we are never going to be 100 percent accurate in estimating expected rates of return. That's because we are trying to measure something that won't stand still! The investment world is dynamic and continuously reacting to a myriad of influences such as those we have described already. What we can achieve, however, is a very useful approximation of expected returns — and that will be good enough for our long-range planning. Remember, *approximately right is better than precisely wrong.*

Experience has shown that *informed* investors have better results than do those who leave everything to fate. We need not spend all our time and energy studying the markets, but it is worthwhile for us have a sense of what is happening and an understanding of why markets move the way they do, particularly if they start to deviate from long-term average returns. For sure, there will be surprises along the way, but our knowledge of the basic nature of investments will prevent the surprises from turning into tragedies.

TAXES

It is not my intention to spend much time on how various investments are taxed for two reasons: first, it is a broad enough topic in itself and, second, I am not a tax expert. In spite of that, it is appropriate here to make just a couple of comments.

The Canadian tax system encourages us to choose one investment vehicle over another by giving us preferential treatment for certain types of income. Interest earned on a Treasury Bill, term deposit or bank account is taxable at full personal rates, whereas dividends are taxed through a tax credit arrangement at a much lower rate. Another advantageous investment from a tax viewpoint is one that generates a capital gain, because under current legislation, only 66 percent of capital gains are taxable. The result is that capital gains are better from a tax perspective than interest but not as good as dividends.

This is a very simplistic explanation and perhaps implies that you should invest only in dividend-generating assets. Indeed, if minimizing taxes were the only consideration, that might well be the best route. However, as I've said several times, there are many things to weigh in choosing appropriate investments. I will explore taxation a little further on when we come to implementing the strategies developed over the next few chapters. For now, my advice is to get yourself one of the many good books on tax or consult an expert.

Summary

* Regardless of the time period under review, unless you invested your money at the precise start and took it out at the exact end of the period, your individual experience is liable to be very different from the long-term averages.
* In the investment world, standard deviation has been used as a synonym for risk because it measures how far above or below the long-term average returns are expected to fall. Investments with high standard deviation are considered riskier than those with low standard deviation.

- One standard deviation gives us approximately a two-out-of-three (65 percent) chance of being accurate while two standard deviations (twice the range) provides us with the experience we are likely to have 95 percent of the time.
- The rate of return I should realistically expect to earn on my investment is a function of three components:
  - Riskless real return
  - Inflation factor
  - Risk premium(s)
- Regardless of how carefully we make these calculations, we are never going to be 100 percent accurate in estimating expected rates of return because the investment world is dynamic and continuously reacting to a myriad of influences.
- Experience has shown that informed investors have better results than do those who leave everything to fate.
- The Canadian tax system encourages us to choose one investment vehicle over another by giving us preferential treatment for certain types of income. The result is that capital gains are better from a tax perspective than interest but not as good as dividends.

6

Developing Your Investment Philosophy

A rational investor will take on greater risk if the anticipated reward is sufficient.

We now have a strong conceptual base from which to build a successful investment strategy. With the foundation laid as to why and how we generally make investment decisions, it is time to become more specific and get down to the real world as it applies to a population of one — you! We now have to zero in on what makes up your personal investment *philosophy*.

We will do this in two stages. First, let's go back to something we discussed at length already — *risk tolerance*. I want to lead you through a couple of exercises to help you more accurately determine your personal risk profile. We've talked a lot about risk and have come to understand its characteristics and impact. As noted, our observations so far have been about investors in general. But how do you, as an individual, react to risk?

Second, we want to get a handle on your investment *personality*. It is as unique as all other parts of your personality. To a certain extent, your behaviour as an investor is a function of your risk tolerance. But there are other considerations.

Arising out of these exercises will be a composite picture of you, the investor. With that in hand, you can set about designing an investment portfolio appropriate for your individual philosophy.

YOUR RISK TOLERANCE

You know from your own experience and observation that some people are willing to take more risk than others are. Certain brave souls will sky dive, race motorcycles and climb sheer rock faces. In their minds, the psychological rewards for having challenged themselves are worth the physical risks.

In investing, as we have already established, a rational investor will take on greater risk if the anticipated reward is sufficient. But just as the adventurers described above wouldn't jump out of airplanes, roar around a race course or scale cliffs without careful planning and the proper equipment, so intelligent investors won't expose themselves to undue risk.

What if I were to offer you a potential return of, say, 50 percent on a highly speculative investment? In all likelihood, you would turn me down, despite the high return, if you thought there were a reasonable chance you would lose all or even part of your money. Similarly, if I presented an opportunity to earn only 2 percent but with minimal risk, you would probably decline that offer as well, confident that you could do better elsewhere. It would be fair to say, then, that somewhere between investments that potentially earn 50 percent but with higher risk exposure and those that pay only 2 percent but don't pose much risk is your "comfort zone." (Realistically, the range is likely to be much narrower than from 2 percent to 50 percent.)

Just how large is your comfort zone, and how can you be more accurate about the types of investments that will fit into it?

Perhaps one way to focus in on the breadth of returns you find acceptable would be to examine how you already have your assets invested. Take a couple of minutes to complete this simple chart. Use net values, if applicable (real estate minus mortgage, for example). Don't worry about being too precise. Round off the dollar values.

A. Lower Risk		B. Moderate Risk		C. Higher Risk	
Dwelling	$ _____	Bonds	$ _____	Stocks	$ _____
Bank Accounts	$ _____	Loans	$ _____	Collectibles	$ _____
Term Deposits	$ _____	Mortgages	$ _____	Real Estate	$ _____
Others(s)	$ _____	Other(s)	$ _____	Other(s)	$ _____
	$ _____		$ _____		$ _____
	$ _____		$ _____		$ _____
	$ _____		$ _____		$ _____
	$ _____		$ _____		$ _____
Total A	$ _____	**Total B**	$ _____	**Total C**	$ _____

Total Portfolio (A + B + C) = $ _____

Lower Risk %   (A ÷ Total) x 100% = _____ %
Moderate Risk %   (B ÷ Total) x 100% = _____ %
Higher Risk %   (C ÷ Total) x 100% = _____ %

Some readers may want to argue that certain assets are in the wrong columns. That's okay. Move them around if you wish. *Perception* of risk is almost as important as the level of risk itself. We are defining *your* comfort zone, so make this exercise meaningful for you.

I suspect, however, that most readers will find themselves very heavily weighted toward the left side of the page. Don't fret if you think, as a result of our previous comments, that you should have greater diversification of risk. Most Canadians are relatively low-risk investors. That's our nature. And besides, this is just an attempt to develop a general idea of how you like to invest. I do caution you, however, to give some thought to how you came to own the assets you have. Is most of your money invested in bonds, for example, because you feel they are the best place to be or simply because they were convenient or the investments with which you are most familiar? In other words, are the assets you own today there by default or as a result of good planning?

Here's the second simple exercise to help get a handle on your risk tolerance. Imagine for a moment that all of your assets have been converted to cash; you sold everything you own and what you have in its place is a pile of dollar bills. Obviously, the larger your asset base to begin with, the greater number of dollars you will have. It doesn't matter; the concept will hold for any amount of money. Now imagine that you live in a world that offers you only two investment choices: you can buy a T-Bill or invest in the stock market. Those are the only options available but you can split the money between them if you wish.

Remember from Chapter 5 that T-Bills will earn an average of 4 percent with a volatility factor of $+3$ percent, so, from 2 to 7 percent. Investing in the stock market, on the other hand, should yield about 12 percent on average but will fluctuate between −3 percent and 27 percent. Given these assumptions, and remembering that you have only two choices, how would you allocate the money?

T-Bills _____ %   Stocks _____%

If you would leave everything in T-Bills (cash), you are best described as a *saver*, not as an investor. If you would place the full amount in the stock market (equities), you would be better identified as a *speculator* — some might even call you a gambler. Most people are not at either extreme and would fall somewhere in between, choosing to allocate a portion of their money to each of the two options.

Although this is far from precise, we might use the following broad asset allocations to describe risk tolerance in general terms:

% Cash	% Stocks	Risk Tolerance
100	0	Very Low
75	25	Low
50	50	Moderate
25	75	High
0	100	Very High

A number of detailed questionnaires and even computer programs are available that can be used to try to pinpoint your risk tolerance, but I don't believe that the 14-page printouts some of them produce will necessarily give you results much more accurate than those you'll get with these two simple exercises. However, you might like to have confirmed what you probably already know intuitively, and these programs will do that.

It is also important to keep in mind that your risk profile can change as your personal situation does, as your responsibilities and liabilities increase or lessen or as experiences shape your attitudes. All you can do is make the best decisions you can, based on the way you feel today. If your tolerance for risk changes at some point in the future, you will have to re-evaluate earlier choices to determine if they are still appropriate. As we proceed, I will be providing you with some guidelines for ongoing review and making changes to your investment strategy. For now, however, in general terms, how would you describe your risk tolerance: high, low or moderate?

YOUR INVESTMENT PERSONALITY

Let's now explore the second aspect of your investment philosophy — that is, your investment *personality*. Again, bear in mind that the way you think, feel and behave as an investor is shaped to a certain extent by your risk tolerance, but there is more to it than that.

I have created a very simple method for assessing investment personality. And like most overly simplified things, it won't give us perfect accuracy, but it will be reasonably indicative. To follow this exercise through, all you have to do is to position yourself somewhere along two lines that describe different dimensions of personality. I've named the two lines *Involvement* and *Spontaneity*. Let's look at them individually.

Involvement

As the word implies, what we're trying to determine with this measurement is the degree to which you want to be involved in day-to-day investment decision-making. The basic question is "Are you an *active* or a *passive* investor?" Do you want to be very involved or are you the type who likes to leave those details to others? Let's consider some extreme examples.

Very *active* investors are those who say or think things like "If an investment catches my eye, it doesn't take long for me to decide to jump in." These people like to be where the action is. They're afraid of being left out and are always asking, "Gee, should I be in *this* or *that?*" Active investors tend to have shorter time perspectives and seek chances to cash in on current trends and the "investment du jour."

At the other end of the spectrum, very *passive* investors really don't want to be involved much at all in the decision-making process. They tend to let other people tell them what is best. In fact, they rely a great deal on the advice of others. They trust their advisers, often to a fault, but once a good relationship is established they're very loyal. The most extreme passive investor would be one who would walk into a financial adviser's office and say, "Here's all my money. Please call me when I'm rich!"

Most investors, of course, fall somewhere between the two extremes. Make an initial attempt to plot yourself on the Involvement line. Do you fall closer to the *active* or the *passive* end? Remember that there is no good or bad place to be; successful investor personalities can be found all along the continuum.

[**Involvement**]

| **Passive** | + — + — + — + — + — + — + — + | **Active** |

[**Spontaneity**]

The second dimension on which I'd like you to rank yourself is *Spontaneity*. This one may require a little more explanation because, unlike the active/passive notion, which is familiar to many activities, the spontaneity theory involves a couple of investment concepts that need to be developed first. They are "market timing" and "money management." Even if you have not run across these terms before, you can probably guess what they mean.

Market Timing

Some people have suggested that market timing is similar to trying to plan a vacation trip to Hawaii during January. You read all the brochures that say the sun shines all the time and, on average, the temperature is 25 degrees Celsius. But somehow, when *you* arrive, you are greeted by a hurricane.

Despite the fact that successful market timing may be even more difficult than predicting the weather, everyone either talks about it or wants to try it, to some degree. And that's because it intuitively makes sense. By definition, market timing means buying low and selling high. And we all know that is the key to successful investing so, in theory, market timing is logical. It is also deceptively simple — buy stocks when the market is going up and sell them when it is going down. Buy bonds when they are increasing in value and sell them when they begin to decline. Use cash holdings as a safe haven when you're not sure. Regrettably, however, as we have repeatedly seen, there is no guaranteed way to predict market movements so most attempts at market timing fail to deliver the hoped-for results.

What causes investors to think they can outguess the market and everyone else? One reason is that, with perfect 20/20 hindsight, I can tell you precisely when a market turnaround *has occurred.* Furthermore, if I look back far enough, I may even see patterns to the market's movements that are repeated sufficiently often for me to become convinced they will occur again, given the same conditions.

That is how complex computer programs that analyze market patterns and anticipate major trends came into being. But just as weather forecasts haven't become very much more reliable over the years despite the extensive use of computer modelling and satellite observation, so no one has been able to *consistently* predict market swings.

Yet the debate continues. People who don't believe in market timing feel that the fundamentals we discussed earlier, such as corporate earnings and interest rates, account for most market momentum. They challenge not only the ability but also the rationality of market timers. Baron Philippe de Rothschild, for example, is often quoted as saying he is quite happy to "let someone else have the top 20 percent of the market as well as the bottom 20 percent." All he wanted was the 60 percent in the middle.

Advocates of market timing point out that you can obviously maximize returns by being 100 percent invested in a market when it is rising and minimize losses by being completely out when it is falling. They don't really care whether companies have good earnings because that can still be the case even when markets are in free fall. Instead, they pore over their charts and computer print-outs looking for signals that the time is right to buy or sell, based on a combination of factors that have preceded a change of market momentum in the past.

There have been innumerable academic studies on market timing and, to date, no conclusion has been accepted in the investment industry at large. Part of the problem is that in a bull market, there is always some sector that is the right place to be at that time. Conversely, you can obviously improve overall returns by being out of a market when it is declining. What is less apparent, however, is that the "opportunity cost" of being out of the market at the wrong time can be substantial. As we noted earlier, market advances tend to be greater in magnitude, more frequent and of longer duration than market declines. The average bull market in Canada, for example, lasts about two and a half to three years, but most of the gains have historically occurred in the first six months or so of the runup. Being on the sidelines, therefore, during the early part of a market advance can be costly.

And bear in mind that market timers have to be right in their predictions twice in a row. They also have to exit the market with consistency just before the downdrafts begin. They have to be adept at identifying peaks and valleys as they are occurring, not after the fact. Some "timers" get caught because what looks like a floor or a ceiling subsequently turns out just to be a temporary resting-place.

Admittedly, there are some market timers who simply take the contrarian approach of buying when everyone else is eagerly selling. They then take their profits when others are busy buying. Remember the truism, often expressed by investment veterans, that "no tree grows to the sky" — sooner or later every market rally fizzles.

Should You Develop a Market Timing Strategy?

There is no doubt that if you were able to come up with a reliable market timing system, you would outperform most money managers. That's because, assuming you are going to have a somewhat diversified portfolio, being in the right market at the right time will have a greater impact on performance than choosing the right individual securities. In fact, a number of studies have shown that even if you pick the worst performing stocks or bonds, you would place yourself in the upper echelon of money managers if you were in and out of the stock and bond market when you should have been. So there is no doubt that market timing can improve results.

The question is "Can you do it successfully?" Recall Rothschild's comment about wanting only the "60 percent in the middle." Although it probably was not what he intended, that attitude is the one adopted by most professional managers who practise market timing. They don't believe they have to pick the absolute top and bottom to be successful. Academic research has shown, however, that they have to be right about 70 percent of the time — and even that is a real challenge.

Market timing requires tremendous discipline. It often means bucking the trend and battling your own emotions. It also requires you to have a reliable group of *indicators* that give you a signal that the market has reached its peak or, alternatively, is just about to blast off. Regrettably, there is no perfect indicator that works every time.

If there were, it wouldn't take long for stories of its success to spread among investors. Everyone would start using it, and once that happened it would no longer be a reliable indicator because markets would react to the impact of the trading activities of the people using the indicator, not to the factors that gave credence to the indicator originally. The very success of the indicator would lead to its destruction as an accurate predictor of market behaviour. Once the secret was out, it would no longer be a secret.

All that having been said and even though market timing is not an exact science and has some shortcomings, I will admit most professional portfolio managers practise it to some degree. They try to be, as we have said so far several times, "approximately right rather than precisely wrong." They vary the percentage holding in cash and equity to try to participate in most market rallies while avoiding major declines. From the perspective of individual investors, however, I am leery of most market timing systems. I find them too much of an all-or-nothing proposition. Being so emphatically in or out of a market means they may miss the brief but strong market up-ticks that can have a dramatic impact on overall results because short-term moves are virtually impossible to predict with consistent accuracy.

Additionally, frequent portfolio changes bring with them the increased cost of trading (commissions, among other charges) and may also trigger taxes, both of which will reduce the net gain.

Market timing comes in many forms. Some are complicated and require diligent monitoring. If that is not how you want spend your time, you might be attracted to the simplest market timing method of all, dollar cost averaging. This is covered in full in Chapter 10.

Money Management

Fully disciplined money managers do not believe that market timing works. Their strategy is to diversify an investment portfolio among the three major asset classes of cash, debt and equities in accordance with an investor's risk profile (much as we did when I asked you to imagine that you had only two ways to invest your money). The rationale for doing so is that diversification will reduce overall risk because it is unlikely that, for example, stocks and bonds will both fall in value at the same instant (although it does occasionally occur for short periods of time). Including cash-type assets which, theoretically, cannot decline in value puts a "floor" under the portfolio to stabilize it. A portfolio diversified among cash, bonds and stocks will have less fluctuation than a pure equity one.

The money management approach also enables investors to satisfy their individual preferences by "fine-tuning" their portfolios. This is accomplished by shifting the weightings of the assets held — for example, holding more equities if the investor wants an aggressive stance or fewer if the investor is more conservative. Typically, money management requires a longer-term perspective on investment results. Money management types are also often strong-willed, but not rash. They are thoughtful persons by nature, frequently doing their own research and usually seeking to avoid volatility.

My Own View

I confess to favouring the money management approach, as perhaps you might have guessed. And the primary reason is that it accounts for the risk tolerance of the investor. The market timing tactic simply attempts to maximize returns without regard for the psychological battering that transferring in and out of the various asset classes inflicts on the investor. In fairness, some investors "savour the action." I don't.

Second, the research I have conducted has failed to convince me that market timing yields any better results over the long term than a simple "buy and hold" strategy. Recall the graph of stock prices from earlier chapters that showed there have been at least 10 significant stock market declines over the past 50 years. Correspondingly, of course, there have been more than 10 major rises. This means that market timers would have had at least 20 opportunities to guess right . . . or wrong, because to be truly effective, they have to get it right twice each time — once getting out of the market and again getting back in. That seems like an incredible challenge to me, and although some professionals insist they don't have to be correct more than half the time to make a difference, I'm not totally convinced of the merit of pure market timing.

There is overwhelming evidence in favour of the money management approach. For example, a recent survey of large pension plans in the United States proved conclusively that over 90 percent of a portfolio's investment results can be explained by the asset allocation — that is, by what percentage the portfolio was invested in cash, debt or equities. Less than 3 percent of the performance could be attributed to market timing and, in some cases, the impact of timing was actually negative.

Furthermore, as we have already pointed out, the average bull stock market in Canada lasts about 33 months — but 60 percent of the market's gain occurs, on average, in the first seven months. The key to success under those conditions, therefore, is clearly to be *in* the market, not *out* of it. In the midst of this debate, I am reminded of a friend's story about purchasing a raffle ticket for a local charity. The prize was to be drawn at the charity's annual social event, and as my friend examined his ticket closely, he noticed these words: "Must be present to win." He felt that might be a good philosophy by which to live his life. On a less grandiose scale, I think it sums up my belief about investing in the stock market.

Is There Any Place for Market Timing?

After reading this diatribe against market timing, you must be asking yourself, "Is there any place for it at all?" Yes, there is. Like most investment strategies, market timing can be practised in degrees, and in fairness, what I have just described as market timing is an extreme. It is often referred to as "tactical" market timing. In fact, somewhere between tactical market timing and equally purist fundamental money management lies a strategic position that would likely serve investors well. That strategy might better be called "timing the market" than "market timing," and this is not a game of semantics. Clearly, if you as an investor are confident in your own intuition, experience, research or the advice of others that a long-term trend is emerging within a particular asset class, you can do your own fine-tuning by shifting the weightings in your portfolio. However, you'll want to be able to make the adjustments easily and inexpensively and be conscious of the risk. Inevitably, the trend will reverse itself, so plan your escape, too! If you were going to attempt market timing, perhaps you would be best to look upon it as a defensive rather than offensive move. When we get to portfolio design and security selection in Chapters 8 and 9, you'll see how this notion of timing the market can be put into practice on a personal level.

PLOTTING YOUR PERSONALITY

Let's get back to our market timing–money management (spontaneity) line. I've shown this one vertically. Plot yourself on this line. Do you favour the market timing or money management approach?

Now let's put the Involvement and Spontaneity lines together and see if we can develop anything useful.

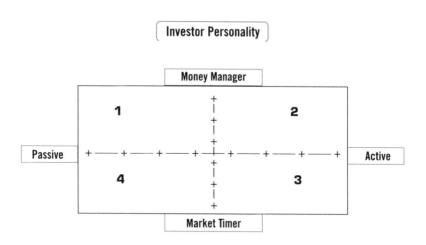

By crossing the two lines, we have created four quadrants. Looking at them in a clockwise rotation from left to right, they could generally be labelled:

1. Passive Money Manager

2. Active Money Manager
3. Active Market Timer
4. Passive Market Timer

Refer back to the positions you initially plotted for yourself on the Involvement and Spontaneity lines when they were separate. Mark those same positions on the four-way diagram. Now, just as on the back of the cereal box, connect the dots! Draw a horizontal line from your spot on the Spontaneity axis to intersect with a vertical line drawn from your position on the Involvement axis, like so:

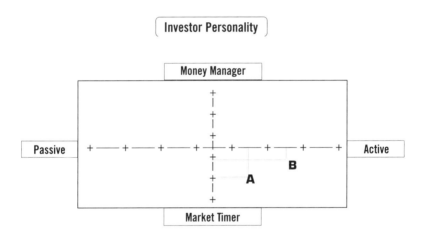

Put a big X on the intersection. This will give you some idea of your investment personality. In the example above, the investor at position A would generally be described as an Active Market Timer. This is not particularly scientific, I know, and again illustrates a tendency only. Most people could not accurately be placed at the extreme outer limits of any of the quadrants. So if you happen to end up, for example, as an Active Market Timer and you say, "That sort of describes me but I'm not really interested in being intimately involved on a day-to-day basis in my investment portfolio," don't worry. This is a general assessment only. Look at position B. That person would also be termed an Active Market Timer but, though investor B obviously wants to be more actively involved than investor A, investor B is less enamoured of market timing. Furthermore, if you disagree strongly with the implications of being in the quadrant where you find your result, go back to the original lines and review how you plotted yourself. Change whenever you wish as long as you're honest with yourself — again, it is your personality we're talking about.

I would expect to find most investors clustered somewhere around the middle of the diagram because very few of us, particularly typical Canadian investors, represent any of the extremes. And remember, there is no right or wrong place to be. Successful investors can be found in all four quadrants. It may also help you if I describe the four personalities a little more fully.

The Passive Money Manager

If you were a television watcher in the 1960s, you surely recall the show *Father Knows Best*. That show's title might be an appropriate description of the way the Passive Money Manager thinks successful investing is accomplished. People with this preference favour a well-thought-out, not-too-spectacular-yet-sound approach. They want advice from someone who has earned their respect by demonstrating an understanding of individual needs and who follows a well-defined methodology. They believe risk management is important and an asset allocation strategy will result in a more consistent rate of return even though that return may not be as "thrilling" as that of a 100 percent stock portfolio during major market advances. On the other side of the coin, returns will not be as devastating when markets decline. Once Passive Money Managers have established a trusting relationship with an adviser, they are quite willing to give that adviser a relatively free hand to carry out the mutually agreed-upon plan. Popular investment choices for this type of investor are asset allocation or balanced mutual funds which invest in cash, bonds and equities at the discretion of the portfolio manager, who normally stays within prescribed ranges in each asset class.

The Active Money Manager

If understanding, control and long-term wealth accumulation are the key features you seek, the Active Money Manager school of thought is the one to which you belong. You'll be able to construct a portfolio which addresses your risk tolerance and, once established, leaves you more or less free to do other things, just checking in once a while to make sure things aren't too far off track.

The disadvantage of this method is that it requires more work. It is vital to spend time assessing your risk tolerance, setting long-term objectives and matching investment alternatives to your needs. This is not a responsibility you can abdicate to someone else if you truly want to make it work for you.

Oh, and one more thing — this approach isn't particularly exciting. It can, in fact, be quite boring. Once the research is done and the plan is put in place, there isn't much more to do, except check in periodically to insure everything is still on track and amend as necessary.

The Active Market Timer

The plus side of the Active Market Timer stance is that it allows investors to take advantage of the latest potential big winner. Provided they are accurate in their timing, they can make some quick money by being in and out of the deal. The challenge, of course, is to know exactly when to get in and out.

Investors favouring this method will often use discount brokers to carry out their stock transactions because the frequency of activity would otherwise lead to unduly high transaction costs. Because they do their own research, however, they do not require the services of a full brokerage firm. They also enjoy flipping real estate, trading commodities and speculating on business deals.

The Passive Market Timer

A combination of simplicity and a promise of excitement appeals to the Passive Market Timers. They want in on the action but don't wish to make decisions themselves about where that action is. They don't want to do their own research so they, too, have found a trusted adviser. On the downside, this approach doesn't easily accommodate the development of a long-term strategy and, consequently, may not truly reflect personal risk tolerance because it focuses on return rather than risk.

Investors of this type are the favoured clients of active brokers and purveyors of penny stocks. Not wanting to be left out of anything that's hot, these people are sometimes easy prey for the get-rich-quick artist. They are also the most likely to subscribe to market timing services or newsletters.

Spelling Out Your Philosophy

By now, you should have a fairly good understanding of your personal investment philosophy. Let's put all three components together and see how things look for you. The three areas for evaluation were:

1. Risk tolerance
2. Involvement (Active/Passive)
3. Spontaneity (Market Timer/Money Manager)

Now I want you to rank yourself on the three scales by writing two or three words for each that describe your view of your investment philosophy:

Risk —

_____
(Very Low ——————————————— Very High)

Involvement —

_____
(Passive ——————————————— Active)

Spontaneity —

_____
(Market Timer ——————————— Money Manager)

Some examples would be:

Risk —

moderately high
_____
(Very Low ——————————————— Very High)

Involvement —

somewhat active
_____
(Passive ——————————————— Active)

Spontaneity —

favour money management
_____
(Market Timer ——————— ——— Money Manager)

THE INVESTMENT STATEMENT — FOUR PARTS

The exercises of the past few pages are leading us toward the creation of what I call the Investment Statement. What we have just completed is the first stage of its development: Level 1 — Personal Philosophy. In total, the investment statement has four parts to it:

Level 1: Personal Philosophy
Level 2: Investment Objectives
Level 3: Asset Allocation
Level 4: Security Selection

If you think this four-part exercise is a little intimidating, please be patient. We'll go through it one step at a time, and you'll quickly sees that it is not that onerous and actually quite useful.

You'll find that a "qualitative and quantitative statement" such as you're going to develop will give you a clear idea of how to construct your portfolio to insure it addresses current needs and long-term objectives. In addition, it will become your "guiding light" by providing a frame of reference for future investment decisions. Whenever something new comes along — a new project, a new investment proposal — you'll be able to evaluate it within the context of the goals you've set. If the new opportunity complements what you're doing, you can feel free to explore further. If it detracts from what you're trying to accomplish, you can quickly reject it. The Investment Statement makes decision-making efficient and effective.

THE INVESTMENT PYRAMID

Before we move on to the next level, it is probably worthwhile to introduce here another concept that may make our progress easier. I am referring to the ubiquitous investment pyramid.

I use the word "ubiquitous" because four out of five investment books you read will have some sort of the pyramid in them. It is used to show the structure of a balanced portfolio and the risk/reward tradeoff, and to detail the steps to building wealth. I'm not too proud to admit that as tired as I am of seeing it, the pyramid is undoubtedly the best way to illustrate all those things — so I'll use it too.

The purpose of my application, ostensibly at least, will be to depict the four levels of the Investment Policy Statement. In doing that, however, I will inevitably touch on the other possibilities. Here, then, is my pyramid:

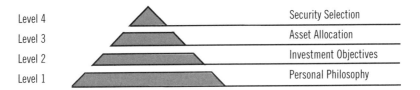

Level 4		Security Selection
Level 3		Asset Allocation
Level 2		Investment Objectives
Level 1		Personal Philosophy

We've just dealt with Level 1, your personal investment philosophy, and we will refer back to it a little later. It is the base, the anchor, the foundation and the strength for everything that rests on top or comes after. Thus it is vitally important that you agree with the assessment of you by you so far. If there is still doubt in your mind that you have thought through the basic questions raised by this chapter sufficiently to have come up with a picture of you the investor, you may want to stop right here, go back and try again.

It is also essential for us to get the order correct here. When we think about the activities in which we typically like to participate as investors, even if only intellectually, it's things like attempting to outguess the market and playing "I wish I had . . ." that are the most fun. Consequently, we'll often want to leap forward to those thoughts before we have adequately established the foundation to our investment strategy. If we want maximum accuracy and effectiveness, however, we must, in this order:

1. Understand how we think, feel and behave as investors (Personal Philosophy).

2. Visualize and verbalize what it is we are trying to accomplish (Investment Objectives).
3. Structure our portfolios to manage the relationship between our goals and our risk tolerance (Asset Allocation).
4. Choose investments that have the best possible chance of meeting our needs and expectations (Security Selection).

There is no point in getting excited about a particular stock or mutual fund if it is outside our comfort zone because of its potential volatility. So we have to base every decision moving up the pyramid on the ones we made for the previous level.

The Investment Statement is extremely useful for that purpose. It is something you're going to refer to, from time to time, to provide an ongoing point of reference for your decision-making. Additionally, if you do work alongside a financial planner or investment adviser on this project, it can become a contract, so to speak, between the two of you. It will spell out the mutual expectations with respect to your investment philosophy, objective, targeted returns and portfolio structure. Because this can be such a valuable tool, it is worthwhile ensuring that it really does reflect the way you feel about the entire investment process. I encourage you, therefore, to review the few words you wrote out earlier about risk, involvement and spontaneity. If you are satisfied with them, take a few minutes to rewrite them in a narrative form. This will complete Level 1 of the Investment Statement. Here are a few sample Level 1 statements to give you an idea of what I am suggesting:

LEVEL 1 PERSONAL PHILOSOPHY STATEMENT

"I am a *moderately risk tolerant* investor who wants to be *somewhat involved* in a *money management* approach to accumulating assets."

"I have *higher risk tolerance* and want to be *very active* with my own *market timing* ideas for maximizing return."

"I am very busy and, thus, *willing to rely on the recommendations* of others. I will let them do what they think is best for me provided they take into account my *need for safety and security.*"

Now try your own:

"My personal investment philosophy could best be described as

_____

_____

_____

_____

_____

_____

_____ "

In the next chapter, let's move on to Level 2 — setting the investment objectives.

Summary

* A rational investor will take on greater risk if the anticipated reward is sufficient.
* Investor philosophy can be measured on two dimensions:
  - *Involvement* — the degree to which you want to be involved in day-to-day investment decision-making
  - *Spontaneity* — *market timing* versus *money management*
* Market timing is logical and deceptively simple — buy when the

market is going up and sell when it is going down. Regrettably, there is no guaranteed way to predict market movements so most attempts at market timing fail to deliver the hoped-for results.

- Money management diversifies an investment portfolio among the three major assets classes of cash, debt and equities in accordance with an investor's risk profile. There is overwhelming evidence in favour of a money management approach.
- There are four investor personalities:
  - Passive Money Manager
  - Active Money Manager
  - Active Market Timer
  - Passive Market Timer
- The Investment Statement has four parts:
  - Level 1: Personal Philosophy
  - Level 2: Investment Objectives
  - Level 3: Asset Allocation
  - Level 4: Security Selection

7 Setting Your Objectives

Investing involves compromise and is often less a matter of what you want than what you are willing to give up.

THE THREE MAJOR OBJECTIVES

If I were to ask you, "What is your investment objective?" how would you respond? Most likely the answer would be something like "I want to retire at age 60" or "I'd like to start my own business within the next five years" or, perhaps, "My wish is to have enough money set aside for my children's education and then I am going to take that back-packing trip around Europe that I missed after university."

We have many different ways of expressing what we are trying to accomplish when we set investment objectives. In my opinion, however, when all is said and done, there are really only three things we hope to do with our investments — *all* objectives, in one way or another, come down to *growth, income* or *liquidity*. We can talk about establishing a second career, retiring, funding the children's education, paying off the mortgage, preserving estate values for the grandchildren and so on, but all of these and anything else we might think of can be distilled down to these three fundamental objectives. We want our assets to *grow in value* — to be worth more at some point in the future than they are today. Then, once we have accumulated whatever amount of wealth we can, we need to be able to convert those assets into *income to replace salaries, wages or business earnings*. And finally, we want to have some sort of *liquid emergency or opportunity fund* so that we don't have to dramatically alter the plans for use of our assets if we need to get through some unexpected crisis or if an unbelievable opportunity suddenly presents itself.

OBJECTIVES CAN CHANGE

Sounds simple enough, doesn't it? *Growth, income* or *liquidity* — take your pick. The truth is, however, that for most of us, our overall investment plan will incorporate some element of each. Few of us will have situations so straightforward that we can think of one objective only. It is also important to remind ourselves that investment objectives are never chiselled in stone — chances are very good that they will change along the way as time passes and new priorities and influences shape the way we see the future. The following table illustrates this point:

Investment Objectives Vary With Life Stage		
Age	Primary Objective	Secondary Objective
20s	Liquidity	Income
30s	Income	Growth
40s	Growth	Growth
50s	Growth	Growth
60s	Income	Growth
70s	Income	Liquidity

Looking at this table from a personal financial perspective at least, I can see that my life has pretty much unfolded this way. For example, when I was in my early 20s, what do you think was my most important financial objective? *Liquidity*, of course — did I have enough money in my jeans on Saturday night to go out and party? My *time horizon* wasn't very long (Saturday to Saturday seemed about right!). Unfortunately, I didn't have any invested assets at the time to provide *income* so I had to invest my time and effort into working at a job to make sure that when Saturday rolled around I could participate in the fun. Today, I must say how delighted I am at the number of young folks I have met during my travels who *have* built some sort of reserve and are using it to pay their tuition, living expenses or as the foundation for a long-term investment program. Many of them are quite knowledgeable and using fairly sophisticated investment strategies to grow their assets and provide income. I wish I'd had their insight and discipline at that age. Which brings me to the next life stage — the 30s.

By the time I got into my 30s, the priorities had changed. While it was still important to have ready access to cash, being in good health and in a blossoming career position, I was less concerned with liquidity. I knew that if I needed some cash beyond my fledgling savings, I could probably get it by simply signing my name on a bank loan application form. A properly designed insurance program would ease the burden of most major catastrophes.

I am not, by the way, advocating here a total reliance on borrowed money for *liquidity* purposes. Prudence dictates that you should have *some* cash available for small financial emergencies. However, I have seen too many financial planning–advice books insist that the readers set aside large cash reserves, such as six to twelve months' income, *before* beginning an investment program. I believe there are better ways to keep emergency and opportunity funds readily available yet more gainfully employed, so to speak. We'll explore this topic further in the next chapter.

The other problem with trying to maintain large cash reserves on hand is that very few of us actually have the discipline to keep those unrestrained dollars in the bank. We *spend* money on things we *need*; we *save* money for things we *want*. Human nature being what it is, however, we are too easily capable of reclassifying *wants* into *needs*. When we see something that we suddenly decide we need and the money is readily accessible, our best intentions can wilt and disappear. As David Chilton, author of the mega-bestselling book *The Wealthy Barber*, says, "A *need* is a *want* your neighbour already has!" It is simply too tempting, in my experience, to keep extra large amounts of readily obtainable cash around.

BORROWING TO INVEST AND MANAGING DEBT

As I have just introduced the notion of borrowing money to meet the liquidity objective, this is an appropriate spot for me to comment on "leveraging" or the use of borrowed money to meet the other investment objectives — in particular, *growth* or *income*. Let's begin with the obvious — any debt has to be *manageable* and used *intelligently*. One of the most valuable assets you will ever have is a good credit rating. There is no doubt that judicious use of credit can accelerate the accumulation of wealth; however, we also have to recognize that financial leverage is a double-edged sword — using other people's money to invest also increases the risk. It's one thing to lose your own money if an investment sours (remember "regret" and "fear" from Chapter 1). It is quite another to lose someone else's, such as your bank's. Bankers tend to be less understanding and patient about an investment misadventure than we might be on our own.

As I am writing this, interest rates are relatively low and we have been enjoying historically high returns in the stock market. Those are the conditions in which leverage strategies become popular. Obviously, if you can earn, for example, 12 percent in the market with money you borrowed at 8 percent, you'll come out ahead. Additionally, under certain conditions, the interest expense is tax-deductible, making your net cost even lower and your net return correspondingly higher. Unfortunately, many investors have tales of woe where the reverse situation persisted, that is, where the cost of borrowing exceeded the investment return even after deducting interest expense. Is leveraging appropriate for you? Here is a handy rule of thumb to help you decide.

The rule is simply this: every dollar you borrow to invest alongside your own increases your risk by 100 percent. If you have $10,000 to invest and you borrow an additional $10,000, you double the risk. Therefore, if the chosen investment would normally yield say, 10 percent, you should expect a return somewhere in the area of 20 percent to account for the extra risk. The mandatory question to ask yourself before making such an investment is "Do I want to invest in something that could potentially earn me 20 percent knowing that it is twice as risky as a 10 percent investment?" In other words, is a 20 percent investment within your comfort zone?

This ratio holds true for leveraged investments of higher or lesser proportion too. For example, if you match each dollar of your own money with another 50¢ from the bank, your expected returns should be at least 50 percent higher than if you went it alone, that is, 15 percent; $10,000 of your own and $20,000 from the bank — 200 percent additional risk — should get 30 percent return, and so on. And then, of course, the really big: none of your own funds with 100 percent leverage. In my opinion, that is at least four times as risky, so, in this example, I'd want to look at a 40 percent minimum potential return and see how that fit with my tolerance for risk.

Let's get back to me and my glorious 30s! With liquidity retreating as the most important financial objective in my life, what moved forward to take its place was *income*. The reason was simple: the decade of my 30s was largely a period of acquisition. Marriage had brought with it a much greater interest than a bachelor would normally perceive as necessary in the comforts of home — things like furniture, a larger car, a well-stocked refrigerator, vacations and, certainly not to be neglected, the house itself!

Unfortunately, all those material goods had to be paid for, and bearing in mind the need for careful use of credit, that meant cash flow or income became the factor that governed how quickly assets of any type could be accumulated.

But something else was happening. Some of that income was being employed to acquire things that actually began to appreciate in value. Most notable was the family dwelling (thanks to a booming real estate market), but there were, whether by good luck or good planning, a few smaller items that also gained in value. We're not talking megabucks here. But the first $1,000 Canada Savings Bond purchased on the payroll deduction plan, a good life insurance program, a minimum monthly automatic bank deposit to an RRSP account — all these things slowly began to add to personal net worth. So *growth* emerged as a secondary objective during that stage of my life.

And now, since I am a few years beyond my 30s, I can speak

about the next significant shift in primary investment objective. This change usually takes place during the 20 or so years between 40 and 60 years old. This period represents, for many of us, our peak earning years, when we are well along in job or career, with incomes progressing toward their upper limits. Financial responsibilities often begin to decline as children become self-reliant, mortgages are paid down or off, most material needs have been pretty much met and disposable income generally rises. Coupled with climbing values of earlier investments and savings plans, this is a time of relative financial easing and probably provides, for most of us, the greatest opportunity to accumulate wealth. *Growth*, therefore, becomes the watchword.

As we move toward age 60, once again there is likely to be a refocusing of purpose. Retirement is edging nearer. We now want those assets that we have been accumulating for the previous 15 or 20 years to be converted to *income* to supplement pensions, government benefits and such. Recalling, though, our earlier admonition about allowing for the inflation that will *not* disappear after retirement, we must have our amassed assets continue to *grow*, at least at a rate equal to increases in the cost of living.

And then, finally, the years beyond age 70 will often prompt us to think about those who will survive us and how we might pass on whatever assets we don't use ourselves to them efficiently, so estate *liquidity* emerges, at least as a secondary objective.

So there you have it — your life (and mine) all neatly laid out. Of course, we know that these things don't always happen in the order or time frame that I have suggested. The life stages described — the ages and their corresponding primary and secondary objectives — are broad generalizations. We all know people who are well along in their wealth-building programs before they reach age 30 and, regrettably, we know others who are not likely to ever accumulate even a small amount of surplus cash.

The essential message is that our objectives can and will likely change over time. Consequently, any investment strategies we develop should reflect our current goals and yet not be so rigid as to preclude altering them if our priorities shift. Suitability and flexibility — that's what we want.

INVESTMENT OBJECTIVES AND THE BASIC ASSET CLASSES

Having now established that, despite the popularity of a thousand other descriptive words, *growth*, *income* and *liquidity* are really the only investment objectives one might have, you may have already jumped ahead and made the connection between those three objectives and the basic asset classes. That linkup looks like this:

Objective	Asset Class
Growth	Equity
Income	Debt
Liquidity	Cash

Again this relationship is not a perfect one. As we noted previously, similar to debt instruments, some equity assets provide income in the form of dividends or rent and certain cash-type holdings yield interest regularly. In general, however, if growth is the primary objective, equities offer the greatest growth prospects. Debt instruments are normally set up to provide regular income flows and cash-type assets are most liquid. We'll explore variations on this relationship when we discuss portfolio withdrawal strategies in Chapter 10.

For now, however, let's reintroduce the sample investments that we have chosen to represent the various asset classes. They line up this way:

Objective	Asset Class	Investment
Growth	Equity	Stocks
Income	Debt	Bonds
Liquidity	Cash	T-Bills

It is also important to restate at this juncture that T-Bills, bonds and stocks were chosen as representative of entire investment classes for convenience only. In real life and as a matter of good practice, a well-designed investment strategy would account for *all* of an investor's assets in their respective asset classes. For example:

Objective	Asset Class	Typical Investment
Growth	Equity	Common stocks, growth mutual funds, real estate, business interests, collectibles, precious metals
Income	Debt	Bonds, mortgages, fixed income mutual funds, preferred shares, loans, pension plan benefits, government benefits
Liquidity	Cash	T-Bills, money market mutual funds, term deposits, GICs, Canada Savings Bonds, bank accounts

In fact, to a certain extent at least, almost all assets could be used for all objectives. It's just that some are obviously better suited than others for a particular desired outcome.

DEVELOPING YOUR PERSONAL OBJECTIVES

In my travels and talks with financial planners throughout North America, there is one concern among them that seems to be universal. They feel there is too large a gap between what their clients want their portfolios to do and what is likely to be possible. In other words, many of their *clients have portfolios that are too small to achieve all their goals given reasonable assumptions about investment performance.* This state of affairs exists for two very simple reasons:

a) Investors have waited too long to begin building assets.
b) As a consequence of (a), the rate of return required to meet the investors' goals is too high. It is either unachievable on a consistent basis or, if pursued, would entail too much risk for the client.

The first of these is easy to understand. The sooner you start to accumulate wealth, the longer the miracle of compounding can work in your favour and the sooner you'll meet your objective. Let's look at a couple of examples (and don't worry if the numbers seem inappropriate for your situation. They were chosen simply to make the arithmetic easier. You can add or subtract zeros to approximate your personal situation):

Example 1 — Targeting Accumulation

Target:	To accumulate $1,000,000 for retirement
Rate of return:	12% per year
Monthly investment:	$500
Age able to retire if started at 25 years old:	52
Age able to retire if started at 35 years old:	62

As you would expect, if you start 10 years later, there will be a 10-year difference in the age by which you'll have met your target. The real difference and the huge advantage, however, become evident if you think about what would happen during that extra 10 years you would be retired, between age 52 and 62, had you started your accumulation program at the earlier age. Obviously, you would have an additional decade to enjoy retirement and enjoy it you could — because you would have 10 additional years of income generated by the $1,000,000 dollars you had accumulated. If, for example, you are able to continue to earn 12 percent per year on your investments after retirement (and if you earned 12 percent up to retirement, there is a good chance you could continue to do so), you could have a $120,000-a-year retirement income without any encroachment on the capital. Let's see — $120,000 a year for 10 years — that's $1,200,000 of income forgone by waiting until age 35 to begin an investment program. That's real money!

Example 2 — Targeting Retirement Age

Target:	To accumulate $1,000,000 by age 60
Rate of return:	12% per year

Monthly investment required for 25-year-old: $200
Monthly investment required for 35-year-old: $625

Again, a startling difference! You would have to contribute more than three times as much money on a monthly basis if you delayed. What's more, the 25-year-old would have put away a total of about $87,000 over the 35 years to age 60; the 35-year-old would have had to set aside about $100,000 more (approximately $187,500 in total) to end up with the same amount of money at retirement.

Example 3 — Targeting Rate of Return

Target:	To accumulate $1,000,000 by age 60
Monthly investment:	$500
Return required if started at 25 years old:	8%
Return required if started at 35 years old:	12%

While one could look at these percentages and easily conclude that

12 percent is as attainable as 8 percent, the point is that 12 percent is one and a half times higher than 8 percent. Wouldn't the risk be proportionately higher as well? For a low-risk investor, even 12 percent might be too ambitious, given what we know about investment returns. Recall that the only investment of the three we have chosen (stocks, bonds and T-Bills) with a long-term track record of about 12 percent was stocks. Should we structure the portfolio of all 35-year-old investors entirely with stocks? I hope you don't believe that, or I have not done a very good job so far in this book of discussing risk management.

THE RISK/REWARD TRADEOFF — A ROLE-PLAY

It doesn't matter which way we look at it, does it? You must set your objectives based on realistic expectations about your ability to save and invest and reasonable assumptions about investment returns.

Perhaps I can illustrate this point more effectively by repeating here a popular scenario from *Risk Is a Four Letter Word*. It is a fairly representative dialogue between a good financial planner or investment adviser and a typical client. It goes like this:

Adviser: *Okay, Bill, we have completed the financial planning part of the process. Now we want to put together an investment strategy that will help you reach your goals.*

Client: Sounds good to me — this is the bit I have been waiting for.

Adviser: *However, before we actually get down to designing your portfolio, Bill, I'd like to do one final check on my understanding of exactly what your goals are.*

Client: You have done a pretty thorough job. I'm confident you understand me quite well. The most important goal is for me to be financially secure so that I can retire early. That's the big one.

Adviser: *Right — and you want to retire in about 15 years — around age 60, with an inflation-adjusted income, excluding government benefits, not too much lower than what you are earning today.*

Client: That's it — around $50,000 a year. I'm 45 years old and in good health. There are quite a few things I want to do in my retirement and most of them cost money. I can't see me really enjoying myself if my income were to drop suddenly.

Adviser: *All right, Bill, let's review what we have concluded about your tolerance for risk in your investments. You felt . . .*

Client: I'm not really a risk taker, remember? I understand now that perhaps I have been a little too cautious in the past and that I'll need to expand my comfort zone, as you called it — but not too far.

Adviser: *Of course not. In fact, on this Investment Statement I had you write out, you describe yourself as "moderately risk tolerant." Do you still feel that way?*

Client: Yes, I think that would be a fair assessment. I had just never thought about managing risk in the way we've talked about it.

Adviser: *And in our earlier review of various investments such as stocks, bonds and T-Bills, we found that "moderately risky" investments had historical returns of, say, between 8 and 12 percent. So could we describe your comfort zone as somewhere between 8 and 12 percent?*

Client: Yes, I think so. I don't believe I would worry too much about investments such as the ones we've talked about with returns in that range. Also, I do remember the "fluctuation factor" impact, so I know that 8 to 12

(115)

percent represents a normal range only. From time to time, returns for investments in that category may be higher or lower, but in the long run they should average somewhere in between, say, 10 percent.

Adviser: *Good! So those are the assumptions on which I'm going to proceed. You want to retire in 15 years with sufficient assets to generate a $50,000-a-year income, adjusted for inflation. So your primary objective right now is growth changing to income at about age 60. And if we start off with a mix of investments that have a past track record of yielding about 10 percent on average with modest fluctuation, you won't lie awake at night worrying about them.*

Client: You've got it.

Adviser: *Okay. Let me plug these numbers into my computer here and see what we get. You have no company pension plan and we are ignoring government benefits because you want them to be a bonus if, in fact, on an after-tax basis, they are worth anything at all to you. You already have investments totaling about $50,000 and you've indicated that you could set aside an additional $500 a month between now and age 60 to help build up your capital. The desired income is $50,000 a year and we will allow 5 percent for inflation. Okay, computer, do your stuff!*

(10 seconds later)

Adviser: *Uh-oh!*

Client: What is it?

Adviser: *Well, it looks like, if we use these assumptions, to meet your stated retirement objectives, we're going to have to earn you an average of 15 percent per year on your investments.*

Client: Fifteen percent — so, can you do it?

Adviser: *Certainly, we do know investments that have earned 15 percent in the past, but that is no guarantee for the future and . . .*

Client: So maybe we should look at those?

Adviser: *But wait a minute, Bill — what rates of return did we decide were within your comfort zone? It was from 8 to 12 percent, as I recall.*

Client: Yeah, but returns in that range obviously won't meet my needs . . . so I have to shoot for better yields and that means taking on more risk . . .

Adviser: *Or rethink your goals. Perhaps they are too high.*

Client: Well, maybe they are a little ambitious — but they are where I'd like to be 15 years from now. Just how risky are those 15 percent investments?

Adviser: *It's hard to say because there aren't as many of them around as there are of the 10 percent variety and we have less historical data on them. I think it is fair to say, however, that if we expect them to generate a rate of return 50 percent higher than the ones we originally considered, we have to be prepared for increased risk of about the same proportion. How do you feel about that?*

Client: I like the 15 percent part — but I don't think I'd be comfortable with that much more risk — one and a half times higher than what I'm used to. But obviously I have to get more than 10 percent or I won't even come close to my objectives.

Adviser: *How high do you think you'd be willing to go?*

Client: I guess I could live with investments that average 12 percent — that's at the upper limit of my comfort zone.

Adviser: *In fact, Bill, you'd have to be willing to expand your comfort zone if we build your portfolio around invest-ments that have* averaged *12 percent because they would also have higher volatility. Are you prepared for that as well?*

Client: I don't really have a choice, do I?

Adviser: *Of course you do. As I said earlier, you could scale down your goals to ones that are achievable with a 10 percent average return . . .*

Client: So, 15 percent will meet my goals, but the risk is too high for my peace of mind. I'm comfortable with 10 percent, but that won't get me where I want to go. It's a tradeoff then, isn't it?

Adviser: *Yes, Bill, that is exactly what it is. What level of risk are you willing to assume to get the reward you want?*

Client: Okay . . . okay. Let's shoot for a 12 percent average. It's in between; I'll give up some potential return for less volatility.

Adviser: *Are you sure? You've got to really believe in this. If even 12 percent is going to bother you . . .*

Client: No. No. I can handle it. Let's look for investments that have earned about 12 percent on average over the long haul. Isn't there anything we can do to reduce the fluc-tuation?

Adviser: *Yes, there is. In fact, I'm hopeful that one or both of two things will happen. You'll end up with more than 12 percent average annual return. Obviously, we can't make any promises or predictions in that regard but if we balance the portfolio properly, we can improve the chances of hitting that target. The other possibility is that you'll find the volatility associated with 12 percent investments isn't too bad at all. You'll come back to me*

> *at some point and say, "I think I can manage a little more risk now." And then we can re-evaluate the investment choices we originally made and perhaps look for something a bit more aggressive. We'll ease into them, as you become more comfortable. How does that approach sound to you?*

Client: Sounds okay. What investments do you recommend?

Okay, it is time to step back into the real world. Although the preceding was obviously an overdramatization, it illustrated a couple of very important concepts:

1. Given reasonable market assumptions, many portfolios are too small to achieve all an investor's goals.
2. It may be possible to structure a portfolio with a target rate of return that will meet objectives, but the volatility (risk) may be too high.
3. It is usually better to focus on *risk* rather than *return.*
4. Once your risk tolerance is established, it sets an upper limit on the portfolio's long-term expected rate of return.
5. If the rate of return is inadequate to meet your objectives, those objectives have to be scaled down or you must be willing to commit more money to the task.

As a matter of interest, in the foregoing example, assuming a 12 percent average rate of return, Bill's retirement objectives could largely be met if he were able and willing to do any one of the following:

1. Invest an additional $68,000 up front.
2. Invest $1,250 a month rather than $500.
3. Retire at age 67 rather than 60.
4. Accept $29,000 a year income instead of $50,000.

Perhaps none of these alternatives by themselves would be desirable. The best answer may be some combination of all four of them, that is, a modification of the objectives overall. Frequently, making investment decisions is often less a matter of what you *want* than what you are willing to *give up*. Except in those rare cases where your assets are greater than required to meet your goals, it is necessary to weigh the options and outcomes. The resulting portfolio should be the one that best balances objectives and tolerance for risk.

In this regard, it is clear that some negotiation has to take place in the mind of every investor — to compromise between what is desired and what is possible. And many people find it difficult to negotiate from both sides of the table, so to speak. They will, therefore, consult a professional financial planner or investment adviser to help them through the process. They feel that the services of a well-trained, objective outsider can go a long way toward improving the likelihood of meeting their aspirations. For example, in our little role-play, we did not consider leverage programs or how to improve after-tax yields as additional methods of moving closer to the targeted returns, yet these are viable alternatives which are best considered under the watchful eye of a competent specialist. I happen to agree that good quality professional advice will help most investors — even the most sophisticated. In today's investment world, however, there are an increasing number of people who belong to the do-it-yourself school of thought. We'll weigh the pros and cons of this debate in Chapter 12.

INVESTMENT STRATEGY AND THE FINANCIAL PLAN

Before we go any further, however, let me emphatically state that, regardless of whether you engage a professional adviser or go it alone, it is impossible to make intelligent asset allocation decisions without *first* considering an overall financial plan. The investments themselves — the stocks, bonds, T-Bills or whatever — are merely *tools,* vehicles for carrying out the financial plan. In developing that plan, you'll set out philosophies, goals, objectives and constraints. In choosing appropriate investments, you must match them to the parameters developed in the financial plan. So, in effect, you will have two types of objectives in the overall process — *financial* and *investment* — even though they may be wrapped up in the same expression. Let's take an example. Say the *financial* objective is to retire in 20 years. The corresponding *investment* objective, then, would be to accumulate assets for 20 years (growth) so they can be systematically liquidated over the next 20 to 30 years of expected retirement (income). The financial plan would identify the amount of income desired at retirement, the available assets with which to work, the manageable ongoing deposits and capital required to meet the object. The investment strategy would determine the asset allocation most likely to obtain rates of return required to meet the target. The portfolio would then have to be adjusted to balance required rates of return and the level of risk you are willing to assume.

Individual investor background will also have a bearing on the asset allocation. It seems pretty clear, for example, that if you are an entrepreneur, the value of your business is a very important asset. It provides income, tax shelter and increasing net worth over time. Your asset allocation, in that case, will be different from, let's say, the much maligned government worker who has a very secure and relatively high-paying job. If I were to ask that person what his or her financial goals were, the response would probably be something like "To retire early" or "To educate my children" or "To pay off the mortgage." In either situation, the tools used to accomplish the objectives — the stocks, bonds, bank accounts or whatever — are just that: tools. By themselves, they're merely different places to put money, but properly aligned with sound, achievable financial objectives, they become powerful building blocks to successful wealth accumulation.

VISUALIZING YOUR OBJECTIVES

This is also the appropriate place to comment a little more about the process of goal setting. Even though we have now accepted that all investment objectives can be distilled down to one or several of *growth, income* or *liquidity*, the procedure we follow to come to those conclusions is important. All too often, when we think about our goals, we aren't specific enough in describing them. Let me give an example. Suppose I say, "My objective is to retire early." What does that mean? What age is "early" — 50, 55, 60 . . . ? What does retirement actually mean to me? What am I doing in retirement? Lying on a beach somewhere or have I taken up archeology and I'm digging in the sand in a desert somewhere?

How much is retirement costing me? Do I have a membership at an exclusive golf club or do I prefer to spend my afternoons playing chess in the park with some long-time friends? If travel is part of the picture, where am I going? How often? With whom? First class or economy?

What about our children? Do they still need financial assistance with the grandchildren's education costs?

Or how about our own parents? Are they still part of our lives and, if so, are they financially dependent on us in some way?

It seems to me that one of the best ways to ensure that we have been thoughtful enough about what our goals are is to take a few minutes, sit back, close our eyes and *visualize* ourselves having achieved the objective. Picture yourself doing whatever it is that you hope to be doing once you've reached that point. Starting a second career? What's that look like? Retired? Where? When? How? With whom? Building your dream vacation home? Where? Type of architecture? Cost?

The bottom-line question is "What lifestyle do we want in retirement and what level of income will we require to maintain it?" That income can then be translated into an amount of capital needed at the date of retirement to generate the desired cash flow.

LEVEL 2 INVESTMENT OBJECTIVES STATEMENT

We have come a long way in this chapter and have now climbed through Level 2 of our investment pyramid.

| Level 2 | Investment Objectives |
| Level 1 | Personal Philosophy |

To maximize the value of what we have just done, go back to the Level 1 part of the Investment Statement you wrote in Chapter 6. Rewrite it here and add a few words for Level 2 — state your investment objective, whether it's *growth*, *income* or *liquidity* or a combination.

Following are samples of Level 2 statements:

"My primary investment objective is *growth* over the next 20 years. I do not anticipate a need for income from my portfolio before that time, although I would like to have some funds available for an emergency or opportunity."

"Within five years I wish to begin receiving an annual income from my investments to supplement my company pension. I also recognize the need for growth beyond retirement to offset inflation."

"My portfolio should largely be made up of *liquid* assets so as to facilitate an efficient transfer to my heirs."

Now add your own Level 2 statement to what you wrote in Chapter 6:

Level 1

_____

_____

_____

Level 2

_____

_____

_____

Now that you have defined your personal investment philosophies and spelled out your objectives with regard to growth, income and liquidity, it is time to move up one more step on the pyramid, to Level 3 — Asset Allocation.

Summary

- When all is said and done, there are really only three things we hope to do with our investments — all objectives, in one way or another, come down to growth, income or liquidity.
- Investment objectives are never chiselled in stone — chances are very good that they will change along the way — as time passes and new priorities and influences shape the way we see the future.
- There is a logical connection between those three objectives and the basic asset classes. That linkup looks like this:

Objective	Asset Class
Growth	Equity
Income	Debt
Liquidity	Cash

- Given reasonable market assumptions, many portfolios are too small to achieve all an investor's goals.
- It may be possible to structure a portfolio with a target rate of return that will meet objectives, but the volatility (risk) may be too high.
- It is usually better to focus on risk rather than return.
- Once your risk tolerance is established, it sets an upper limit on the portfolio's long-term expected rate of return.
- If the rate of return is inadequate to meet your objectives, those objectives have to be scaled down or your willingness to commit more money to the task must be increased.
- It is impossible to make intelligent asset allocation decisions without first considering an overall financial plan.
- One of the best ways to ensure that we have been thoughtful enough about what our goals are is to take a few minutes, sit back, close our eyes and visualize ourselves having achieved the objective.

8

Don, Harry, Gary and the Boys

The problem with asset allocation is that it works whether you want it to or not.

BROADER DIVERSIFICATION INCREASES RETURN

Most investors by now understand that diversification reduces risk. The old adage "Don't put all your eggs in one basket" has been drilled into us for years. In fact, that wise advice has been around forever, it seems. Way back somewhere between 1200 B.C. and A.D. 500, the Talmud counselled, "Let every man divide his money into three parts and invest a third in land, a third in business and let him keep a third in reserve." A little later, in 1605, Miguel de Cervantes, the author of *Don Quixote*, stated it directly when he suggested that "'tis the part of a wise man to keep himself today for tomorrow and not venture all his eggs in one basket." Of course, both our world and the investment markets have gotten more complex over the past couple of centuries but the wisdom of diversification remains sound.

In more recent times, we have extended the "eggs in one basket" theory to now suggest that we should also have "more than one basket." We briefly talked about this in a previous chapter by suggesting that *building a portfolio that was spread among several asset classes could reduce market risk*. The modern-day terminology to describe this strategy is *asset allocation* and that's what I want to discuss now.

Asset allocation has become the buzzword of the financial services industry. Today, it seems everyone is writing about it, talking about it or offering a product or service built on its concepts. My first book, *Risk Is a Four Letter Word*, was even subtitled *The Asset Allocation Approach to Investing*. Unfortunately, with so many people trying to describe the process of asset allocation, its meaning has now been extended (and distorted) to include everything from "black box" computer-driven portfolio optimization to market timing. I don't think we need to be that complicated. To my more fundamental way of thinking, asset allocation is simply a strategy that answers two basic questions:

• What type of assets should I have in my portfolio?
• How much of each should I have?

The graph at the top of the next page shows a broadly diversified portfolio. Again, I'm not suggesting that your portfolio needs to look like this one; it is just an example to make the point that portfolios can be as varied as the people who own them. You can include anything you want in your personal investment portfolio — whatever makes sense to you to meet your objectives while staying

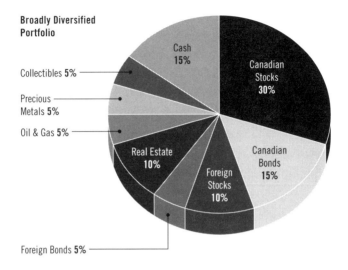

Broadly Diversified Portfolio

Cash 15%
Collectibles 5%
Precious Metals 5%
Oil & Gas 5%
Real Estate 10%
Canadian Stocks 30%
Canadian Bonds 15%
Foreign Stocks 10%
Foreign Bonds 5%

within your tolerance for risk. My assignment is to give you confidence that the choices you make are the right ones for you.

We are going to spend a fair bit of time on this portfolio construction issue because, quite frankly, how you answer the two questions posed above will be more important than just about anything else you might do in the investment process. There is an academic background to this, which we will get to soon enough. For now, let's just remind ourselves that in every major field of study or practice, occasionally there occurs a rare but vitally important breakthrough in thinking that moves that field forward to the next level of understanding or application. It has happened in medicine, molecular structure, mathematics and manufacturing, to name a few. It has happened in the profession of investing as well, and we should all know about that too. Before we get to those Nobel Prize–winning findings, however, I'd like to take a less academic approach to demonstrating the power of diversification to *improve return* and *reduce risk simultaneously*. Sound impossible? Let's see.

Suppose you have $100,000 in cash and I offer you two options for investing the money. One choice is to put the entire $100,000 into a secure investment, perhaps a long-term government bond with a yield of, say, 8 percent. The second option is to split the $100,000 into equal amounts of $20,000 and diversify among five investment opportunities with varying degrees of risk from, say, extremely risky to very conservative and with potential returns ranging, let's say, from zero to 15 percent. Specifically, the alternative investments are:

Amount	Investment	Expected Return
$20,000	Las Vegas	?%
$20,000	Under the mattress	0%
$20,000	Term deposit	5%
$20,000	Corporate debenture	10%
$20,000	Mutual fund	15%

If you choose the diversification route, you get to take $20,000 to Las Vegas and have a wonderful time. You might win but, if your experience is like mine, the casino will likely come out ahead. You might think it odd for me to include a suggestion to gamble in Las Vegas in a book about investing for "peace of mind" but the profit potential there is really no worse than it is for a number of investments I have been exposed to and better than some. At least you can have some fun in Vegas as you lose your money! But if you accept my offer of diversification, this is part of the deal: you have to throw away the first 20 percent of your money! But then, realizing that you just blew twenty grand (albeit in search of a potentially big payoff), you conclude that you had better be sure of *some* of your money, so you stuff the next $20,000 under your mattress to be left there until the day you need it. Obviously, money in such a "safe" place will not generate any return, but at least it will be there when you want it.

The third $20,000 you put into a term deposit at your bank, assuming it will yield about 5 percent over time. Then, on the recommendation of your broker, you buy a good quality corporate debenture with an interest coupon paying 10 percent, using up another $20,000 and finally, you allot the remaining $20,000 to a growth mutual fund that invests internationally and has a long-term track record of about 15 percent.

Given these two opportunities, which would you choose — the $100,000 bond investment earning 8 percent — or the diversified approach, knowing that you are going to lose the first $20,000, make nothing on the next $20,000, only 5 percent on the third, 10 percent on the fourth and 15 percent on the last $20,000?

At first glance you might think, "Well, I enjoy Las Vegas but 'better a steady dime than a rare dollar'," so you select the non-diversified investment and, indeed, that might well be the best alternative for your risk profile. However, let me add one more element to our equation: the time horizon is 25 years. Would that make a difference? I hope you are nodding your head because you now agree that the longer the time horizon, the better choice certain investments, such as stocks (represented by the mutual fund in this example), become. So let's look at the results of choosing either of these options.

	Amount	Investment	Return	Value in 25 Years
A)	$100,000	Bond	8%	$648,500
B)	$ 20,000	Las Vegas	−100%	0
	$ 20,000	Mattress	0%	$ 20,000
	$ 20,000	Term deposit	5%	$ 67,725
	$ 20,000	Corporate debenture	10%	$218,600
	$ 20,000	Mutual fund	15%	$658,375
	$100,000			**$964,700**

By following the diversified approach, you would end up with about 40 percent more money despite the fact that the first two choices you made were, at best, duds! I admit, again, to choosing numbers that make the arithmetic work out more easily for me. The message is clear — diversification among properly chosen assets can increase return!

BROADER DIVERSIFICATION REDUCES RISK

The second part of the statement I made earlier with respect to the power of diversification was that it reduces risk. Let's see if I can demonstrate that as well.

Suppose you have two investments that are identical in pattern of returns, that is, they fluctuate to the same degree and as one goes up or down, so does the other. The only difference is that one has a higher rate of return than the other does. (Mathematicians refer to such a relationship as "perfectly *positive* correlation.") You are probably asking why we would bother to have two investments with equal risk when one has a greater reward. Why not just own the better one? And indeed, that is the correct line of thinking because what we will end up with by keeping both investments is the *weighted average* of their returns, like this:

Investment	Return	% of Portfolio	Weighted Return
Investment 1	8%	50%	4%
Investment 2	12%	50%	6%
Total		**100%**	**10%**

This simple diagram shows graphically what we're talking about. All we have done in this example is put our eggs in two similar baskets rather than one. We get the average return of them both with no reduction in volatility despite the supposed diversification between two investments.

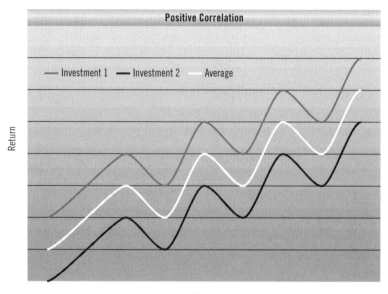

Time

EXPECTED PORTFOLIO RETURN

What we can see from this example is how we can estimate the *expected return* of a portfolio. It is simply the weighted average of the returns of the individual holdings. Here are some simple calculations to illustrate:

Investment	Return	% of Portfolio	Weighted Return
Treasury Bills	4%	25%	1.0%
Bonds	8%	25%	2.0%
Stocks	12%	50%	6.0%
Total Portfolio Weighted Return			**9.0%**

Based on our expected returns for the three basic asset classes using T-Bills, bonds and stocks as representative investments, we would expect a portfolio comprising 25 percent cash assets, 25 percent debt assets and 50 percent equities to yield us 9 percent average return over the long term. But what if 9 percent won't meet our objectives? What if we want a higher return? Well, obviously, we would have to increase the proportion of assets with higher returns, for example, trading cash assets for debt assets or equities.

Let's assume we want a return of 10 percent. The following combination would work.

Investment	Return	% of Portfolio	Weighted Return
Treasury Bills	4%	10%	0.4%
Bonds	8%	30%	2.4%
Stocks	12%	60%	7.2%
Total Portfolio Weighted Return			**10.0%**

In this example, we have reduced the T-Bill holdings from 25 percent of the portfolio to 10 percent and allocated an additional 5 percent to bonds and 10 percent to stocks. Alternatively, we could choose the following allocation:

Investment	Return	% of Portfolio	Weighted Return
Treasury Bills	4%	15%	0.6%
Bonds	8%	20%	1.6%
Stocks	12%	65%	7.8%
Total Portfolio Weighted Return			**10.0%**

In this scenario, the stock portion is further increased to 65 percent of the portfolio at the expense of bonds while the cash (T-Bill) position is strengthened. So it is possible to target a desired rate of return in several ways by mixing and matching various weightings of the individual investments to meet the objective. What's the difference among the portfolios? It would appear to be risk, wouldn't it? Higher expected returns are achieved only by including greater proportions of more aggressive assets. I am going to come back to this topic shortly with some really good news but for now, let's continue this part of the discussion.

How high can we go? Only to 12 percent, which would be a 100 percent equity portfolio. Does that mean we will actually earn the 9 or 10 or even 12 percent every time with these portfolio constructions? Of course not! We are talking about *expected* returns over the long haul. As we have discussed already, returns will fluctuate on an annual basis within some fairly large ranges. What this exercise does point out, however, is the importance of the asset allocation decision — and that leads me to introduce Gary Brinson. His research undertaken in the late 1980s has become one of the cornerstones of modern-day investment management.

Brinson focused his investigation on the question "What are the major contributors to investment success or failure?" He was able to identify three primary influences:

- ◆ Investment Policy (Asset Allocation)
  - The ratio of cash, debt and equity holdings in a portfolio
- ◆ Security Selection
  - The quality of the stocks and bonds held
- ◆ Market Timing
  - Being in or out of a market at the right time

The next chart illustrates his findings and shows that he concluded one influence was more important than any of the others.

More than 90 percent of a portfolio's performance could be attributed to the investment policy decisions or how the assets were allocated, that is, the weighting among cash, debt and equity assets. Slightly less than 5 percent was accounted for by the actual securities held in the portfolio and less than 2 percent was due to market

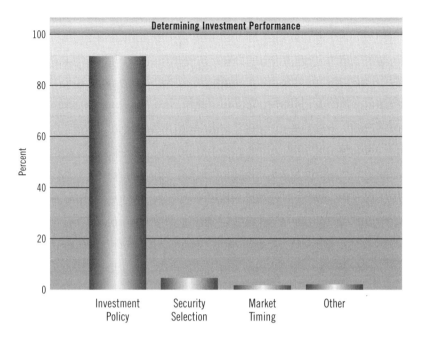

timing. In fact, in several instances among the portfolios studied, the impact of market timing efforts was actually negative! Note that there was also approximately 2 percent (labelled "Other") that could not be identified specifically. That was chalked up to luck. With this knowledge, I find it almost amusing to think about the things that we, as investors, typically want to spend most of our time doing. Isn't it trying to figure out which are the best investments to hold (security selection) and whether it is the right time to buy them (market timing)? Those are the fun activities, aren't they? Yet, if we look at the results of Brinson's study, we see that the *asset allocation decision is ten times more important* than everything else put together.

The message is clear. Time spent determining the correct asset mix for our portfolios will have a substantially greater impact on our ultimate results than any other activity. Furthermore, if we think about all the influences on investment returns, the asset allocation decision is the only one over which we have complete control. Things like whether stocks are giving us better returns than bonds, whether markets are going up or down, or the social, political and economic conditions that affect the investment environment are all beyond our influence. So it is prudent and important to spend whatever effort is required to come up with the appropriate asset mix for our personal objectives and risk tolerance.

And that is a neat segue into a discussion of the other half of the investment equation — risk. We've shown how reward is calculated as the weighted average of the holdings. Let's look now at the volatility of a portfolio and see if we can arrive at an expectation for it in a similar manner.

ESTIMATING PORTFOLIO VOLATILITY

For this part of the discussion, let's suppose we were confined to investments with the same potential returns but those returns come at exactly *opposite* times, that is, as one goes down, the other goes up. (As you might expect, this relationship is technically called a perfectly *negative* correlation.) The following diagram illustrates that situation. Again, the return would be the weighted average of returns of the two investments but the risk now *would be completely eliminated*! All the negative returns of one would be off-set by the positive returns of the other. What a marvellous situation! Regrettably, in the real world, such a combination of investments doesn't seem to exist. If it did, smart investors would never choose so-called risk-free assets such as Treasury Bills. Instead, they would look for two very risky investments with potentially high returns occurring under exactly opposite market conditions. Putting them together would result in maximum return with no risk. In actual practice, the more likely situation is that larger portfolios

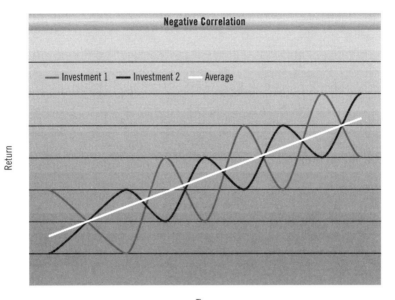

will have a number of assets with *differing*, but not necessarily opposite, patterns of returns. Then the results would resemble the graph at the top of the next page.

Once more, the overall yield of the portfolio is the weighted average of the individual assets, but the fluctuation — the risk — is dampened. In fact, if the assets are well chosen, the volatility can be reduced to the point that it is actually *possible to achieve a higher rate of return without increasing the risk*. This is the fundamental, exceptionally powerful argument in favour of diversification. It is accomplished by building a portfolio of multiple assets with low *correlation*, that is, varying patterns of performance. To fully appreciate this phenomenon of simultaneously reducing risk and increasing return, we should review the second but most important breakthrough in investment management thinking. It started back in the 1950s and the star player is another Nobel Prize winner, Harry Markowitz. The Nobel Prize, by the way, wasn't awarded to

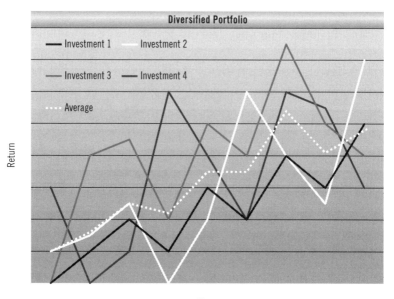

him until 1990. It takes a long time for genius to be recognized, I guess.

It is not my intention to make you into a professional investment manager nor to bore you with academic jargon and gobbledegook. Markowitz's work, however, is considered the foundation of Modern Portfolio Theory, and it is now the basis for many investment decisions made by professionals. Furthermore, the feedback I have received from investors and financial advisers alike suggests to me that at least a basic understanding of this concept goes a long way to helping decide on appropriate asset mixes — finding the right balance between desired return and potential risk. It is also the core of many software programs that perform *portfolio optimization* used by professional advisers. Additionally, the designers of most of the *managed money* products available in the marketplace today, such as "wrap" accounts or "private wealth management" services, rely on Modern Portfolio Theory to structure their recommended portfolios. We'll talk more about these products in Chapter 11. For now let's return to Harry Markowitz and see what he discovered.

REDUCING RISK WHILE INCREASING RETURN

Markowitz's major contribution to investment management thinking was to take what we have conceptually described above and render it as a mathematical formula. (Don't fear — I'm not going to inflict the formula on you!) With that statistical ability it is possible to estimate expected return *and* expected volatility of a diversified portfolio. The expected results of virtually any number and combination of assets can be estimated so that investors can choose the combination that is best for them. Most significant, Markowitz concluded that it is possible to identify the optimal portfolio mix that:

1. yields the highest rate of return for a given level of risk, or
2. has the lowest level of risk for a targeted rate of return.

As a consequence of knowing what optimal portfolios look like, in many instances *it is possible to simultaneously increase the reward and decrease the risk of a portfolio by combining various amounts of certain asset classes*. I am going to try to describe this more fully without getting lost in the statistics. For those readers who have studied these concepts in depth before, forgive some of the liberties I will take in explaining them. My objective, again and as always, is to be *approximately right rather than precisely wrong*.

First of all, Markowitz confirmed something we covered earlier — that the expected *return* of a portfolio is the weighted average of the individual assets' returns. He found, however, that the expected *volatility* of a portfolio wasn't quite so straightforward. Recall that I previously introduced the notion of *correlation* of returns. I said they could be *positive*, meaning they move more or less in lock step with each other, or *negative* in that they move in opposite directions. The mathematical expression of this relationship is the *correlation coefficient* and it is written as a decimal number and interpreted as a percentage. For example, a *perfectly positive correlation* of returns between two investments would show a value of +1.000, which would indicate that the two assets move up and down from their average returns in 100 percent tandem. A *perfectly negative correlation* would have a value of –1.000, meaning that they were 100 percent opposite in their movements — as one goes up, the other goes down. In between is the full range of correlation. Two investments with a correlation coefficient of, say, +0.600, would mean that as one moves up or down, the other moves in the *same* direction (because it is a positive number) but only moves 60 percent as far. A correlation coefficient of, say, –0.750, would imply a 75 percent movement in the *opposite* direction and so on. With this insight, Markowitz was able to calculate the expected volatility of a portfolio by mathematically combining the individual asset weightings, standard deviations and the correlation of returns among them. Again, I'm not going to suggest in any way that we all need to know how to do this stuff — but I do think the background helps us appreciate that successful investing is more than just technical skill or good luck — there is a little science in it too.

As a matter of interest, at the top of the next page is a table of correlation coefficients among a number of popular asset classes.

Among other details, you can see that the correlation between Canadian and U.S. equities is relatively high (+.740) while the correlation between Canadian and international equities is relatively low (–.020). Based on what we have just discussed, *from a risk reduction standpoint,* we would achieve a better result combining international equities with Canadian equities than by putting U.S. and Canadian equities together. Real estate has a low correlation with just about everything except cash, so it would likely be a good

Correlation Coefficients

	T-Bills ($CA)	T-Bills ($U.S.)	Bonds ($CA)	Bonds ($Int'l)	Stocks (CA)	Stocks (U.S.)	Stocks (Int'l)	Real Estate
T-Bills ($CA)	1.000	+.862	+.307	+.268	−.100	−.100	−.090	+.389
T-Bills ($U.S.)		1.000	−.100	−.230	+.003	−.090	−.120	+.529
Bonds ($CA)			1.000	+.712	+.075	+.326	+.304	−.250
Bonds ($Int'l)				1.000	+.087	+.275	+.380	−.150
Stocks (CA)					1.000	+.740	+.741	−.020
Stocks (U.S.)						1.000	+.891	−.200
Stocks (Int'l)							1.000	−.160
Real Estate								1.000

addition to a portfolio if we were trying to reduce risk, and so on.

From these findings, Markowitz determined that investors should do more than try to maximize expected return in their portfolios because that would be ignoring the risk reduction that could be obtained from diversification. He demonstrated that, for various levels of risk, it was possible to identify particular combinations of assets that had the best return potential. Consequently, we should all *look for that combination that gives us the greatest potential return for the level of risk we are prepared to accept.* Markowitz went on to describe these "superior" combinations as "efficient," meaning that they did the best job of matching risk and reward. He then proceeded to plot these combinations on a graph that he called the "efficient frontier." Let me illustrate by showing what happens when we mix just two of our three major asset classes. I'll use Treasury Bills and stocks in this example.

Suppose we start with a portfolio of 100 percent Treasury Bills. In the graph on the next page, that is represented by Portfolio A in the lower half, just right of centre of the diagram. Now we add a small amount of stocks to the portfolio, say 5 percent to begin with.

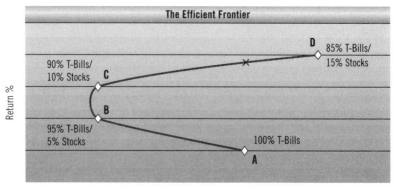

Surprisingly, when we run this combination through a computer model that incorporates expected return, asset weightings and correlation coefficients, we find that the anticipated risk actually *declines* while the expected return *increases*, as is shown by Portfolio B. As a rational investor, I would prefer Portfolio B over Portfolio A because it gives me the best of both worlds — improved returns and lower risk! Hard to imagine, isn't it? We can actually reduce risk by adding so-called risky assets to our portfolio.

How far can we go with this? Is there a limit? The answer, of course, is "Yes," and we can begin to see that if we increase the stock portion by an additional 5 percent, to 10 percent (C). The result is a further rise in the expected return, but notice that this time the risk expectation doesn't change. Portfolio C has the same standard deviation as Portfolio B. Again, I would prefer to have the better performing asset mix — that of Portfolio C — over Portfolio B because the expected returns are higher and, although there is no reduction in risk this time it doesn't increase either.

It would appear, however, that we have now turned the corner on the opportunity to maximize return for a given level of risk. If we continue the process, we see that expanding the stock portion to 15 percent (Portfolio D), for example, has the effect of further improving return, as we would expect, but the risk reverses its declining trend and starts to increase. Clearly, then, there is a portfolio mix somewhere between Portfolio C and Portfolio D (X marks the spot) where we will achieve a higher expected return than a 100 percent T-Bill portfolio yet have no greater risk. Following Markowitz's advice, if our objective was simply to get the maximum return for the least amount of risk, we should structure our portfolio with a mix that approximates the one represented by position X.

The diagram just shown is an exaggerated or very closely detailed illustration of the actual risk and return changes that occur with various combinations of stocks and T-Bills. It's like one of those "insert" sections of a roadmap that provides close-up street information for key areas that cannot be adequately shown on the full-scale version. For your interest, here is the actual efficient frontier for the full range of combinations of T-Bills and stocks. The framed area at the left end of the graph is the "insert."

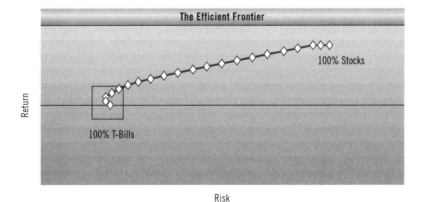

In the real world, many investors are willing to take on something more than the least amount of risk. You're more likely to choose a portfolio somewhere further along the efficient frontier, that is, at a point beyond Portfolio D (85 percent T-Bills/15 percent stocks).

Also bear in mind that so far we have dealt only with a simple portfolio of two assets. This process can become as detailed and sophisticated as we want it to be. Recall our diagram of portfolio possibilities back in Chapter 3? It included 18 different types of investments as an example of a very broadly diversified portfolio. You can imagine the number of calculations of weightings, standard deviations and correlation coefficients that would be required to come up with an optimal portfolio. That is why this work is left to computers. It is also one of the reasons we are not going to go any further with this discussion. As I stated at the beginning, I don't want to get mired in the technicalities of this but to provide a basic understanding of the underlying concepts of Modern Portfolio Theory. The important message and the lesson we learned from Harry Markowitz is that *broad diversification among assets with varying patterns of return will improve return and decrease risk.* We knew this intuitively and now we have scientific proof.

ALLOCATING YOUR ASSETS IN THE REAL WORLD

Now I'd like to show you how, in the real world, you can structure your portfolio without the aid of high-powered computer programs and arrive at an approximate asset allocation that will meet your financial objectives and be aligned with your personal tolerance for risk. Compared to what we have just described with respect to the work of Harry Markowitz, you are likely going to be surprised at how uncomplicated this process can be. In fact, you might even wonder if something so simple really works. Believe me, it does. While the computer has enabled us to take the science of investing to a higher level, good old-fashioned common sense and intuition can still do a pretty good job.

Before we get started on the process itself, I want to say that I hope you are aware that we are developing a process for making investment decisions that will serve you well, not only now, but for many years to come. Whatever decisions you make must be appropriate for today and yet flexible enough to meet your needs, as they will inevitably change over time. It is vital, therefore, that each step be thoroughly completed before the next is begun. It's like building our pyramid; you can't start at the top and work down because each level has to be solid enough to support all those above it. I also hope it is clear that, as I take you up the pyramid, you're making the transition from *general* notions to *specific* tactics. Level 3 — Asset Allocation — takes the concepts developed so far and puts them into action. The asset allocation decisions you make in this chapter will be the framework for constructing your portfolio, but their long-term usefulness will be directly related to the strength of the underlying assumptions about your personal philosophy and objectives.

With these thoughts in mind, let's look at the asset allocation step. Simply, it is a matter of answering the following question:

"Given my personal philosophies (risk tolerance and investor personality) and my objectives, what percentage of my assets should be allocated for *growth*, what percentage for *income* and what percentage for *liquidity*?"

Another way of asking this question is "Based on what I said in my Level 1 and Level 2 statements about who I am and what I am trying to accomplish, how should I structure my portfolio?"

The first question focuses on the investment *objective*. It could also be restated by substituting the name of the asset class that we identified earlier as being most appropriate for each objective:

"Given my personal philosophy (risk tolerance and investor personality) and my objectives, what percentage of my assets should be allocated to equities, what percentage to debt, and what percentage to cash?"

Or distilling it even further, using the three specific investments on which we have relied so far, you could ask something like this:

"Given my personal philosophy (risk tolerance and investor personality) and my objectives, what percentage of my investments should be held in *stocks*, what percentage in *bonds* and what percentage in *T-Bills*?"

You're going to come to the same result, regardless of the approach you take. The important thing to note here is that we did not, in any of the above examples, waver from the underlying assumptions with respect to philosophy and objectives. The asset allocation decision is founded on those two fundamentals, which are unique to you.

So here is the secret of successful asset allocation — *figure out what it is you are trying to accomplish with your investment strategy and then organize your portfolio in the way that is most likely to make it happen.*

What does that mean?

Let's start with something we developed in the last chapter and that is: there is a direct and obvious link between our objectives (growth, income or liquidity) and the three major asset classes. It looks like this:

- Growth — Equity
- Income — Debt
- Liquidity — Cash

The asset allocation decision, then, is pretty straightforward. If my primary objective is *growth*, I should include a significant amount of equity in my portfolio because *equities have historically shown the highest rate of growth*. If it is to provide *income*, I should have considerable *debt-type assets* because *they offer the most consistent income flow* and if the objective is *liquidity*, *cash-type assets* should probably dominate, as *they are most liquid*. Pretty simple, huh?

The next question is "How much of each?" The answer is a familiar one — it depends on your risk tolerance. Let me use myself as an example.

At my age, my primary investment objective continues to be *growth*. I am not yet at the stage that I want to draw income from my portfolio and I do not have large liquid cash needs because I have a good credit rating and can readily borrow funds for an emergency or opportunity should one of those contingencies arise. Consequently, it makes sense for me to make up a substantial portion of my portfolio with equity investments. Does that mean 100 percent equities? The answer is an emphatic "No" because my risk tolerance won't permit me to do that. Despite the fact that I have been in this business for many years and I know that over time equities will outperform, I still find peace of mind in a more diversified or balanced portfolio. So I have to ask myself, "With what percentage of equities *would* I be comfortable?" Suppose the answer is 70 percent. I should be prepared, then, to allocate 70 percent of the value of my portfolio to equity-type investments.

What about the 30 percent that's left?

Having dealt with the primary objective of growth first, I would likely jump to the *least* important objective next, which, in my instance would be *liquidity*. Now I would ask myself, "What percentage of my portfolio do I want available in liquid form for emergencies or opportunities?" Knowing, as I said earlier, that I am probably able to obtain money for such occasions fairly easily, I would opt to keep only a minimum amount of my assets in the relatively low-yielding cash-type assets — say, 10 percent. I do want some money here so I don't have to run to the bank for every little thing and it also helps when borrowing if you have some of your own funds to commit as well.

So far, then, my asset allocation looks like this:

- Equity   70%
- Cash   10%
  Total **80%**

Having used up 80 percent of my portfolio, there is now only one place left to put the balance and that is in the debt category. The final asset allocation, then, is:

- Equity   70%
- Debt   20%
- Cash   10%
  Total **100%**

Broadly speaking, the asset allocation decision does not need to be any more complicated than that — determine what you want to do, weight the portfolio in favour of the asset class most likely to meet that objective and balance it for your risk tolerance. In the next chapter, I am going to show you how to make this more complicated but, believe me, even such a naïve approach to asset allocation will improve the overall performance results of many investors. Recall Gary Brinson's findings that more than 90 percent of a portfolio's performance is determined by the asset allocation. Get that even approximately right and the race is won from the start!

DETERMINING EXPECTED RETURN AND EXPECTED VOLATILITY

Not everyone would be happy just leaving things at this point with the broad diversification. Most of us would also want some idea of the return and risk we can expect from the mix we have chosen. That's easy because we have already been through this.

Calculating Expected Return and Risk — The Easy Way

Earlier in the chapter, we saw how the expected return of a portfolio is the *weighted average* of the individual assets' returns, like this:

Investment	Return	% of Portfolio	Weighted Return
Treasury Bills	4%	25%	1.0%
Bonds	8%	25%	2.0%
Stocks	12%	50%	6.0%
Total Portfolio Weighted Return			**9.0%**

We went on to say that it would not be entirely accurate to follow the same approach when trying to estimate volatility because we would be overstating the risk. Volatility would actually be reduced owing to the *correlation* of returns among the assets. Just for fun, though, let's do it anyway. The result would be:

Investment	Volatility	% of Portfolio	Weighted Volatility
Treasury Bills	±3%	25%	±0.75%
Bonds	±9%	25%	±2.25%
Stocks	±15%	50%	±7.50%
Total Portfolio Weighted Risk			**±10.50%**

Now let me run that same mix through the computer to see how it calculates the overall portfolio risk. The result is a volatility expectation of ±9.0 percent. So . . . we get ±9.0 percent using the sophistication of a portfolio optimization program or ±10.5 percent using the simple weighted average approach. Hmmm . . .

I say, who cares? Over the long term during which I am going to be managing my portfolio, how much difference is it going to make to me if my returns normally fluctuate *on an annual basis* by ±9.0 percent or ±10.5 percent? I suspect that it won't matter very much at all. If you have access to asset allocation software, on your own or through your financial adviser, use it. You will get more accurate results. On the other hand, don't let not having that software prevent you from putting together a portfolio that matches your objective and risk tolerance. Use the simple weighted average method to calculate both expected return and expected volatility.

What's the worst that will happen? You'll overestimate the risk. Is that so bad? I'd much rather err on the conservative side — overestimating risk — and then be pleasantly surprised. Wouldn't you?

JUGGLING RISK AND REWARD

Here are the steps in the asset allocation process so far:

1. Determine primary objective.
2. Determine secondary objective.
3. Balance portfolio for risk tolerance.
4. Calculate expected return.
5. Calculate expected volatility.

As we have seen previously, it is possible to come up with a number of asset mixes that yield the same return. As you might expect, you can also create several combinations of assets that will have approximately similar anticipated volatility. You may want to do some trial-and-error number crunching to end up with the blend that is best for you. It is also quite likely that you will end up making a tradeoff between risk and reward. If you find yourself in that situation, here are the rules to follow:

Rule 1 — *All other things being equal, if the expected returns are approximately the same, choose the portfolio with the lowest expected risk.*

Of course, that makes sense, doesn't it? Why take on extra risk with no prospect of enhanced reward?

Rule 2 — *All other things being equal, if the expected risk is about the same, choose a portfolio with the highest expected return.*

Do we have a conflict here? I'm suggesting that you choose, on the one hand, the portfolio with the least risk and on the other, the portfolio with the greatest expected return. Of course we have a conflict. That's what this whole exercise is about. To whatever degree of accuracy you desire, you can come up with a portfolio that approximates the level of risk you are willing to assume or the target rate of return necessary to meet your objectives. It is most likely, however, that these two portfolios will be mutually exclusive because, as we know, low risk and high returns are seldom found in the same asset allocation.

If you have two choices — to target return or to match risk tolerance — which one should you choose? Both will work; however, as you might suspect, my preference is to approach the asset allocation decision from the risk management side rather than trying to put together a portfolio with an expected rate of return sufficient to meet my objectives. Here's my reasoning, which relates back to the quest for "peace of mind" investing.

Target Risk Rather than Return

Let's suppose that you have a net worth of $10,000. You are sitting at home one evening reading the newspaper when you discover that your ticket in the provincial lottery just won $10,000. Your psychological well-being is going to be increased by your discovery. Right? Of course, you just doubled your net worth from $10,000 to $20,000! But what if your net worth was, say, $1,000,000, when you won the ten grand? Your net worth, in that instance, would have increased by 1 percent to $1,010,000, so your psychological well-being will still go up — but not by as much as if you had a $10,000 net worth. More money is always better but the psychological lift we get from each additional dollar gets less and less. In other words, the dollar we already have is worth more to us than the dollar we have yet to receive.

Economists refer to this as the "declining marginal utility of wealth" — more money is always better but it is better at a diminishing rate. In an investment context, if we have the prospect of either gaining a dollar or losing one, we'd likely prefer to avoid the loss. In fact, earlier we noted that behavioural scientists have concluded that, on average, it takes a $2 gain to psychologically compensate us for a $1 loss. For the sake of our peace of mind, then, I prefer to do my asset allocation by focusing on risk rather than return. *By setting an upper limit on the amount of risk you are willing to assume, you automatically put a ceiling on the rate of return you can realistically expect to earn from your portfolio.* It is then a fairly straightforward matter of calculating the capital requirements necessary to meet your objectives using that rate of return. If the requirements are too onerous, objectives have to be scaled down, risk tolerance expanded or some combination of both implemented.

There is one final point regarding asset allocation: it works whether you want it to or not! By definition, a diversified portfolio will always underperform one or more of the asset classes contained within it. This may be obvious but when one asset class is generating substantially higher returns than normal, it is easy to be lured into thinking that the asset mix should be changed to "chase" those higher returns. This would mean increasing the weighting in the outperforming area by decreasing it in others. The immediate effect, of course, would be to change the long-term risk/reward profile of the portfolio, and if the changes are radical, chances are you would fail to meet your ultimate objective with regard to volatility or return. The real value of a good asset allocation strategy is that it protects us from ourselves!

With this background knowledge, it is time for you to take a shot at writing out your Level 3 statement, identifying the basic asset allocation you feel will be within your risk tolerance and yet still address your objectives. I say "take a shot" because it is quite possible that the proportions for the three basic asset classes you set out now may well be changed just a few pages further along in this book. Don't be alarmed by this. There is some trial and error to this process as we narrow our attention down to the specific assets you will have in your portfolio. That is why each time I asked you to write a part of your Investment Statement, I also suggested that you go back and review what you did for previous levels. As you gain more insight into the asset allocation concept, you'll probably fine-tune your thinking. So for now, draft the fundamental asset allocation which, based on what we have done so far, seems appropriate for your portfolio. Complete your Level 3 statement by answering our question:

"Given my personal philosophy (risk tolerance and investor personality) and my objectives, what percentage of my assets should be allocated growth (or equities), what percentage for income (debt) and what percentage for liquidity (or cash)?"

You will note that I have asked you to make this statement with regard to your objective for the three major asset classes only. We will identify the specific assets in Level 4. Following is a table of suggested portfolio balances, ranked by age, as compiled by one of Canada's leading accounting firms, to help you out a little further in deciding what might be the appropriate asset allocation for you. These percentages are guidelines only, reflecting an academic view of the population at large. You must assign your own values in light of your personal Level 1 and Level 2 statements. Again you might find it a useful reminder to re-state those comments below. I have also offered some sample Level 3 statements.

	Suggested Asset Mix by Age		
Age	Cash	Debt	Equity
20s	35–50%	20–30%	20–35%
30s	10–15%	15–25%	60–80%
40s	5–10%	25–35%	70–80%
50s	5–10%	30–40%	50–60%
60s	20–30%	35–50%	20–35%
70s	30–50%	40–60%	20–35%

LEVEL 3   ASSET ALLOCATION STATEMENTS

"My portfolio will be composed of 20 percent liquid, 30 percent income and 50% growth assets. With this combination, I expect a long-range average return of approximately 10 percent and an average volatility of ±11 percent."

"My portfolio will consist of 15 percent cash, 40 percent debt and 45 percent equity investments. This should result in an average return of 10 percent over time with annual volatility in the range of ±11 percent."

Now write out yours.

Level 1

_____

_____

_____

Level 2

_____

_____

_____

Level 3

_____

_____

_____

Let's climb to the top of the pyramid now and select some securities.

- Asset allocation is simply a strategy that answers two basic questions:
  - What type of assets should I have in my portfolio?
  - How much of each should I have?
- More than 90 percent of a portfolio's performance can be attributed to the asset allocation decision (Gary Brinson).
- It is possible to simultaneously increase reward and decrease risk of a portfolio by combining various amounts of certain asset classes (Harry Markowitz).
- We should all look for that combination that gives us the greatest return for the level of risk we are prepared to accept.
- The "secret" of successful asset allocation is to
  - Figure out what it is you are trying to accomplish with your investment strategy.
  - Organize your portfolio in the way most likely to accomplish it.
- By setting an upper limit on the amount of risk you are willing to assume, you automatically put a ceiling on the rate of return you can realistically expect to earn.

9 Selecting Your Securities

Whatever method you use to pick securities, your ultimate success or failure will depend on your ability to ignore the worries of the world long enough to allow your investments to succeed.
— PETER LYNCH, *BEATING THE STREET*

The final step in the portfolio design process is to choose the specific investments we want to include among our holdings. By now you have a good understanding of the relative merits of cash, debt and equity assets. You also know how to arrive at the percentage weightings to be given to each of those asset classes, keeping in mind your objectives and risk tolerance. Now let's continue this narrowing process — from those more general decisions to the very specific ones about which securities to own.

As I've said, this is the part of the investment process on which many of us want to spend most of our time because it is the most fun. It is also where we think we can have the most impact. Every day the newspapers, radios and TV are filled with details about the success or failure of one company or another or the rise and fall of bond prices or mortgage rates. Then there is page after page of columns of mutual fund performance data. It is no wonder that we have come to feel this is where we should spend so much of our energy. However, as Gary Brinson proved with his famous study of the determinants of portfolio performance, security selection explains only a small portion of the final results we achieve. Nevertheless, it does have strong psychological importance to us, so let's look at a couple of approaches for handling this part of the process.

Let's stick with the example of my personal objectives and asset allocation as set out in the last chapter. Recall that my primary investment objective was *growth* but that I wasn't prepared to own a 100 percent equity portfolio due to my risk tolerance. I had decided on the following mix:

* Equity   70%
* Debt   20%
* Cash   10%
  Total   **100%**

THE SIMPLEST APPROACH — A PACKAGED SOLUTION

We can choose our securities to put together a similar portfolio in a number of ways. Let's start with the simplest, which would be to find a *balanced mutual fund* where the fund portfolio is made up of those approximate percentage holdings. We'll discuss mutual funds in more detail in a later chapter, but for now, let's acknowledge that there are mutual finds available that invest in fixed percentages of the three major asset classes. Almost all mutual funds maintain some *cash* to handle redemptions — frequently in the 5 to 10 percent range. Once the cash component is allocated, many so-called *balanced* funds have prescribed percentages allocated to debt and equity securities. This could be 50 percent of the remainder of the fund to each or 60/40, 70/30 and so on, depending on the fund's investment philosophy. These percentages (or specific ranges within which they must be kept) are often prescribed in the mutual fund's prospectus. Searching through a mutual fund database or looking to your professional adviser for advice, it would not be too difficult to find a fund that came very close to most popular asset allocations. The mutual fund manager would then do the security selection in these funds for you. This means selecting the stock and bonds he or she felt would perform consistently. The manager would periodically trade some of those securities for performance reasons or to maintain the balance among the asset classes according to the fund's investment philosophy as described in the prospectus.

For smaller portfolios, and particularly for investors who adhere strictly to the Passive Money Manager approach described in Chapter 6, these funds may be just the ticket. However, if you are looking for something slightly more aggressive than a fixed percentage balanced fund, you might be interested in the *asset allocation* mutual funds available in the market. The strategy employed by the managers of these funds could generally be considered a refinement of the first approach in that the fund managers do try to maintain a balance between cash, debt and equities but the mix is not as rigidly enforced. The managers are normally free to adjust the percentages in each asset class depending on their view of the market. When they become optimistic about the stock market, for example, they may increase the equity portion; when they are less enthusiastic, they may increase their bond or cash holdings. Some managers are given more leeway than others to adjust the asset allocation. The more aggressive funds are often described as "tactical" asset allocation funds while less aggressive ones are frequently called "strategic" asset allocation funds. In the latter case, the managers are frequently constrained to maintain a minimum percentage in each asset class regardless of how they feel about the markets so that the funds can legitimately be labelled as "balanced" or "asset allocation" funds rather than "market timing" funds. They would seldom be allowed to have 100 percent of the portfolio in any single asset class or to completely exclude one.

To further our discussion, let's assume that you want to be more actively involved in the selection of the securities you will hold in your portfolio. Alternatively, even if you decide to use one of these "packaged" approaches described above, the following process may assist you in deciding which one to choose.

THE SECURITY SELECTION PROCESS

Step 1

Let's return to my sample portfolio of 70 percent equities, 20 percent debt assets and 10 percent cash. In determining which specific securities to include, I'd normally concentrate on the equity portion first because it is the largest and, therefore, the most important component. In keeping with my fundamental philosophy, I'd try to address the issue of risk before I did anything else. To do this, I might begin by dividing the equity part of my portfolio into the risk categories of conservative, aggressive and speculative. Then I'd assign weighting to each of these categories to parallel my risk profile. For simplicity, let's assume my assets available for investment total $100,000. Given that, I may choose to organize the equity portion something like this:

Equity Groups	% of Equity Portfolio	% of Total Portfolio	$ Value of Total Portfolio
Conservative	50%	50% x 70% = 35%	$35,000
Aggressive	30%	30% x 70% = 21%	$21,000
Speculative	20%	20% x 70% = 14%	$14,000
Totals	**100%**	**70%**	**$70,000**

This arrangement puts half of my equity component in conservative securities and half in aggressive-to-speculative choices. As a result, when I look at my *overall* portfolio, I see that slightly more than one-third of my total portfolio would be invested in conservative equity securities and the same amount in aggressive-to-speculative choices.

Step 2

I would next say to myself, "Okay, I want 70 percent of my portfolio in equities. Now, with what type of equities am I familiar and comfortable?" From that question, I might end up with a list that looked something like this:

- Growth mutual funds
- Individual common stocks
- Real estate
- Business interests
- Collectibles
- Options

Your list might be longer or shorter depending on your own experience and preferences. Bear in mind that whatever securities you choose should give you some confidence that they will meet your needs and be within your tolerance for risk. I may like the potential return of investing in real estate because I have had success in doing so before. But if I had been burned in one of the numerous real estate boom-bust cycles we have experienced across Canada, I may be considerably less willing to include that type of security in my portfolio again, even if I felt it had a good return potential. The psychological discomfort may outweigh promise of reward. For our purposes right now, let's assume the above is my list of eligible securities.

Step 3

The next step would be to evaluate the list of potential investments in relation to *my perception* of their risk by matching each choice to the descriptions I have developed. For example, I included growth mutual funds as one type of equity security in which I would be interested. But growth comes in many disguises in the world of investing. Mutual funds invested in well-known, multinational companies with large stock market presence (capitalization) are, in a long-term market history, generally considered *conservative* equity investments. On the other hand, funds that invest exclusively in one major field, such as biotechnology, telecommunications, precious metals or single country funds that focus on developing countries are broadly deemed more aggressive. Yet all of these funds could be labelled as growth funds. Consequently, this may require me to subdivide the broader groups into something more definitive, particularly if my portfolio is large enough to permit me to diversify across some of the sub-asset classes as well as the three major ones. I would then be able to weight these more specific types of securities into my *equity* component. The result may look like this:

Equity Groups	Security Selection	% of Portfolio	$ Value of Portfolio
Conservative ($35,000)	Large Cap Canadian Equity Mutual Fund	20%	$20,000
	Large Cap. U.S. Equity Mutual Fund	5%	$ 5,000
	IBM	5%	$ 5,000
	TD Bank	5%	$ 5,000
Aggressive ($21,000)	Canadian Special Equity Mutual Fund	10%	$10,000
	Asia Pacific Equity Mutual Fund	5%	$ 5,000
	Microsoft	6%	$ 6,000
Speculative ($14,000)	Amazon.com	7%	$ 7,000
	Wayne Gretzky Memorabilia	7%	$ 7,000

So in the conservative equity category, I have diversified by choosing a Canadian and a U.S. large cap fund and two blue chip stocks.

For the more aggressive position, I have chosen a more narrowly focused Canadian fund that invests in smaller, specialized industry companies along with a foreign fund concentrated in one geographic area of the world known for its superior return potential which is often accompanied by higher volatility. I have completed the category by including a relatively young, fast-growing, yet enormously successful global firm.

Finally, on the very aggressive or speculative front, I am going to try to ride the wave of dot.com stocks with one of the major players in that explosive field. And finally, speaking of players, I have decided that memorabilia connected with the world's greatest hockey star is going to multiply in value now that he is retired from the game, so I am going to try to speculate on that. Anyway, if it doesn't work out, I'll be the proud owner of a couple of sweaters bearing the number 99 along with a few autographed hockey sticks! (Investing can be fun too!)

So that is how we might go about completing the *equity* security selection. Let's move to the next largest component — *debt*. The process is the same. Only the subdivision, if applicable to my portfolio size, differs. In our example, I have subdivided the debt portion of the portfolio by maturity date of the potential holdings. It may look something like this:

Debt Groups	Security Selection	% of Portfolio	$ Value of Portfolio
Short-Term (1–2 years) ($5,000)	Bank Term Deposit	5%	$5,000
Mid-Term (3–5 years) ($5,000)	3-Year GIC	5%	$5,000
Long-Term (5 years+) ($10,000)	Canadian Bond Mutual Fund	5%	$5,000
	International Bond Mutual Fund	5%	$5,000

Finally, we'd address the *cash* component in a similar way:

Cash Groups	Security Selection	% of Portfolio	$ Value of Portfolio
Very Liquid ($5,000)	Bank Account	5%	$ 5,000
Liquid ($5,000)	Money Market Fund	5%	$ 5,000

So there we have it — the security selection is complete. Obviously, I have left out entirely the part where you evaluate the merits of the various securities themselves. Though important, I ignored that step for two reasons; first, because I wanted to emphasize the *process*, not the products, and second, because security evaluation is such a broad topic that it would fill a book itself. Determining *which* large-cap Canadian equity fund is the right one for you or whether you should own Microsoft stock rather than Intel stock is a matter of your own preference or, perhaps, the recommendation of your professional adviser. My mission is to provide you with a framework you can use while you carry out that investigation. On that note, here is a summary worksheet that you might find useful. Modify it in any way that makes it more meaningful to you. For simplicity, I have tried to maintain some consistency with the examples we have used so far. Regardless of the number and descriptions of the categories and divisions you use, the procedure is essentially the same:

1. Start by filling in the dollar amount of your total (100%) portfolio at the top of the chart.
2. Divide that amount into percentages and dollar amounts for each asset class according to the allocation decisions you made in the previous chapter (first column).
3. Subdivide as appropriate for your situation (percentages and dollar values).
4. Select your preferred securities and assign dollar values.

Total Portfolio (100%): $

Asset Class	Asset Allocation	Name of Security	$ Amount
CASH (%)	Very Liquid (%)	1.	
$	$	2.	
	Liquid (%)	1.	
	$	2.	
DEBT (%)	Short-Term (%)	1.	
$	$	2.	

Total Portfolio (100%): $ _____

Asset Class	Asset Allocation	Name of Security	$ Amount
	Mid-Term (%)	1.	
	$	2.	
	Long-Term (%)	1.	
	$	2.	
EQUITY (%)	Conservative (%)	1.	
$	$	2.	
		3.	
		4.	
	Aggressive (%)	1.	
	$	2.	
		3.	
		4.	
	Speculative (%)	1.	
	$	2.	
		3.	
		4.	
		Total	**$**

A word of caution: if you use this worksheet, the total dollar value at the bottom right should equal the one you started with at the top of the chart. Don't allocate more money than you have!

WORKING WITH LARGER PORTFOLIOS

You can also see that the worksheet allows for two specific securities in each of the cash and debt groupings and four in each of the equity categories. That is just for convenience and illustration. You may not use all the spaces on the worksheet or you may wish to add more. This leads to the question of how to deal with a substantial portfolio in which it is possible to achieve a much broader diversification. And, as shown earlier, broader diversification is generally better over the long term. Not surprisingly, the *process* with a larger portfolio is identical — the difference is just that you have more options from which to choose for the specific securities to include. Let me illustrate by comparing our original example of a $100,000 portfolio with a $1,000,000 portfolio. We'll consider the conservative equity component only for simplicity, knowing that the same procedure could be applied to the aggressive and speculative equity portions as well as to the cash and debt holdings.

Conservative Equity (35%)	Total $ Value	Securities	$ Value
$100,000 Portfolio	$35,000	Large Cap Canadian Equity Mutual Fund	$20,000
		Large Cap U.S. Equity Mutual Fund	$ 5,000
		IBM	$ 5,000
		TD Bank	$ 5,000
$1,000,000 Portfolio	$350,000	Large Cap Canadian Equity Mutual Fund 1	$ 50,000
		Large Cap Canadian Equity Mutual Fund 2	$ 50,000
		Large Cap Canadian Equity Mutual Fund 3	$ 50,000
		Large Cap Canadian Equity Mutual Fund 4	$ 50,000
		Total	*$200,000*
		Large Cap U.S. Equity Mutual Fund 1	$ 25,000
		Large Cap U.S. Equity Mutual Fund 2	$ 25,000
		Total	*$ 50,000*

Conservative Equity (35%)	Total $ Value	Securities	$ Value
$1,000,000 Portfolio (cont'd)		Conservative Stock 1	$ 10,000
		Conservative Stock 2	$ 10,000
		Conservative Stock 3	$ 10,000
		Conservative Stock 4	$ 10,000
		Conservative Stock 5	$ 10,000
		Total	*$ 50,000*

Clearly, this is a dramatic oversimplification, and there would be issues surrounding how you make choices like those outlined above, such as concentration and duplication. For example, many equity funds that invest in Canadian companies with large stock market capitalization will, by necessity, end up owning the same stocks. This is simply because the Canadian large-cap market is highly concentrated among a fairly small number of companies and most portfolio managers with a mandate to invest in that market would want to include the best performing ones in their funds. There are ways around this issue, such as seeking out managers who follow a value approach to investing and pairing them in your portfolio with managers who follow a growth approach. I'll have more to say about this in Chapter 11 when we discuss the subject of professionally managed money. For now, the important point to be made is that the process of security selection may become more *extensive* as the size of the portfolio increases, but it doesn't have to be any more complex.

LEVEL 4   SECURITY SELECTION STATEMENT

We have climbed to the top of the pyramid. It is time for you to write out your Level 4 Statement on security selection. Depending on your preferences, it can be as simple or detailed as you wish. Here is a relatively uncomplicated rendering from our earlier example:

"My portfolio will have the following types of securities:

Cash	—	Very Liquid	5%
	—	Liquid	5%
			10%

Debt	—	Short-term	5%
	—	Mid-term	5%
	—	Long-term	10%
			20%

Equity	—	Conservative	35%
	—	Aggressive	20%
	—	Speculative	15%
			70%"

Or you could be more specific and include a worksheet such as the one presented earlier in this chapter — whatever amount of detail appeals to you. One point here: the more specific you are, the more frequently you are going to have to review your Investment Statement. As I have stated (and, I hope, proven), the Level 4 Security Selection is the easiest part of the process because the foundation was laid by all the decisions that went before it regarding philosophy, objectives and asset allocation. Consequently, Level 4 is the part of your Investment Statement most likely to change. As time passes, you will develop new preferences or alternatives for some of your original investments and want to incorporate or substitute them into your portfolio. If you spell out exactly what your holdings are, you will have to rewrite the Level 4 part of the Investment Statement each time you change securities. But that isn't all bad and, in fact, it may be worthwhile to impose such discipline on yourself, because it should also cause you to at least reflect on your Levels 1, 2 and 3 comments to ensure that they remain current and relevant. If you think, however, that you are going to be a fairly active trader of securities, keep your Level 4 Statement quite broad and schedule a review of the other three parts of the Investment Statement on at least an annual basis.

Recall that I suggested in the last chapter that you might want to fine-tune your Level 3 notes once you have a little more information, particularly as it applies to a multiple-asset portfolio. Here is your chance to do that.

Level 1

_____

_____

_____

Level 2

_____

_____

_____

Level 3

_____

_____

_____

Level 4

_____

_____

_____

KEEPING TABS ON YOURSELF

You should now have a complete four-part Investment Statement. I encourage you to date and sign it, for a number of reasons. First, it will remind you of the time and context within which you made the decisions contained in it. If your thinking changes or any of the assumptions on which you based your choices subsequently become invalid (for example, the expected return or expected volatility of any of the assets turns out to be very different from what was anticipated), you will have a reference point from which to consider amendments. In addition, as new investment opportunities present themselves, you will be able to evaluate them in light of what you have written. If something appeals to you as an investment but doesn't seem to fit into the original plan, you can go back to the time and circumstances under which you constructed the portfolio and see if anything has altered that would now permit you to include the new investment in your portfolio. Once again, I repeat — this is your plan. It is not chiselled in stone and can (and will likely) be amended as time passes. The paramount thing is that it be meaningful and relevant in light of your current goals and investor personality.

And finally, if you are going to use the services of a professional financial planner or investment adviser, both of you will welcome a written statement as a point of reference for your intentions and as a benchmark for performance. In Chapter 12, I am going to introduce an Investment Policy Statement similar to one you should expect to receive from a professional adviser, so I'll have more to say on this subject there.

We have gone through all four levels of the pyramid, spelling out your personal philosophy, setting objectives, determining asset allocation and selecting appropriate securities. Let us now do a quick review of the steps followed in designing your strategy and portfolio.

[Level 1 | Investment Philosophy]

Through a process of determining your personal *risk tolerance* and *investor personality*, you carry out one of the mandatory requirements for anyone giving investment advice, that is to "know the client." Since you are the client, it is imperative that you "know yourself."

[Level 2 | Investment Objectives]

Deciding whether your priority should be *growth, income* or *liquidity* or some combination of all three is the second step in getting to "know yourself." This basic decision usually reflects your current stage in life and, therefore, is influenced by age, career, family situation and financial planning objectives.

[Level 3 | Asset Allocation]

Considering the objectives you set for yourself, what would be the best allocation of your assets into the three major categories of *cash, debt* or *equities*? The weightings will be largely determined by the level of risk you are willing to assume, which will then set an upper limit on the rate of return you can realistically expect from your portfolio. Expected return and risk can be quantified to the extent that good information is available about the individual holdings. Diversification among well-chosen investments can yield a higher rate of return overall with less risk.

[Level 4 | Security Selection]

All the securities that you might own or wish to own should be considered within their respective asset classes. As your portfolio size increases, it may be appropriate to subdivide the asset classes into more specific descriptions. The more active you expect to be in trading securities, the more generalized your security selection statement should be.

Summary

- Security selection is a narrowing process — from general decisions to specific ones about which securities to actually own.
- Security selection explains only a small portion of the final results we achieve. Be that as it may, it does have strong psychological importance to us.
- The Security Selection Process:
  - Divide each asset class into meaningful components and assign a weighting to each category to parallel your risk profile.
  - For each category, develop a list of securities with which you are comfortable.
  - Evaluate the list of potential investments in terms of *your* perception of risk.
  - Assign dollar values to each chosen investment.
  - Repeat for each asset class.

10 | Implementing Your Strategy

Keep only those assets you would buy today if you did not already own them; sell everything else.

You now have a completed Investment Statement that tells you what to do as far as putting together an appropriate investment portfolio. The next question is how you go about implementing the decisions you have made. Obviously, if you were starting from scratch with only *cash* holdings, which you were now going to diversify among the securities you had chosen, the task would be much simpler than if you had a collage of existing investments to try to incorporate into your plan.

Well, if having a portfolio composed entirely of cash would make life easier, why don't we assume that is exactly what you have? Why not begin by *theoretically* converting all your existing assets to cash? Then you can deal with the asset allocation and security selection decisions from the ground up, so to speak. Calculate the total dollar value of your investments and then compare where you are with where you want to be. Following is an example of what we mean, using a hypothetical $100,000 portfolio:

Current Portfolio

Security	Asset Class	Dollar Value	% of Portfolio
Bank Account	Cash	$ 5,000	5%
Money Market Fund	Cash	$20,000	20%
Total of Asset Class		**$25,000**	**25%**
GIC (5-Year)	Debt	$20,000	20%
Term Deposit (3-Year)	Cash	$20,000	20%
Total of Asset Class		**$40,000**	**40%**
Growth Mutual Fund	Equity	$20,000	20%
Shares in XYZ Ltd.	Equity	$10,000	10%
Stamp Collection	Equity	$ 5,000	5%
Total of Asset Class		**$35,000**	**35%**

So this portfolio is made up of:

Cash	$ 25,000	25%
Debt	$ 40,000	40%
Equity	$ 35,000	35%
Totals	**$100,000**	**100%**

But let's suppose that after going through the exercises in the previous chapter and completing your Investment Statement, your desired allocation is:

Cash	$ 10,000	10%
Debt	$ 30,000	30%
Equity	$ 60,000	60%
Totals	**$100,000**	**100%**

To get from where you are to where you want to be, you must somehow reduce the cash holding by $15,000 and the debt portion by $10,000, then shift the combined amount of $25,000 from those two asset classes to your equity component. Sounds simple enough, doesn't it? You can just cash in half your GIC or term deposit for $10,000, take $15,000 out of your money market fund and buy $25,000 worth of stocks or growth mutual funds. Right? Well . . . maybe not. Aside from the practical implications of such moves, including the fact that the GIC or term deposit may not be readily cashable and that there are tax implications to consider, a number of other questions have to be answered first.

TIMING OF PORTFOLIO ADJUSTMENTS

From a psychological perspective, there are two sides to the argument as to how quickly a transition to a new asset allocation should take place. On one side are those who might say, "Listen, I've gone to all this work; I know what I want to do, so let's get on with it." The counterpoint to that is "I agree with the plan I've outlined, but I would like to implement it over a period of time so I can gradually get used to the idea of having almost half of my portfolio in equity-type investments."

DOLLAR COST AVERAGING

Both approaches are valid. If the new mix you propose doesn't threaten your peace of mind too much, go for it right away. If, on the other hand, you think more along the lines of the latter, more cautious group, the best strategy may be a planned transfer, over a period of time, of equal amounts from one asset class to another. This approach is called *dollar cost averaging* and makes particular sense for re-allocations into the equity category. Following is an example of dollar cost averaging at work, assuming you wanted to move, say, $25,000 into an equity mutual fund. You could take as long as you like, within some obvious practical limits given the amount of money you wish to re-allocate. In this example, you might take a year or two to complete the transfer by making your purchases in amounts of approximately $1,000 or $2,000. Here is a possible outcome of a 12-month purchase plan:

Timing	Amount	Fund Unit Price	Units Purchased
Month 1	$2,000	$5.00	400
Month 2	$2,000	$4.00	500
Month 3	$2,000	$3.33	600
Month 4	$2,000	$4.00	500
Month 5	$2,000	$5.00	400
Month 6	$2,000	$4.44	450
Month 7	$2,000	$4.00	500
Month 8	$2,000	$3.64	550
Month 9	$2,000	$4.00	500
Month 10	$2,000	$4.44	450
Month 11	$2,000	$4.00	500
Month 12	$3,000	$5.00	600
Totals	**$25,000**		**5,950**

By the end of the year, you would own 5,950 units, for which you paid a total of $25,000. That averages out to $4.20 per unit, which demonstrates the major advantage of dollar cost averaging: by making regular purchases of equal amounts, you purchase more units when prices are low and fewer when they go up. In month 1, for example, your $2,000 bought 400 units at $5.00 per unit. As the price fell through months 2 and 3, the same dollar amount purchased more units. Conversely, as the price began to rise, your $2,000 deposit bought fewer units. This works best for assets with fluctuating prices, such as growth mutual funds or common stocks. As you can see from our example, *even though the unit value declined immediately after you started your scheduled buys and never recovered to a level any higher than the one at which you started*, you still managed to make a profit. By the end of the year, in this example, you would own 5,950 units at a current price of $5.00. That adds up to $29,750 or $4,750 more than you invested. Again, I have purposely chosen these numbers to make my points but the theory is sound as long as the value of the unit does not continue to decline indefinitely. Then it is simply a bad investment choice and regardless of how many units you buy at any price, you will lose money.

There is also a very valid psychological value derived from dollar cost averaging. It becomes apparent if you think about the volatility that might occur in the short run with equity investments. As you know, short-term returns can be quite different from the long-term projections on which you built your plan. "Averaging into the market" will normally dampen the volatility, making the shorter-term experience more like the longer-term expectation. A good rule of thumb, therefore, might be *the more volatile the target asset is, the more time you should take to get there*. In some cases, it may take as long as a year or even two years to reach the desired asset allocation.

WHAT ABOUT RRSPS?

Moving money into and out of a Registered Retirement Savings Plan is not as straightforward as transfers among non-RRSP assets are because there are restrictions on annual contributions and tax implications or penalties for early withdrawal. However, in general, it is quite permissible to re-allocate to a different asset class as long as you remain under the RRSP umbrella. For example, you could transfer from your trust company RRSP, which might be invested in a term deposit, to an RRSP-qualified stock mutual fund, or vice versa. Properly documented, there would be no adverse tax effect as a result of that transaction. It is beyond the scope of this book to comment at length on financial planning strategies employing Registered Retirement Savings Plans, but several excellent books are available on that topic; in addition, a knowledgeable financial adviser can assist enormously in this area. I will, however, make a couple of suggestions from the viewpoint of investment strategy.

Although, for most people, RRSPs will be part of their longer-term strategy, they may not be the ideal place for long-term investments, such as equities. RRSPs are the most valuable tax concession available to Canadians. However, to derive the maximum tax-deferral benefit, you will want to shelter within your RRSP investments that generate the most taxable income — and that may not be your equity holdings. As I briefly commented in Chapter 5, our tax regulations provide preferential treatment to investments that generate capital gains compared to those that yield interest. This is accomplished by taxing only 75 percent of capital gains. The following table illustrates the relative tax position of investments in the three basic asset classes. Note that rates vary among provinces and that this table is a simplified approximation. Again, good professional advisers can really earn their keep when it comes to something as complex as the Income Tax Act.

Tax Rates on Investment Income

Taxable Income	to $30,000	$30,000–$60,000	Top Rate
Interest	27%	42%	52%
Dividends	7%	25%	35%
Capital Gains	18%	27%	36%

So if you are not normally going to put equities into your RRSP, what are you going to include? As stated already, look first to those assets attracting the highest level of tax, which are most likely to be the interest-generating investments found in the *debt* category. Of course, you will also be earning interest on the *cash* component of your portfolio, but if those assets are to serve their purpose as a source of liquid funds, you will not likely want to restrict access to them, which the tax consequences of a withdrawal from an RRSP might do. So your debt assets, such as GICs, term deposits, mortgages and bonds, will largely fund your RRSP.

The procedure for allocating assets to your RRSP is:

1. Make all of your asset allocation decisions as if there was no such thing as an RRSP. Tax considerations should always be secondary to sound investment strategy.
2. Evaluate the specific investments you have chosen to include in your portfolio as a result of the asset allocation decision to identify the one that attracts the highest rate of tax for each dollar invested.
3. Put this investment into your RRSP first.
4. If the dollar value of that particular asset does not take you to the maximum amount you are permitted to hold in your RRSP, choose the investment that attracts the *next* highest rate of tax and add it to the RRSP. Keep repeating the process until the RRSP is fully invested.

AND HOW ABOUT PENSION PLANS?

There is a tendency to ignore our company pension plans in putting together an investment strategy because we assume there is little we can do to influence their performance and, in many cases, involvement in them is obligatory as an employee. However, if you're a member of a pension plan, it is worthwhile to scrutinize the plan to determine the specific investments within it so that you can allocate the value of the plan to its rightful asset class. Otherwise, you may actually have a total investment portfolio that has a very different asset allocation from what you originally intended. Commonly, many pension plans will have large bond or mortgage holdings in them so plan members will have a significant *debt* asset class position whether they want or not. So if, for example, your pension is invested largely in Government of Canada bonds, you will want to include a value for it in your *debt* allocation; mostly blue-chip Canadian stocks would obviously be an *equity* asset and so on. Then you can direct the money over which you *do* have control to balance the portfolio toward your intended allocation.

So how do you determine the value of a pension plan so you can include it as part of your total investment strategy? There are a number of sophisticated ways for an actuary to do that, but for us humble mortals a simple capitalization of the projected income stream will suffice for our purposes. Here's how the calculations can be done.

1. Your annual Employee Benefit Statement will often show a projected monthly income assuming you continue to work until normal retirement age. If it does not, ask your Employee Benefit administrator for the figure.
2. Multiply that number by 12 to obtain a yearly income projection.
3. Convert (capitalize) the annual income to the amount of money you would theoretically have to have in your portfolio to gener-

ate the same income. To do this, simply divide the annual income by a conservative interest rate obtainable in the market today and multiply the result by 100. Here's an example:

Monthly Income	$ 1,000
Annual Income	$12,000
Current Government Bond Interest Rate	8%
Capitalized value of pension	($12,000 ÷ 8) x 100 = **$150,000**

So now you can include the value of your pension as part of your total portfolio. When you do your asset allocation, prorate that value to the appropriate asset class. For example, if your pension is invested 100 percent in bonds and mortgages (as many are), allocate all of it to the *debt* category. If it is balanced equally between bonds and stocks, allocate 50 percent to *debt* and 50 percent to *equity* and so on.

The same sort of consideration should be given to any other asset over which there's some limit to your ability to deal with it directly. Shares in your company, trust funds or deferred compensation would be additional examples.

DEALING WITH ASSETS YOU DON'T WANT ANY MORE

One of the challenges you may face in making the transition from an existing portfolio structure to the newly desired one is what to do with the assets you already own that don't fit into the revamped portfolio. This is a particular problem if today they are not worth what you paid for them. In other words, you have lost money on them but you are still holding them, just waiting for the day when the price gets back to the level of your initial investment. *Then* you intend to sell! Somehow we convince ourselves in these situations that we haven't really lost the money until we actually dispose of the asset. It's the old "paper loss" theory. Well, guess what? If that piece of real estate or stock has a current value lower than what you paid for it, you have lost money!

What do you do about it? Obviously, you are not going to sell *everything* that has declined in value because, presumably, some of it does have potential to not only regain what it lost but also add some profit. Here's how you might solve the dilemma. Ask yourself this question: "If I did not own this asset today, would I buy it?" In other words, "Knowing what I do about this investment, do I have enough confidence in it that I'd buy it all over again?"

If you can honestly answer that question with a "Yes," then, assuming the asset is appropriate for your target portfolio, hang on to it. On the other hand, if your response is something like "Heck no! This thing is a dog . . . as soon as it gets back up to what I paid for it, I'm outta here," sell now and replace it with something in which you *do* have confidence!

The converse to this approach also applies when you have an asset that has increased substantially in value as you have owned it but it doesn't fit in the new portfolio structure. A frequently encountered example of this would be shares in the company for which you work. They may have been a great investment but now, when considered in the context of a new asset allocation, they mean you have too much equity exposure in your portfolio overall. The question to ask yourself in this situation is "If I didn't own this asset today, would I buy it?" Sound familiar?

Alternatively, if you simply have a security that has increased in value so substantially that you are waiting for what you believe will be its inevitable decline, ask again, "If I didn't own this asset today, would I buy it?" If your answer is "No way . . . it isn't worth today's price," sell it! As a practical matter, you may have to delay the sale for a period of time or structure the disposal in a certain way to minimize the tax consequences. In the case of an inappropriate asset, however, the general rule is *keep only those assets you would buy today if you did not already own them; sell everything else.*

REBALANCING THE PORTFOLIO

I have made the point several times that the asset allocation decisions you make initially are not chiselled in stone — they can be changed at any time and, indeed, should be re-examined on a regular basis. In particular, if your personality as you defined it in Chapter 6 tends toward the passive side of the Involvement line, you might think it less important to review your program once it is set up. That is because many investors equate a passive approach with a "buy and hold" strategy when, in fact, those investors who want to be less involved in the investment process are often the ones who need to be most conscious of shifting asset allocations that may, over time, cease to reflect their risk tolerance. Let me expand a little more on this very important point.

If, as we agreed earlier, equities will outperform all other assets in the long run, it is inevitable that, over an extended time horizon, the *equity* portion of your portfolio will grow faster than the *debt* or *cash* components. Therefore, the equity side, if left unchanged, will gradually represent more and more of your total holdings. Here's a simple example of a portfolio that starts off with half of its assets combined in cash and debt and the other half in equities.

Asset Class	Initial Value	% of Portfolio	Growth Rate	Value in 5 Years	% of Portfolio
Cash	$ 20,000	20%	5%	$ 25,525	16%
Debt	$ 30,000	30%	8%	$ 44,080	28%
Equity	$ 50,000	50%	12%	$ 88,110	56%
Totals	**$100,000**	**100%**		**$157,715**	**100%**

At the end of five years, the combined *cash* and *debt* holdings fell from 50 percent to 44 percent of the total while the *equity* class increased from 50 percent to 56 percent of the overall portfolio. You may argue that such a small difference doesn't really matter, and you could be absolutely correct — if the slight increase in risk, from having 50 percent of your portfolio in equities to having 56 percent is still within your comfort zone. However, this example assumed fairly normal expected rates of growth for the three asset classes. What if, in the space of five years, you experienced some unusual market conditions? Following is an example in which the equity market has a higher-than-expected return.

Asset Class	Initial Value	% of Portfolio	Growth Rate	Value in 5 Years	% of Portfolio
Cash	$ 20,000	20%	5%	$ 25,525	13%
Debt	$ 30,000	30%	8%	$ 44,080	23%
Equity	$ 50,000	50%	20%	$124,415	64%
Totals	**$100,000**	**100%**		**$194,020**	**100%**

In this scenario, the equity portion of your portfolio would have jumped from one-half to almost two-thirds of the total — while your time horizon *decreased* by five years. That may still be acceptable to you — having the potential volatility increase simultaneously with the shrinking of the time horizon, *provided your risk tolerance has expanded* over that same period. If it hasn't, however, you will want to "rebalance" the portfolio. How do you rebalance? You pretend you are Robin Hood by stealing from the rich to give to the poor — that is, you take from the best-performing asset and give to the under-performing ones, as shown in the chart at the top of the next page.

The specifics of this example are that you should sell $27,405 worth of your best performing holdings, which were equities, to buy more cash and debt investments, prorating the purchase of

Asset Class	Current %	Current Value	Desired %	Target Value	Difference	Action
Cash	13%	$ 25,525	20%	$ 38,804	$ 13,279	Buy
Debt	23%	$ 44,080	30%	$ 58,206	$ 14,126	Buy
Totals	**36%**	**$ 69,605**	**50%**	**$ 97,010**	**$ 27,405**	
Equity	64%	$124,415	50%	$ 97,010	$ 27,405	Sell

each to return the portfolio to the balance you desire. Psychologically, this can be a very difficult thing to do if you have had an experience like the example above. I am suggesting you need to sell off the asset that has given you the best return to buy more of the ones that have not performed as well! However, if you want to maintain the risk profile of your portfolio, that's *exactly* what you must do. And, of course, the theory also works the other way around — when the equity portion of the portfolio falls below its initial allocation, you have to sell some cash and debt assets to buy more equities. Otherwise, the inflation-fighting potential of your portfolio will be curtailed.

The other major advantage of the rebalancing tactic is that it disciplines us to adhere to one of the key tenets of successful investing, that is "buy low — sell high." Rebalancing a portfolio on a periodic basis automatically forces us to do that.

I suggested earlier that investors who tend toward the passive personality are the ones who should be on guard the most against a shifting risk profile of their portfolios. For those who are more active in their investment management, the theory still applies, of course, and particularly if some degree of timing the market is being practised. For any kind of investor, however, I recommend that you set *ranges* for the amount you wish to have in each asset grouping rather than specific percentages. For example, instead of setting the target precisely at 15 percent, plan to keep between 10 and 20 percent in *cash*. Rather than, say, 30 percent in *debt* assets, make the range 20 to 40 percent and, perhaps 40 to 60 percent in equities rather than a prescribed 50 percent. This will assure that a minimum is always kept in each class and yet it also provides flexibility to over-weight or under-weight any category as conditions change and one class becomes more or less attractive. I listed some suggested weighting (by age) in Chapter 8.

When to Rebalance

As I explained how to develop an Investment Statement, I made the comment that any change in the pyramid would automatically require a review of all higher levels, that is, a change of *Philosophy* (1) should prompt you to re-examine your *Objectives* (2), *Asset Allocation* (3) and *Security Selection* (4) to see if they are still appropriate. Altering your *Objectives* (2) would necessitate a look at your *Asset Allocation* (3) and *Security Selection* (4) and so on. Obviously, then, just about any change in your thinking or the assumptions on which you based your decisions about portfolio structure should lead you to at least look at the asset allocation.

Alternatively, I believe that an annual review is a good idea. Do it near the anniversary of the date on which you initially made the plan or select a specific day each year, perhaps your birthday! Wouldn't it be a nice present to yourself to confirm that your investment strategy remains on track?

MEASURING PERFORMANCE

As you review the asset allocation on a regular basis, you also want to determine how well the portfolio you have put in place is doing for you. Obviously, you can easily measure the absolute return simply by adding the present value of all your assets and comparing that to the value at the start of the period. But to gauge the effectiveness of your asset allocation you should compare your actual results with the expected returns and volatility you spelled out in Level 4 of your Investment Statement. If your target was, say, 12 percent average return with a "fluctuation factor" of ±10 percent and the actual results are –30 percent or +30 percent, try to determine the reason. Is the variance just a short-term aberration or was something grossly over- or underestimated from the beginning?

Don't be too quick to judge or make changes because short-term volatility is to be expected. However, as an additional measure, compare the performance of the specific securities you've chosen against benchmarks for the asset classes. For example, if the *equity* component of your portfolio is represented by growth mutual funds invested in Canada, plot their return against that of the Toronto Stock Exchange (TSE 300) index results; U.S. stocks can be compared to the Standard & Poor's (S&P 500) index and so on. The financial newspapers regularly publish statistics on the returns of various investments, especially interest yields on T-Bills, bonds and mortgages, stock market returns and mutual fund performance, so you can make relatively accurate comparisons if your portfolio is composed of those assets.

Needless to say, you must choose benchmarks that are relevant to the type of investments you own. For example, don't measure your international mutual funds against the TSE. The appropriate benchmark in that case may be the MSWCI (Morgan Stanley World Capital Index) or, perhaps, the EAFE (Europe, Australia, Far East), depending on how global the fund actually is.

The more esoteric your investment choices are, however, the more difficult it will be to find a relevant benchmark, so you will have to rely on your initial Investment Statement estimates. There's nothing wrong with that — if your portfolio results are meeting your needs and expectations, it doesn't matter very much how well your portfolio is doing compared to an alternative allocation. The long-term goal of this process is to achieve your financial objectives, not necessarily to beat the market.

GETTING MONEY OUT OF YOUR PORTFOLIO

If you're one of the millions of Canadians who have had the "Don't put all your eggs in one basket" advice repeated to you over and over again, you have probably also been warned to "never spend the principal" when converting assets to income. The intention of this latter counsel is sound — if you can live off the earnings from your investments, you'll never run out of money. The problem is that while your income may continue forever, the ability of that income to buy you the goods and services you want or need may well be deteriorating. We're talking about the ravages of inflation. Inflation has often been referred to as a "double demon" because it has two serious ramifications for investors. First, it destroys accumulated wealth and, second, it reduces the purchasing power of income. I'll repeat here the chart from Chapter 2 so we can refer to it as we proceed with this section.

Year	Capital @ 6% Inflation	Income @ 8% Return
Now	$500,000	$40,000
12 Years	$250,000	$20,000
24 Years	$125,000	$10,000
36 Years	$ 62,500	$ 5,000

Now let's imagine for a moment that you are retiring, in good health, at age 60. Your normal life expectancy would be another 20 to 25 years. Let's also suppose that you have an accumulated investment portfolio of $500,000; you want to use it to provide you with the maximum amount of income it can. However, because your parents admonished you to "never spend the principal," you elect to reconstruct your portfolio with investments that generate regular income payments without tapping into the capital. Considering the three representative investments we have used throughout this book as examples, you rightfully conclude that something in the *debt* asset class, like long-term government bonds, has the highest expected regular income flow. Let's assume the return is about 8 percent for this illustration. So that might be a good choice. Invested entirely in bonds, then, your $500,000 would provide $40,000 of interest income in the first year.

But let's look 12 years down the road — when you're age 72. If, during the intervening years, inflation were a modest 6 percent, you would see the value of your capital fall, in terms of today's worth, to about half — $250,000. (Did you ever learn the Rule of 72? Divide the number 72 by the inflation rate and you will know approximately the number of years it takes for capital values to be *cut in half*. Alternatively, divide 72 by any rate of return and you'll have the approximate number of years it will take for your investment to *double* in value. But enough of that for now.)

More important is the impact on income. As a retiree attempting to live on interest only, if inflation remains in the 6 percent range, you'll see the *purchasing power* of your income fall by 50 percent as well, to $20,000, *even though you are able to earn a return greater than the rate of inflation*! If you are fortunate enough to survive another 12 years to age 84, which is becoming increasingly likely given advances in medical technology, you would have the pleasure of seeing your income cut in half again, to the equivalent of $10,000. If you made it all the way to age 96, you'd be trying to get by on an income with the purchasing power of only $5,000 in today's dollars!

What's more, by converting all your assets into interest-generating ones, you automatically lower the overall expected return from your portfolio because you have eliminated all the higher performing equity investments. It has been said several times before and warrants repeating here: portfolios with long time horizons need *equities* in them, and someone retiring at age 60 certainly has a time horizon sufficiently long for it to be appropriate to include equities. In setting up your portfolio to provide income, you must think of *total return*, which includes dividends and capital gains from equities, interest and perhaps some capital gains from debt-type assets as well as the interest produced by cash holdings. *It is better to spend a little principal from a portfolio with a higher total return than to design one with maximum "interest only" income but lower overall yield.*

How Much to Withdraw

The next big question on your mind should be "If I am going to spend part of the principal, how much can I take out of my portfolio and still have confidence that I will never run out of money?" Regrettably, there's no simple answer to that because no one knows how long he or she is going to live and, thus, how long the money has to last. Obviously, too large a withdrawal can have devastating effects. Even with only modest levels of persistent inflation, the purchasing power of a portfolio can significantly erode over time if too much of its average total return is used to meet expenditures.

The ideal way to preserve purchasing power is *to limit your withdrawals from the portfolio to the earnings in excess of the rate of inflation.* For example, if your portfolio earns 12 percent and inflation is 5 percent, you should withdraw only the difference, which is 7 percent. As the years pass, you would be able to increase the actual dollar amount withdrawn annually because the total value of the portfolio would rise each year by the net amount allowed for inflation. In real life, however, this rule might prove to be a real challenge to implement if the difference between the portfolio return and inflation does not generate sufficient income to maintain the standard of living desired in retirement. For example, if you want an income of $1,000 per month ($12,000 annually) from a $100,000 portfolio, it would require a return of 12 percent + *the rate of inflation* just to keep the same income level and purchasing power. On the other hand, $1,000 per month from a $300,000 portfolio requires a return of only 4 percent + inflation, which is likely to be much more achievable and sustainable. In any event, some good advice is to try as best you can to get by on something less than the total returns generated by the portfolio. Then there will always be at least a partial hedge against inflation. Once more, here's where a good financial planner can assist in coordinating all your government and employee benefits with your personal retirement income sources. Below is a table that illustrates the withdrawal strategy just described, assuming an initial income requirement of $1,000 monthly with various income yields and allowances for inflation.

Year	Beginning Value	% Return	$ Income	Inflation Rate	Inflation Allowance	Net Income	Portfolio Balance
1	$200,000	10%	$20,000	4%	$ 8,000	$12,000	$208,000
2	$208,000	8%	$16,640	3%	$ 6,000	$10,640	$214,000
3	$214,000	6%	$12,840	3%	$ 6,000	$ 6,840	$220,000
4	$220,000	12%	$26,400	5%	$11,800	$14,600	$231,800
5	$231,800	15%	$34,320	6%	$13,900	$20,420	$245,700

As you can see, the income would have fluctuated over the five-year period while the size of portfolio continued to grow. In the real world of volatile returns and inflation, sticking to a consistent withdrawal would have required that you spend a little principal in the scenario described above. Otherwise, your income would have declined in Years 3 and 4. We would hope there would also be times when the portfolio would yield quite a bit more than was needed to offset increases in the cost of living (Years 4 and 5). In those years, you could give yourself a raise! Regardless, the advice is the same — try to avoid withdrawing all of the income as it is earned.

IS THERE A BETTER WAY?

In my opinion, there is a better alternative than simply converting all your assets to bonds and living off the interest as it is generated. And in describing how to go about improving the situation, I am going to avoid distinguishing between Registered Retirement Income Funds (RRIFs), Life Income Funds (LIFs) and non-registered investments. RRIFs and the like have minimum income rules that have some bearing on what you can and cannot do to meet your income needs. However, the strategy for getting to your money on a regular basis is essentially the same. Nor am I going to discuss the tax aspects of this procedure. Both of these topics should be reviewed with a competent adviser. And while this discussion is more properly included in a later chapter on professionally managed money, I want to introduce it here because it relates so specifically to living with your portfolio and the asset allocation decisions you have already made.

THE MUTUAL FUND WITHDRAWAL PLAN

One of the most underused investment products available in the marketplace today is the *mutual fund withdrawal plan*. Perhaps the name has something to do with it — it sounds painful! Yet in reality the automatic withdrawal arrangement is the most intelligent and flexible method for converting assets into income.

Quite simply, it works like this: you invest your money in a mutual fund or group of funds, then ask the manager or group of managers to send you a cheque or make a deposit directly into your bank account on a regular basis. You determine the amount of the cheque and the frequency of payment. You can increase (or decrease) the payout at any time. You don't have to worry about whether your portfolio is generating interest from its debt-type holdings, or dividends and capital gains from your equities. The fund manager simply redeems a sufficient number of your units each period to provide whatever amount of cash you have requested.

Why would this be such a tremendous benefit? Recall my comments earlier in this book about the danger of abandoning equities in favour of "less risky" investments such as bonds as you approach retirement? The consequence is erosion of purchasing power due to inflation. Yet as a practical matter, if you have all your money invested in the stock market, for example, how do you arrange things so that you can receive an adequate regular income from those assets? Recall that the average dividend payout from common stocks in Canada is only 2 to 3 percent. It would take a substantial portfolio of common stocks to generate a reasonable income if all that was available was the 2 to 3 percent dividend stream. And I don't think your stockbroker would welcome your instruction (every month) to "sell 11 shares of my IBM stock and send me a cheque for $1,000." The natural tendency, noted previously, is to think about changing your growth assets into income-producing ones. The problem with that strategy, as we already know, is that you will lower the overall portfolio rate of return. With a mutual fund withdrawal plan, you don't have to do that.

If you are happy with the portfolio mix you had before retirement, you needn't change it to have greater weighting of income-producing assets. You instruct the fund management company as to which funds you want to systematically redeem and how much is to be withdrawn from each. The fund manager then automatically converts a portion of your holdings to cash each month and sends it off to you at your condo in Florida! What remains in the portfolio after each withdrawal continues to compound as if you were not touching the money. That allows you to increase the withdrawal amounts as you go. The only concern you should have is that the portfolio continues to earn sufficient return to provide the level of income you desire and that your withdrawal amount is reasonable.

Beyond that and the tax implications of cashing in *any* investments, the withdrawal plan idea is a sound one. Most important, you don't have to alter your portfolio at retirement, although you are free to do so at any time. Chances are, however, that the mix you had between the ages of 30 and 60 could also serve you well between 60 and 90 with, perhaps, some modest adjustment to account for a shortened time horizon. But don't forget the longevity tables we looked at earlier. Many of us will spend as many years living off our investments as we did accumulating them, so our asset mix may not have to change too much if it was right for us in the beginning.

On the next page is an illustration of the actual results for a well-known small-cap growth fund in which an initial amount of $100,000 was invested and $1,000 per month, that is, 12 percent annually of the original amount, is withdrawn. The withdrawals are then indexed to increase by a theoretical inflation rate of 5 percent per year for 20 years. For comparison purposes, there is also a column showing the result of the withdrawal had an alternative investment yielding 15 percent been used instead of the fund. Note also that the fund had negative returns in four years, which resulted in the portfolio's value declining from year to year. In four different years, the fund had a return less than the original 12 percent target. In other words, at least 40 percent of the time, the fund under-performed. Yet, after 20 years, the value of the fund is still *19 times* the amount of the original investment *and* $366,000 has been withdrawn. I am not trying to promote this particular fund, which is why I have not identified it. You can do some research on your own or with your financial adviser and you will come up with a number of funds that have had similar experience. We all know that "past performance may not be indicative of future performance" but I use this simplified example to illustrate the concept and the potential power of the mutual fund withdrawal plan.

Year #	Annual Return	Annual Withdrawals	Total Withdrawals	Remaining Cash Value	15% Investment
1	N/A	N/A	N/A	$100,000	$100,000
2	41.6%	$12,000	$12,000	129,600	103,000
3	33.7%	12,600	24,600	160,675	105,850
4	23.6%	13,230	37,830	185,365	108,498
5	30.9%	13,892	51,722	228,751	110,881
6	53.5%	14,586	66,308	336,546	112,927
7	53.1%	15,315	81,623	499,937	114,550
8	−11.4%	16,081	97,704	426,863	115,652
9	38.2%	16,885	114,589	573,039	116,114
10	33.3%	17,729	132,319	746,132	115,802
11	−0.2%	18,616	150,935	726,024	114,556
12	34.9%	19,547	170,481	959,859	112,193
13	9.7%	20,524	191,006	1,032,442	108,498
14	−2.4%	21,550	212,556	986,113	103,222
15	8.9%	22,628	235,184	1,051,249	96,078
16	21.2%	23,759	258,943	1,250,355	86,730
17	−5.4%	24,947	283,890	1,157,888	74,793
18	41.9%	26,194	310,084	1,616,849	59,817
19	11.7%	27,504	337,589	1,778,516	41,285
20	9.5%	28,879	366,468	1,918,596	18,599

In all likelihood, with this experience, the investor would have increased the amount of the monthly withdrawals even more than the 5 percent originally set as the years passed and it became evident that the fund was growing at a rate faster than it was being depleted by the income payout. By Year 20, for example, a $29,000 withdrawal represented less than 2 percent of the total fund value.

Obviously, I chose a fund with a very good long-term track record to dramatize my point; however, I believe the convenience and flexibility of a mutual fund withdrawal plan is clear. All of the features, advantages and benefits of mutual funds (described more fully in the next chapter) that make sense in the accumulation of wealth can be continued through the conversion of that wealth to income.

Summary

* Begin by theoretically converting all your existing assets to cash and then comparing where you are with where you want to be.
* Dollar cost averaging is a planned transfer, over a period of time, of equal amounts from one asset class to another. It makes particular sense for re-allocations into the equity category.
* Make all of your asset allocation decisions as if there was no such thing as an RRSP and put the assets that attract the highest rate of tax for each dollar invested into your RRSP first.
* Keep only those assets you would buy today if you did not own them; sell everything else.
* Rebalancing a portfolio on a regular basis automatically forces us to buy low — sell high.
* The long-term goal of asset allocation is to achieve your financial objectives, not necessarily to beat the market.
* It is better to spend a little principal from a portfolio with a higher total return than to design one with a maximum interest-only income but lower overall yield.
* Limit your withdrawals from the portfolio to the earnings in excess of the rate of inflation.
* The automatic withdrawal arrangement is the most intelligent and flexible method of converting assets into income.

11 Managed Money

In calm water, every ship has a good captain.
— Swedish proverb

This chapter is about *managed money*. So what, you say, hasn't the entire book so far been about managing my money? And the answer is "Of course it has." When the investment community talks about *managed money*, however, it is referring to the care and investment of other people's funds by professional managers, such as those employed by mutual fund and other similar *institutional* organizations. In other words, it is you giving your money to someone else to make the investment decisions on your behalf. They become your *money managers*.

In the old days (way back in the 1960s and 1970s!) the practice of having someone else manage your portfolio was less popular and a lot simpler. Professional money management was generally restricted to those with multimillion-dollar portfolios or, for a few adventurous souls, a handful of mutual funds or investment products offered by some life insurance companies. The past few years, however, have seen what seems to be an unending onslaught of new product and service offerings from just about every financial institution as they scramble to get and retain control of the investing public's wallets and wealth.

The race among investment product suppliers has also caused a revolution in design, features and benefits that has added to the complexity of choice. Underneath all that, however, the concepts and philosophical foundation upon which these products are based have remained consistent. Those principles are:

- Pooling of assets
- Instant diversification
- Professional management

The major *managed money* product classifications are:

- Mutual funds
- Segregated funds
- Wrap accounts
- Private wealth management services

Each of these adheres to the three basic principles listed above, with varying degrees of constancy. Additionally, each offers unique benefits and appeals to certain segments of the investing population. So let's first look at the similarities by following the fundamental strategies of pooling of assets, instant diversification and use of professional management through an example. Then we'll come back to identify the differences among the major product categories.

POOLING OF ASSETS

Suppose that you and I each had $10,000 to invest. We both know from some reading we've done that, over the long term, stocks will deliver greater returns than cash- or debt-type investments, so we decide to purchase shares in publicly traded companies. Before we select which stocks to buy, however, we think it prudent to do a little research. You, because you have a more *active* investor personality, have been studying all the financial newspapers and have even requested the annual reports of a couple of companies that caught your attention. I, on the other hand, being more *passively* inclined, have simply been asking for recommendations from a few people who I know are experienced investors.

As a result of our individual research we make the following choices:

You: 2,000 shares of ABC Ltd., a fast-growing computer software company, at $5 per share

Me: 100 shares of XYZ Inc., a large, well-established conglomerate, at $100 per share

Periodically, we play golf together and, inevitably, the conversation turns to our investments with each of us expounding on the wise choice we made. (Remember our need for "bragging rights"?) You talk about the excitement of owning ABC Ltd. Its price is now $6.50 per share, an increase of 30 percent from your purchase price — but it has also dropped to as low as $3 while you owned it. You believe the long-term prospects remain bright but the stock does have a history of high price volatility so you could be in for a bit of a wild ride along the way. By comparison, my experience with XYZ Inc. has been rather boring. Its price has never fallen below what I paid for it and, in fact, it has risen unceremoniously to $110 per share — an increase of 10 percent. I don't think about it very often and I assume it will continue to perform in a similar manner for many years to come.

Over a post-game refreshment in the clubhouse one day, we quietly admit to each other that we wouldn't mind if our respective investments exhibited more of the characteristics of the other's. You would welcome some of the price stability exhibited by XYZ Inc. and I wouldn't be unhappy with a higher return, such as you have experienced with ABC Ltd. We agree that the easiest way to combine the lower volatility of XYZ Inc. with the superior returns of ABC Ltd. in our portfolios is for each of us to own shares in both companies. There are two ways to accomplish this. I could sell some of my XYZ Inc. and use the proceeds to buy shares of ABC Ltd. You, of course, could do the reverse. Instead, we decide to form a simple partnership, with each of us contributing our respective holdings and sharing, on a pro rata basis, in the overall profits. In other words, we *pool our assets* so that we jointly now own 2,000 shares of ABC Ltd. and 100 shares of XYZ Inc. (For simplicity, I will ignore the relative profits earned to this point.)

By doing this, we have achieved two things. First, we have created a larger capital base with which to work. If, some time down the road, we decide to sell our holdings in ABC Ltd. and XYZ Inc. in favour of buying something else, we will, presumably, have about twice as much money to re-invest. This will give us much more flexibility in choosing alternative investments because some of the other opportunities we might examine may be available to us only if we have a minimum amount of cash to commit. For example, if we decided to abandon stocks altogether and buy real estate, the more money we had in total, the wider the choice of properties we could consider.

INSTANT DIVERSIFICATION

The second and most important consequence of pooling our assets is that we get to enjoy the power of *diversification*. We have already discussed at length the tremendous benefit that can be derived combining two or more assets with different performance characteristics. Following this example through, we would expect our new "two-stock" portfolio (one-half ABC Ltd. and the other half XYZ Inc.) to have a more consistent return than one that contained only ABC Ltd. and a higher yield than one holding XYZ Inc. exclusively. As our portfolio grows and we are able to include additional, carefully chosen investments, we now know that we could actually increase total return within a given risk level or, alternatively, maintain the same expected return while lowering the overall risk profile or, in fact, do both. That is exactly what money managers do — they automatically diversify your investment dollars over a larger number of assets than you could likely purchase on your own. For example, as I am writing this, if you had $10,000 to invest in the Canadian stock market, you could buy any of the following:

500,000 shares	— Adda Resources (Mining), or
100,000 shares	— Voyager Films (Media), or
10,000 shares	— Brick Brewery (Food and Beverage), or
1,000 shares	— Air Canada (Transportation), or
500 shares	— Power Financial (Financial Services), or
250 shares	— Imasco (Consumer Goods), or
100 shares	— Daimler Chrysler (Automotive), or
65 shares	— Rothmans (Tobacco), or
30 shares	— JDS Uniphase (Internet)

By comparison, if you invested in a well-known Canadian equity mutual fund, your same $10,000, as part of a large pool of investors' money, could purchase the following diversified portfolio:

Canadian Equities

Financial Services (12.46%)

Bank of Montreal	$182
Bank of Nova Scotia	$199
Canada Life	$ 76
Mackenzie Financial	$ 99
Manulife Financial	$103
Royal Bank	$242
TD Bank	$345

Communications and Publications (4.35%)

Astral Communications	$ 32
Cogeco Cable	$ 45
Quebecor Printing	$ 62
Rogers Communication	$103
Seagrams	$104
Thomson Corporation	$ 89

Consumer Products (2.10%)

High Liner Foods	$210
Imasco Limited	$ 18
Richtree Inc.	$ 3
Sleeman Breweries	$ 26
Vincor International	$ 32

Paper and Forest Products (1.54%)

Donahue Inc.	$154
West Fraser Timber	$108

Gold and Precious Metals (3.19%)

Barrick Gold	$161
Franco Nevada Mining	$114

Placer Dome	$ 44

Industrial Products (28.63%)

ALI Technologies	$ 20
ATI Technologies	$148
ATS Automation	$ 67
Ballard Power	$ 40
Bombardier	$ 88
C-Mac Industries	$130
Celestica Inc.	$ 57
Cognos Inc.	$108
Delano Technology	$ 6
Ensign Resource	$ 21
Epic Data	$ 11
Geac Computer	$ 42
Genesis Microchip	$ 15
Intertape Polymer	$ 41
JDS Uniphase	$281
MDSI Mobile Data	$ 39
Magellan Aerospace	$ 31
Magna International	$154
Nortel Networks	$999
Open Text	$ 75
Potash Saskatchewan	$ 40
Prudential Steel	$ 78
Royal Technologies	$ 37
TecSyn International	$ 20
Teknion Corporation	$ 49
Descartes Systems	$133
Wcstaim Corporation	$ 31
Tritech Precision	$ 32
Unican Security	$ 69

Resources Services (0.16%)
    Precision Drilling $ 16

Merchandising and Retailing (2.16%)
    George Weston Ltd. $ 72
    Metro-Richelieu $ 53
    Sears Canada $ 91

Metals and Minerals (3.78%)
    Alcan Aluminum $161
    Falconbridge $ 18
    Noranda $ 96
    Rio Algom $103

Conglomerates (0.85%)
    Edper Brascan $ 19
    Power Corporation $ 59
    Quorum Growth $ 7

Oil and Gas (8.97%)
    Alberta Energy $ 58
    Berkeley Petroleum $ 25
    Canadian Hunter $ 59
    Canadian Resources $ 81
    Crestar Energy $101
    Petro-Canada $168
    Rio Alto Exploration $ 43
    Suncor Energy $180
    Talisman Energy $182

Pipelines (0.89%)
    Enbridge $ 89

Real Estate and Construction (1.83%)

Brookfield Properties	$ 72
Oxford Properties	$ 72
TrizecHahn	$ 56

Utilities (8.30%)

BCE Inc.	$812
Teleglobe Inc.	$ 18

Transportation and Environment (0.31%)

Laidlaw Inc.	$ 31

Health Care (5.25%)

AnorMED	$ 24
BioChem Pharma	$ 56
Biovail Corporation	$305
DC Diagnostic	$ 5
Hemosol Inc.	$ 35
Inex Pharmaceuticals	$ 53
Lorus Therapeutics	$ 5
TLC Laser Eye Centres	$ 42

Foreign Holdings — Various (13.80%)

France	$144
Spain	$ 90
United States	$734
United Kingdom	$381
Netherlands	$ 18
Italy	$ 12

Cash	$159
TOTAL	**$10,000**

It is easy to see that a single purchase of some type of pooled fund can immediately create a very broadly diversified portfolio.

PROFESSIONAL MANAGEMENT

So far we have looked at two of the key features of managed money: *pooling of assets* and *diversification*. To explore the third feature, *professional management*, let us return to the golf club where you and I are discussing our joint investment holdings. As we do, either on the course itself or at the "19th Hole," chances are that a few of our golfing buddies will hear some of the conversation and it won't be very long before they are offering suggestions as to good investment opportunities. Some of them might even want to join us in our pooling arrangement, and before we know it we could have a small investment club with each member contributing ideas and cash to buy more investments on a shared basis. As the number of people and the amount of money increases, we'll probably want to meet more formally from time to time, to make decisions about which stocks to buy or sell and to distribute any profits. We may also have to find a volunteer to account for the assets of the club, negotiate commissions with brokers and deal with the paperwork that comes with buying and selling stocks. Periodically, we could even invite a specialist to one of our gatherings to educate us on specific investments or to provide us with research to aid in our decision-making.

If we follow the natural life cycle of a group of investors such as I have just described, the day will come when someone stands up in one of the meetings and says, "This thing has just got too big to continue in such an informal way. The paperwork has become a burden, we all have our own ideas about the investments we should be making and none of us has the time or skill to sort it all out in a way that can maximize return without exposing us to too much risk. I would like to propose that we hire a manager to look after all those details. We can find a professional who has the same *philosophy* (remember? — risk tolerance + personality = *philosophy*) as we do, with a *good track record* in choosing stocks, *knowledge of the regulatory requirements* and the *administrative capability* to handle our affairs. I would be willing to pay that manager a small portion of our total assets as compensation." From statements such as those the money manager is born!

In addition to meeting our needs as outlined above, is there anything else should we expect from a money manager? In my opinion, that person's first responsibility should be to communicate his or her *investment philosophy* so that we could decide if there was a match between our philosophy and that of the money manager. Does he, for example, subscribe to the "market timing" school of thought or take a "money management" approach? Is she a "value investor" who searches for stocks with prices that appear to be below the actual value of the company? Conversely, does he seek "growth" stocks with good long-term prospects? (I must admit that I've never met a portfolio manager who wasn't interested in *both* "growth" and "value," but the investment industry has created these labels to differentiate between approaches.)

Alternatively, does she employ a "top-down" strategy, first determining broad economic outlook by answering questions such as "Is the country in an expansion or a contraction phase?" Or "Are interest rates headed up or down?" or "What are the prospects for inflation?" and then selecting companies she expects to perform best under the anticipated economic conditions?

Once the philosophy is determined, the professional manager must develop an investment strategy that keeps the portfolio on a consistent track toward its objective. That might be long-term capital appreciation for equities or above-average income with preservation of capital for bonds or high short-term yield for money-market investments. Investors want to have confidence that the strategy won't change (without their permission) after they have entrusted their money to the manager. The industry jargon for subtle changes in strategy is "style drift."

Then the manager must buy and sell assets to execute the strategy, keep account of all the transactions, handle investors' purchases and redemptions, distribute profits, issue tax statements and receipts, comply with the innumerable regulations and report to investors on a regular basis.

In Canada, hundreds of firms provide the services I have described, ranging from large, international mutual fund complexes to "boutiques" that handle only a few select clients. Choosing the one appropriate for you can be somewhat daunting. I have alluded to some of the factors you should consider with respect to philosophy and objectives, and we'll come back to additional selection criteria in just a bit. For now, we should acknowledge that, in many cases, these organizations are better equipped to provide the level of professional expertise required for successful investing than we are individually. And what's more, they do it all at what I believe to be a most reasonable cost, typically 2 to 3 percent of the dollar value of the assets they manage. I believe that is a real bargain when one considers the enormous responsibility this is and the infrastructure and personnel needed to carry out the task.

ADVANTAGES

Let's move on to the advantages that managed money products or services can exhibit over many other investments. There is no particular priority to the following list. A wide range of investors is drawn to these offerings by different advantages.

Liquidity

Most money management organizations can normally redeem all or part of your investment for its cash value in the few days it takes to process the request. (With some of the private wealth management services where you can hold individual securities as well as pooled funds, it may take more time to dispose of the individual assets.) In practice, a number of firms, particularly the mutual fund companies, can also provide same-day emergency redemption, including electronic transfer of the proceeds to your bank. Managed money is not as liquid, therefore, as your savings account because you cannot typically walk into a local office or branch and withdraw the cash you need on the spot, although some fund companies do offer limited chequing privileges. However, you are able to access your money much more readily than you can, say, any investment you might have in a mortgage, limited partnership, a piece of real estate or your own company shares.

Diversification

A couple of pages back I showed the difference between what $10,000 would buy if you invested in a single stock and what you would own if you purchased a well-known Canadian mutual fund with the same dollar amount. That example clearly illustrated the diversification effect of pooled funds, but in fact the advantage can be far more substantial. In *Risk Is a Four Letter Word,* I described the "triple safety net" that comes with using a number of mutual funds to carry out your investment strategy. For consistency, I'll continue with the mutual fund example, but note that these concepts apply to almost all managed money products.

The first level of safety is the diversification within a single fund itself. Most equity mutual funds, as we noted in an earlier chapter, will own anywhere from 40 to more than 100 stocks, depending on the size of the fund and its investment objective. Consequently, if stocks of firms in the retailing business, for example, aren't doing too well, the energy stocks might be, and so on. Bond funds might hold 10 to 15 different issues; real estate funds may own 20 to 30 properties or more. The basic notion of diversification as a means of reducing volatility and increasing return can be found in a single mutual fund.

But what if the stock market is in a slump and equities in general aren't performing in a particularly exciting manner? This is where the second line of defence comes into play. By owning funds that are invested in more than one asset class, you can extend the value of diversification even further. Why not have your portfolio made up of funds that specialize in each of cash, debt and equity investments? To emphasize the point, note that in Canada, we at present have more than 2,500 different mutual funds available to individual investors. Can you believe it? The breakdown, according to asset class, is:

Cash	178 funds	
Debt	349 funds	
Equity	1,494 funds	
Total	**2,021**	

In addition, more than 500 "balanced" or "asset allocation" funds include all three major asset classes in them. The hot products of the late 1990s were "clone" funds that use financial derivatives such as stock index options or futures to mirror the performance of other funds in the same fund family that would normally be classified as foreign content for RSP purposes. So it is quite possible to have a second level of diversification by constructing a portfolio with mutual funds that are diversified not only among securities but among asset classes. As we also noted earlier, owning a number of securities reduces *business risk* while asset class diversification shrinks *market risk.*

The third "safety net" is put into place when you select funds with different investment managers. There are approximately 200 mutual fund–sponsoring companies in Canada and many of them offer competing products — most of them offer an equity fund that specializes in Canadian stocks, for example. Chances are that among a couple of hundred independent investment managers there will be some difference of opinion as to how money should be invested at any particular moment. Some will believe that interest rates have farther to fall and will include in their portfolios companies that typically profit from declines in interest rates. Others will think the rates have bottomed out and are set to rise. Consequently, they will look to invest in companies with good prospects under those conditions. Some who are more "market timing"–oriented may anticipate a general downward movement in the stock market and will, therefore, increase the cash component of their portfolios to avoid having all their capital in the market as it declines. They will also want to have money available to purchase stocks at the expected lower prices. The more fundamental money managers may feel that their mandate calls for them to always be invested in equities, so they will look for companies that represent long-term value regardless of short-term market fluctuations.

All of these managers can be successful even though they have differing philosophies. So why not *diversify among managers* to minimize the risk that the single management firm you've chosen might be wrong from time to time? As Sir John Templeton, patriarch of the mutual fund industry, writes in his foreword to Roger Gibson's excellent book, *Asset Allocation: Balancing Financial Risk*, "To diversify your investments is clearly common sense so that those which produce more profits than expected offset those which produce less. Even the best investment professional must expect that no more than two-thirds of his decisions will prove to be above average in profits. Therefore, asset allocation and diversification are the foundation stones of successful, long-term investing." There is no "all-weather" manager who performs well under every market condition, so diversifying among managers would give you the combined yet independent expertise of a number of professionals.

Full-Time Management

The value of having a full-time, dedicated professional looking after your portfolio can perhaps best be illustrated by repeating here a story I told in *Risk Is a Four Letter Word*. It describes an experience I had a few years ago. One day, an elderly gentlemen appeared at my office unexpectedly and asked for a few minutes of my time. At that stage of my career, I was working with a well-established mutual fund management company that had a very good long-term track record for its Canadian equity fund. The gentleman, whom I'll refer to as Mr. B., told me that he had been following the results of my firm's fund and wanted to invest some of his money in it. I had to tell him that our funds were distributed through brokers and independent mutual fund advisers only and, therefore, it was a policy of our firm not to accept direct investments. I went on to say that I would, however, be happy to introduce him to several good representatives from whom he could choose one who seemed best able to provide the level of expertise he required and with whom he could establish a good rapport. When he somewhat reluctantly agreed, I suggested that if he told me a little about his situation, I could narrow the list of potential advisers down to a few whose philosophies and methodologies could accommodate his needs.

Here is Mr. B.'s story. He had been an employee of a national transportation company for over 40 years, beginning as a yard helper and retiring at age 65 from a position as a department supervisor. His income, very modest at first, had risen steadily as he progressed through the firm, but it had never been what one might call generous. At this point, I will admit to you that I was taken aback when Mr. B. next told me that, despite limitations on his disposable income, he had an investment portfolio that was worth $1.2 million! He went on to say, "Investing has been my hobby since I was a teenager; in fact, it has been an obsession with me. I have spent 20 to 30 hours a week for the past 50 years playing the stock and bond markets and managing my investments. As my portfolio has grown, I've had to dedicate more and more time to just keeping up with the paperwork and now, quite frankly, I'm a little tired. I still enjoy the thrill of analyzing companies, interest rate trends and such, but I'd like someone else to take on a large part of that responsibility for me. And I'm willing to pay them to do that." (Sound familiar?)

"What's more," Mr. B. went on to say, "my wife has never been too crazy about all the time I've spent with our investments rather than with the family. And certainly, should anything happen to me, she wouldn't have a clue about what to do with all the stocks and bonds and mortgages in the portfolio. So what I was hoping to do was to take $1 million of the $1.2 million total and put it into a few good mutual funds, to let the professionals manage it for me, and for my wife if I'm not around. The balance of $200,000 I intend to keep as my 'play money.' I will continue to do what I have been doing because I enjoy it, but I'll do so on a much smaller scale."

The happy conclusion to this story is that Mr. B. built a close relationship with a competent financial adviser who not only allocated the money among several good mutual funds but also assisted Mr. B. with his estate planning. However, perhaps the more telling sequel came to me a few weeks later when I was expounding the virtues of long-term investing in mutual funds to another, much younger person. I was able to illustrate, with the performance of a very popular common stock fund, how a $10,000 investment in 1954 would, 40 years later, be worth $2.1 million with all management fees accounted for. Most important, *the investor would not have had to even look at it since the day it was invested!* All the time that someone like Mr. B. devoted to managing his portfolio could have been spent doing something else for personal enjoyment, family, faith, community or whatever. I understand that investing was Mr. B.'s passion and he got considerable psychic reward from the time and effort he employed in the activity. I also know that $10,000 was a lot of money to start with in 1954. But the point is still valid — in the majority of cases, a professional manager is likely to be in a better position to do the things necessary for successful investing, leaving you free to spend your time on other, more personally appealing pursuits. And chances are good that you'll end up with a better performing portfolio overall.

The other advantage to having professional managers on your side is that they are on the job full-time. The myriad responsibilities of a professional money manager can be carried out by a team of specially trained experts who do nothing else all day long but look after your money. Furthermore, they don't take phone calls! "So what?" you say? Let me ask you, "How many 'hot investment tips' have you received and how many of them have turned out as promised?" I'm willing to bet that not many have come even close to the claims the tipsters made. Well, professional portfolio managers don't act on "hot tips." They rely on sophisticated research, a massive data bank, specialist advisers and a proven methodology for making intelligent, considered investment decisions. Can we realistically hope to outperform them by ourselves?

Flexibility

I have already mentioned several times the considerable flexibility of investment options available through the use of managed money products and services. Let me expand a little more on some of the key ones with another example. How would you react if you were an investment adviser and one of your clients made the following request?

"I'd like to open an investment account so I can begin to accumulate wealth in an organized way. My intention is to set aside, say, $500 a month for the next 20 years. And here's what I'd like you, my friendly adviser, to do for me. Each month, please automatically withdraw the $500 from my bank account because I don't want to have to send you a cheque every four weeks or so. However, from time to time, I may want to stop and subsequently restart the withdrawals or change the amount. I'll try to give you a couple of weeks' notice but I'm not sure when or even if I will want to make that change. Periodically, I may drop in a few extra bucks in a lump sum or I may have to dip into my account for some cash.

I'd like one-third of my investment to go into income-producing assets such as bonds or mortgages for my RRSP, 25 percent into Canadian blue-chip stocks, $100 a month into Japanese securities and the balance into some sort of cash account with interest calculated daily and credited to my account on a monthly basis. I'll take a look at the asset mix and the results every six months or so and may want to shift some of my holdings from one investment to another. I know that $500 is not a lot of money compared to some 'big time' investors; nonetheless, I expect you to treat me exactly as you would them, buying the same quality stocks, bonds, Treasury Bills or whatever and paying as much attention to my portfolio as you would to a multimillionaire's.

When I retire in 20 years or so, I'm sure I'll want to keep investments similar to those I've used to build my portfolio but then, of course, I'll want you to start sending a cheque to me at my condo in Florida every month, making the appropriate deduction for taxes. Oh, yes, I'd also like a regular report on the unit value of each investment I own and a full accounting for all purchases, sales and transfers at least annually."

I think we can stop here because the message should be clear. If you were the investment adviser in this example, your only sensible response would be "There's just one way we can do all those things for you, and that is by using the services of a professional money manager."

Another Benefit — Peace of Mind

Peace of mind is one of the basic priorities of this book, and we began talking about it in the very first pages. At that point, we were referring to the psychological comfort that comes from using an asset allocation approach to investing. Now, however, I want to apply the "peace of mind" notion to managed money. The link should be fairly clear — the asset allocation decisions you made earlier can, in most instances, be implemented entirely through the use of managed money products. There are pooled funds that match every *philosophy*; that is, they fit every level of risk tolerance from highly conservative to very aggressive. There are funds to meet every *objective* — liquidity, income or growth — and *asset allocation* can be accomplished among cash, depth and equity funds by making *security selections* from T-Bill, bond, mortgage, dividend, common stock, international, real estate, precious metal, balanced and asset allocation funds. I am not suggesting that managed money is the only investment alternative to be considered. I'm just repeating my earlier statement that, for many of us, using professional money managers could be our best choice for meeting our investment objectives.

DISADVANTAGES

The question I hope you're asking right now is "Are there any *disadvantages* to having my portfolio made up of pooled funds managed by other people?" And the answer, of course, is "Yes." For one thing, it can be boring — leaving most of the security selection decisions to someone else (remember, that is the fun part!). So it doesn't serve our need for "bragging rights" particularly well.

For another, these products and services cost money. They all come with fees for the professional management I claim is so valuable. For example, even though some mutual funds may call themselves "no-load," someone has to pay the people who run and distribute them, so costs are often "buried" in the management fee and are indirectly reflected in the overall performance. That is not to say that some managers don't do a better job of controlling costs than others or that some distributors, particularly large institutions, can't keep costs low by using existing facilities to distribute or manage funds along with their other products and services. The challenge for you as an investor is to find the right mix of expertise, convenience, variety and performance at a cost that is commensurate with the level of service you desire. For some readers, that will mean engaging a financial planner, full-service broker or product specialist who has the facilities and can afford to respond to your needs for active management of your account. For others who feel they don't require such personal involvement, the services offered by a discount broker, bank teller, phone-in direct marketing firm or over the Internet may be sufficient. Of course, there are many levels in between. Just be sure you understand what you're getting or giving up for the price you pay.

The other major problem with investing in managed money products is the "complexity of choice" — there are simply too many options. We saw earlier that there are more than 2,500 mutual funds available in Canada and new ones are being launched every month. Add to that number the "sophisticated client" departments that now exist in all major banks and the hundreds of less publicly profiled independent money managers offering private wealth management services and it is easy to be overwhelmed by the choices. Further compounding the problem is the fact that "all portfolio managers are not created equal" so analysis of philosophy, personnel and performance is essential. I'll have more to say about choosing managers shortly.

Right now, though, let's build on the conceptual basis of managed money as we have already described it by differentiating among the four major classifications introduced earlier, specifically, mutual funds, segregated funds, wrap accounts and private wealth management services.

MUTUAL FUNDS

Mutual funds are, in my view, the best investment choice for a large number of Canadians and, apparently, an increasing number of investors share that opinion because sales have skyrocketed over the past 10 years. Canadian mutual fund managers now look after more than $300 billion of our money, an increase of about 4,000 percent since the mid-1980s. That pace of sales growth and the large number of books available that describe in detail all the technicalities of mutual funds suggest to me that many people are familiar with them. Therefore, I'm not going to spend very much time discussing how they work but rather I will try to explain the unique features that may suggest why they have such appeal. We'll also want to stay within the context of what we have already said about managed money products in general without repeating the obvious.

Guaranteed Price — Guaranteed Buyer

On the assumption that most Canadians will purchase publicly traded, open-end mutual funds (which are far and away the most popular), the most beneficial feature is the fact that when the time comes to redeem them, there is a guaranteed buyer! That's what "open end" means. The mutual fund itself will always buy back the units you own, without question and with no argument as to how much they are going to pay you because the values of the fund units are published daily in all major newspapers. Whenever you decide to sell your mutual fund, you can look in the *Globe and Mail*, *National Post*, or, in many cities, your local newspaper for the daily unit value, call your broker or financial product specialist and know that your fund will be disposed of at that price.

In recent years, a new purchase arrangement called the "deferred sales charge" has become commonplace. Here there is no sales commission deducted from your deposits, but there is a fee for early redemption, usually within six to nine years of the initial purchase. This may affect the total proceeds you receive if you redeem your fund but has nothing to do with the selling price. It is simply a commission similar to the one you would pay if you were selling many other investments, such as stocks, bonds, mortgages, real estate or works of art.

Variety

I have already made the point that there are over 2,500 mutual funds available in Canada and that they cover the three basic asset classes. Closer examination reveals that the diversity is even greater. We can tabulate the mutual funds available in Canada as follows:

Managed Money

Asset Class	Fund Type	Sub-Group	No. of Funds
Cash	Money Market	Canadian	157
		U.S.	17
		Foreign	2
Debt	Bond	Canadian	191
		Foreign	78
		Short-Term	35
		High-Yield	16
	Mortgage	Canadian	23
Equity	Canadian	Canadian Diversified	267
		Large Cap Diversified	96
		Small Cap Diversified	61
		Canadian Dividend	66
		Canadian Growth	38
		Canadian Value	32
		Large Cap Growth	4
		Small Cap Growth	35
		Large Cap Value	12
		Small Cap Value	8
		Labour-Sponsored Venture Capital	16
	U.S.	Large Cap	75
		Diversified	34
		Mid Cap	32
	Foreign	Global (may include Canada)	200
		International (excl. Canada)	78
		Europe	67
		Emerging Markets	35
		Asia Pacific	35
		Japan	20
		Asia Pacific (excl. Japan)	10
		North America	14
		Latin America	11
		China	4

Asset Class	Fund Type	Sub-Group	No. of Funds
Equity		India	2
(cont'd)		U.K.	1
		Germany	1
	Specialty	Global Science & Technology	45
	Sectors	Canadian Science & Technology	3
		Canadian Natural Resource	33
		Canadian Precious Metals	13
		Global Natural Resource	6
		Global Precious Metals	3
		Canadian Real Estate	10
		Global Real Estate	5
		Currency	4
		Financial Services	11
		Miscellaneous Specialty	47
	Balanced	Canadian Balanced	304
		Global Balanced	102
		Canadian Asset Allocation	66
		Global Asset Allocation	10
		Canadian High Income	27

Source: Morningstar Canada Inc.

These fund types can be defined even further. For example, about two-thirds of the funds listed above qualify as RRSP investments. Some funds make monthly distributions of income; others do so quarterly or, most commonly, on an annual basis. The smallest fund has about $150,000 invested in it while the largest has more than $11 billion. Some have very low volatility and some very high. One-year rates of return range from +188 percent to –39 percent and 10-year compound average returns vary from more than 23 percent to a loss of 9 percent. (Note: At the time of writing, only 625 [about one-quarter] of the funds currently available have been around long enough to establish 10-year performance track records. Fewer than half have existed for more than five years; about one-third weren't on the market three years ago and a whopping 25 percent have been introduced in the past 24 months.)

Most funds can be purchased under an automatic bank withdrawal agreement or with lump-sum deposits. Some restrict themselves to direct sales to members (and their families) of certain professional or trade associations. The best-known funds are available through stockbrokers, independent mutual fund representatives, banks and trust companies, insurance agents and other "one-company" salespeople, as well as on a direct-purchase basis by mail, telephone or over the Internet.

The sales commission or "load" structure among the funds is as follows:

Type of Load	Description of Charges	No. of Funds Available
Front or Back	Can be purchased with either "front" or "back" end load*	1,029
Deferred	May charge fee when funds are redeemed**	362
Front	Charge fee when funds are purchased	150
Back	Charge fee when funds are redeemed	16
None	Does not charge fees on purchase or redemption	838

Source: Morningstar Canada Inc.

* Front-end loads may be reduced (in percentage terms) as the size of the investment increases.
** Deferred loads may decrease as the time elapsed between purchase and redemption lengthens.

It is easy to see that the number of options available to investors using mutual funds is enormous and overwhelming! You can choose funds representing each asset class or have someone else diversify among the classes for you by purchasing a balanced fund or a fund where the manager does the overall asset allocation. Your RRSP contribution can be made into a mutual fund and you can make regular deposits from your bank account to take advantage of dollar cost averaging. If income is the objective, it can be received on a monthly, quarterly or annual basis. You can select funds with a history of providing the levels of return you need to meet your goals and a volatility factor that is within your comfort zone. Large, well-established funds with long-term track records of stable returns can be mixed with smaller, more aggressive choices to increase overall return potential. For total variety, mutual funds are difficult to match. They can be bought through just about every financial intermediary, in almost any amount, under numerous purchase arrangements — *there is a mutual fund to meet every financial objective.*

Record of Performance

So far I have not discussed at any length the performance of mutual funds compared to other investment options. I will provide some general guidelines on the aspects of performance to consider in choosing any managed money product. Rates of return, however, should not be the only criterion in choosing a fund, and there is a great deal of information available on mutual fund performance. As noted already, mutual fund prices are published daily in most major newspapers, so you can track their progress as frequently as you wish. Additionally, it is possible to obtain, from weekly, monthly or quarterly summaries in the same newspapers, the one-, three- and six-month rates of return as well as longer-term track records for one, two, three, five and 10 or more years if the fund has been available for that length of time. All mutual fund managers will provide performance data on request for most periods and certainly any good mutual fund adviser will be well acquainted with the results of the various funds they offer (and many that they don't offer). I'm not aware of any other investment that makes its performance results so readily available and permits an investor to compare one offering to another with such accuracy.

Once again, though, the standard caveat applies that "past

performance is no guarantee of future results." Combined with other relevant data, however, knowing how an investment has performed in the past can definitely improve your chances of selecting one that will come close to meeting your objectives or, conversely, eliminating from consideration those least likely to help you achieve your goals.

Taxation

I have avoided discussing taxation in any great detail several times throughout this book because it really is a subject unto itself and could easily fill several hundred pages. However, it is worthwhile to highlight briefly the tax advantage enjoyed by mutual fund investors. In fact, the majority of the following comments also apply to the other types of managed money products.

Reducing the taxation issue to its simplest terms, all income realized by an investor is subject to tax with only one exception, that being earnings inside a tax-sheltered plan such as a Registered Retirement Savings Plan (RRSP), Registered Pension Plan (RPP), Deferred Profit Sharing Plan (DPSP) or some other such special legal arrangement. When we come to discussing the tax advantage of mutual funds, the operative phrase is "income realized" because not all earnings of a mutual fund are immediately realized and thus not immediately taxable. Stick with me on this and I'll try to make some sense of a complex topic.

Basically, a mutual fund earns profits from three sources: *interest* on the cash balance not invested in specific assets, *dividends* from stocks or interest payments received from such things as bonds in the portfolio and, finally, net *capital gains* for any assets sold at a profit. Most mutual funds are structured in such a way that the net amount of those earnings (after fund operating expenses are paid) "flow through" to the investor. The consequence of this "flow-through" is that the individual investor, not the fund, is liable for tax. What do not pass on to the investor, however, and are therefore not taxable until received are the capital gains that have accrued to assets in the portfolio that have not yet been sold for profit. That's where the "unrealized" part comes in. Until the stocks are actually sold, the profits are not "realized." I'm over-simplifying this description somewhat but it is accurate enough for our needs. An example will help clarify this.

Suppose you hold units in a hypothetical mutual fund that, at the beginning of the year, had only three assets in its portfolio: $10 million of short-term cash invested in T-Bills, a $10-million government bond and $10 million worth of stock in the Apex Corporation. With such a portfolio, the earnings possibilities are as follows:

Asset	Possible Earnings Type
T-Bills	Interest
Bond	Interest and capital gains
Stock	Dividends and capital gains

Let us further assume that about halfway through the year, the fund made its only transaction: selling the bond that it purchased for $10 million for $10.1 million. Interest at the rate of 10 percent was earned on the bond up to the date it was sold and the T-Bill also generated interest income of 8 percent to the fund. Apex Corp. paid a dividend equivalent to 6 percent of its beginning-of-the-year share value. The shares of Apex also increased in market value through the year from $10 million to $11.5 million. The fund has 1,500,000 units issued in total and its operating expenses for the year were $500,000. What are the tax consequences under this scenario? The following tabulations show the earnings and "flow-through" to the mutual fund investor.

Income to mutual fund

Interest on T-Bill (12 months @ 8%)	$ 800,000
Interest on bond (6 months @ 10%)	$ 500,000
Capital gains on sale of bond	$ 100,000
Dividends from Apex (6% x $10,000,000)	$ 600,000
Total income	**$2,000,000**

Expenses of mutual fund

Operating	$ (500,000)
Net income	**$1,500,000**

"Flow-through" ($1,500,000/1,500,000 units) = $1.00 per unit

If your holdings in the fund were 1,000 units, you would receive a tax "slip" for $1,000 ($1.00 × 1,000 units). If the legal form of the mutual fund was a "trust," which is the most common, you would receive a T-3 and the $1,000 would be proportionately allocated by the fund manager to interest, dividends and capital gain types of income, which you would correspondingly include on the appropriate line of your tax return. If the mutual fund were set up as a "corporation," all the income you receive from it would be reflected on a T-5 as "dividend income" or capital gains and would be taxable as such. Note, however, that regardless of the legal form the mutual fund takes, the capital gains from the increase in the value of the Apex shares — that is, from $10 million to $11.5 million — does not get passed through to you because those gains have not yet been realized. When the stock is ultimately sold by the fund, any resulting profit will be passed along to the unit holders, but not until then. In this example, the total earnings for each unit were actually $2.50, made up of $1.00, calculated as above, plus $1.50 in unrealized capital gains. There is, then, a tax-deferral advantage associated with mutual fund investing: much of the gain is not taxed until the time when the stocks are ultimately sold for profit. Furthermore, capital *losses* from other stocks in the portfolio that might have been sold for less than its purchase price will be offset against those gains — leaving only the "net" gain taxable.

One final point should be made which, although it is not really tax related, does fit with our comments on distributions from mutual funds. The daily prices shown in the newspapers or quoted elsewhere *include all net earnings of the fund as they occur,* that is, *realized* and *unrealized.* If through the year a fund had income over and above its expenses of $1.00 per unit and unrealized capital gains of $0.50 per unit, the published unit value would have gradually risen by $1.50. So a fund with a unit value of the start of the year of, say, $5.00 would grow to $6.50 by year's end in this example. If you redeemed the fund just prior to the distribution, you would receive $6.50 per unit. If you held on to the fund until its distribution was made, normally at year-end, you would see the published unit value fall by the amount of the distribution. Each year, at the time of annual distributions, mutual fund companies are flooded with calls from investors who want to know why their funds suddenly lost so much value in a single day. In fact, investors didn't lose anything.

Using $5.00 as a starting unit value again, if that fund's price rose to $6.50 over the year as interest, dividends and capital gains (realized and unrealized) were reflected and then a distribution of $1.00 per unit were made to flow through the net income earnings to investors, the next day's price in your newspaper would be $5.50 ($6.50 – $1.00). You would be in the same net position because your units would be worth $5.50 and you would have received $1.00 cash for every unit you owned on the date distribution was made. Mutual funds accrue all earnings on a daily basis, so when some of those profits are paid out to the unit holders, the price has to fall by the amount of the distribution. In practice, most investors who are not using their mutual funds to provide income take advantage of the "automatic reinvestment of distribution" option available from most managers. Under that arrangement, the dollar value of the distributions is automatically reapplied by the management company to purchase additional units in the fund on the investor's behalf. The investor winds up with more units at a lower price, but the *total value* of his or her investment remains the same as it was before the distribution.

Whew! Am I glad that's over. I have said far more about tax than I ever intended to and once again, my advice is to talk to a professional.

SEGREGATED FUNDS

Segregated funds became the darlings of the managed money field during the latter part of the 1990s despite the fact that they had been around for decades as part of the product offerings of the life insurance industry. The term "segregated" comes from the legal requirement of the insurance industry that these funds be held separately — in other words, segregated — from the other assets of the insurance company. They cannot be used as part of the "reserves" that insurance companies must maintain to actuarially ensure they have adequate funds on hand to meet policy-holder obligations. The assets purchased by these funds must be kept exclusively for the benefit of their investors.

That difference aside, segregated funds function pretty much like conventional mutual funds do. They have similar investment philosophies and their managers buy and sell the same types of securities. Segregated funds are purchased and redeemed on a like basis, under familiar commission arrangements. Unit values are published in daily newspapers and long-term track records are available for performance comparisons. Most of the major brand-name mutual fund companies in Canada have now partnered with life insurance companies to offer segregated funds, hence their increased popularity.

Return of Capital Guarantee

The "return of capital guarantee" is the feature of segregated funds that has captured the hearts and minds of so many investors in recent years even though, as indicated, it has been available for decades. The life insurance industry apparently only recently learned that, by teaming up with major mutual fund companies, they could offer this benefit to a far larger marketplace. Here's how you make the "guaranteed" part of a segregated fund contract work for you:

- Invest in a segregated fund.
- Wait 10 years.
- After 10 years, if the value of your investment is not at least 75 percent of the amount you deposited, cash it in.
- The insurance company guarantees to pay you at least 75 percent of the amount you invested.

In fact, today the more popular segregated funds have improved on the 75 percent guarantee and now promise to pay you 100 percent of your deposits!

Sound too good to be true? Well, it's true enough but the bigger question is "What's the catch?" Actually, there is no catch but there are a couple of things to keep in mind. First of all, the chances of your investment's being worth less than you paid for it 10 years in the future are slim. In fact, my research indicates that there has never been a 10-year period over the past 50 years when an investment in a diversified Canadian portfolio of stocks (the TSE specifically) would have lost money. So a 75 percent or even a 100 percent return of capital guarantee isn't too big a gamble on the part of the insurance or mutual fund company from that perspective. Nevertheless, there is always the chance that some 10-year period will see disastrous market conditions and that guarantee will be worth real money. But there's more to this. The much more important benefit of this guarantee feature is that it also applies in the event of the death of the investor. That's where the insurance company comes in. If the investor dies within the 10-year period and the value of the fund is less than the original investment, the beneficiary or estate will receive 100 percent (not 75 percent) of the initial value. Obviously, if the value of the fund were greater than the initial investment, the payout would be for the higher amount. A friend of mine has suggested that the chances of dying in any 10-year period are greater than the chances of the market having an overall negative return over that same time. I don't know if that is statistically sound reasoning, but I do believe that because death is an uncertain event, this insurance benefit has considerably more value than a 10-year performance guarantee.

There is even more good news. I mentioned earlier when talking about mutual funds that the competition among firms has led to some quite interesting product innovations. The same has occurred on the segregated fund front. Imagine this scenario. You are 10 years away from your planned retirement age and you decide to invest in a segregated fund offered by a well-established mutual fund company — perhaps one you have been supporting for years because of their great long-term track record. As you hoped (and expected), the value of your fund has risen steadily for seven or eight years and is now worth twice as much as you originally invested. (A 9 percent annual return would double your money in eight years — remember the Rule of 72?) Then the markets take a serious tumble, losing 30 percent for each of the next two years. Now, not only have your gains been wiped out but your investment is actually worth a few dollars less than you paid for it and you are only a year or so away from retirement. How do you feel?

Fortunately, most of the popular funds have recognized how upset people would be if something like that occurred, so they have come up with an interesting twist to the 10-year guarantee.

They will permit investors to "lock in" the value of their fund, for purposes of the performance guarantee, at any higher amount resulting from market gains. Here's a simple example:

Original Investment	$10,000
Average Annual Return	10%
Value after 5 Years	$16,105
New "guaranteed" amount after "lock-in"	$16,105

So your gains are protected. You simply inform the fund provider at any time that you want to lock in your profits so that, in the event of your death or your investment's maturity, that minimum value is preserved, rather than the lower amount of your initial investment.

Most companies will allow you to lock in a number of times each year but there is small catch. Every time you lock in a value for your fund, the 10-year period starts over. That's only fair to the issuing company. Asking them to guarantee your accumulated value without the opportunity for the long-term returns of the market to work on their behalf would be unreasonable.

Creditor Protection

Another distinguishing feature of segregated funds is that they are considered "insurance policies" by the regulators rather than investment securities. This could be important to investors who encounter financial difficulty so severe that it results in their declaring personal bankruptcy. Because segregated funds are classified as insurance policies, they cannot normally be included among the assets that creditors or bankruptcy trustees can attach for unpaid debts or other obligations. Conventional mutual funds are deemed part of one's assets and, therefore, assailable. There are rules against "last-minute" deliberate use of segregated funds to avoid creditors, and several cases remain before the courts for interpretation, but, in general segregated funds offer greater creditor protection than most other investments.

Still sound too good to be true? Do all these benefits — the guarantees at death and maturity, the lock-in privileges and creditor protection — come without cost? The answer is "No." Segregated funds have higher management-expense ratios (MERs) than regular mutual funds — usually about 1 percent more. So whereas the average MER of a conventional mutual fund is approximately 2 percent, segregated funds would be in the 3 percent range. That's the cost of the "insurance" and it will have an effect on overall return as management expenses have to be paid before gains are passed on to the investors. So the decision is the same one you would make in any other investment situation — how much risk are you willing to assume for the return you expect? You can "self-insure" and have that extra 1 percent working for you or you can transfer some of the risk to someone else and accept a lower overall return. That decision is yours to make.

It is also worth noting that the arrangements between most mutual fund companies and life insurance companies are not perpetual — they are contracts that can be changed under certain terms and conditions. Theoretically, an insurance company that had heavy losses as a result of honouring some of the "guarantees" could terminate its agreement with the fund company. I am not suggesting that this will occur or that mutual fund companies do not have contingency plans in place, but in deciding whether segregated funds offer value you should be aware of this risk too.

Note also that the number and variety of segregated funds offered today is nowhere near the range of conventional mutual funds. Consequently, many of your portfolio choices arising from the asset allocation decisions you make may not be available in the form of a segregated fund. However, despite the increased cost and limited choice, segregated funds may be an appropriate addition to the portfolios of many investors.

WRAP ACCOUNTS

The wrap account is another type of investment that has been around for a while, 10 years or so, but has become popular only recently. Like many other fast-rising investment vehicles, the definition of a wrap account has been stretched to include a wide range of products. Let's see if we can bring some order to the confusion.

To begin with, we should note that the term "wrap" originally referred to how the fees for this type of investment were charged to investors. Rather than assessing individual transaction fees (commissions) each time a security or mutual fund was bought or sold, the adviser or adviser firm "wrapped" everything up in one annual charge, usually 2 to 3 percent of the total value of the assets under management. Presumably, this did two things:

- It simplified the process of buying and selling. With no need to consider transaction costs, investors could structure and alter their portfolios as they saw fit.
- It reduced the overall cost to investors, particularly those with a more active personality.

Furthermore, it eliminated any concern that investment recommendations by an adviser were being made in an effort to generate additional commissions. Under the rules of operation for most wrap accounts, there is unlimited trading for the same fee, so it makes no difference how many trades are processed. We should note, however, that some programs, particularly where the entry level is relatively low, do have an annual cap on the number of transactions that are permitted under the "one fee." In those cases, a nominal charge will be assessed for each transaction over and above that number.

Regardless of the terms and conditions, most wrap accounts offer similar features, such as:

- Financial planning
- Risk assessment
- Asset allocation
- Customized (or semi-customized) portfolio design
- Money management services (account transfers, chequing, etc.)
- Personalized reporting
- Safekeeping of securities

Some add in estate and tax planning, although these benefits are often found only in the higher end programs that we'll describe in the next section on private wealth management services.

Wrap accounts can generally be categorized by two criteria:

1. The minimum amount of money the client must invest
2. The degree of customization permitted

Not surprisingly, it works like this — the more money you have, the greater your ability to customize the product and services to your needs. Who says money doesn't talk?

Bearing in mind that every firm offering wrap accounts adds its own features to the product for competitive reasons, here is a broad breakdown of the industry.

Entry Level

There was a time when you could not participate in a wrap program unless you had several hundred thousand dollars to invest.

Competition and technology, however, have driven that number way down. Today, you can join for as little as $2,000. As noted, however, you won't get much in the way of customization at that level. Where you will typically find your money invested is in a "mutual fund wrap" account, through which you have access to a number of pre-packaged mutual fund portfolios. These portfolios are structured to recognize varying levels of risk tolerance among investors. So all "conservative" investors, for example, will have the same portfolio of funds; similarly, all "very aggressive" investors will have the same portfolio, and so on. The funds within each portfolio are pre-selected by the management firm, according to their assessment of risk/return potential, to match typical investor profiles. The chosen funds are normally brand names but there is no opportunity for clients to mix and match funds.

The process requires investors to complete a questionnaire of some sort. The answers given about personal situation, risk tolerance, investment experience and so on are scored and the resulting score dictates which portfolio you are offered. You don't have to accept that one but if the questionnaire is well structured, there should be a reasonable match between your preferences and at least one of the packaged portfolios.

Mid-Level

The process for the next level of wrap accounts is very similar to the first one just described. The questionnaire might be slightly more detailed but the end result is still a recommended portfolio dependent on your risk/return profile and needs. The big difference is that there is an opportunity to tailor the portfolio more toward your personal preferences. This type of account uses pooled funds as well, as opposed to individual securities, but may also offer access to funds or money managers that aren't normally available to individual investors. The actual funds are almost always held in what is called "nominee" form — that is, in the name of the investment dealer, not the client. This doesn't mean that it isn't your money. Of course it is and the dealer cannot make any trades or changes to the portfolio without your permission, although it would not be uncommon for investors to give their brokers limited discretionary trading authority. "Nominating" the dealer to act on your behalf facilitates transactions on short notice and substantially reduces the paperwork.

The ante to get into this game can be as high as $50,000 to $100,000 or even more, depending on the philosophy and reputation of the firm offering the product and the number of extra "bells and whistles" you get. There is more competition in this segment of the managed money market than any other so, as noted, firms are being increasingly innovative and flexible in their efforts to attract and retain clients. If this type of program appeals to you, it can really pay to shop around for the package of products and services best suited to your needs.

Upper Level

Usually requiring a minimum portfolio size of $150,000 to $500,000, this is where wrap accounts originally started. This is also the entry level for separately managed accounts that characterize the wealth management services we'll review in the next section. By "separately managed," we mean that the securities are in the name of the investor, not nominee form as described above. In addition to a virtually unlimited choice of pooled funds, investors using this stage of wrap account service can include stocks, bonds, mortgages and many other popular investments in their portfolios. Again, the degree of customization can vary among firms.

PRIVATE WEALTH MANAGEMENT SERVICES

The purest form of managed money is found among the firms that dedicate themselves to meeting the needs of investors with a very high net worth. Often insisting on a minimum portfolio of $1 million to $10 million, these specialists offer the highest level of service and flexibility. As a result of the larger account size, private wealth management firms are able to have a much more personalized relationship with their clients. Whereas under the wrap account scenario the client's contact person is normally the stockbroker or investment adviser, in the private money manager world, there is normally a direct liaison between the client and the person who actually manages his or her money. Consequently, many firms in this arena limit the number of clients they have so as to maintain the level of service appropriate for (and often demanded by) wealthier investors.

Fees for private wealth management services are normally scaled down as the portfolio size increases, for example, starting at 1.5 to 2 percent on the first $1 million; 1 percent on the next $1 million; 0.5 percent on the next, and so on.

Again, there can be significant variance among firms as to the number and calibre of services they offer, but at a minimum, private wealth managers should provide everything that wrap account managers do with more personalization and attention. In particular, clients should expect to receive a comprehensive Investment Policy Statement derived from some fairly in-depth discussions with the management firm about personal situation, goals, risk, security preferences, etc. (I've included a sample IPS in the next chapter.) That is not to say that wrap account managers don't care or are less attentive than private wealth managers — but you should get what you pay for as you move up the ladder, don't you think?

Some private wealth managers have really taken the role to heart and have moved beyond simply managing their clients' money.

They have become "life managers" and offer to arrange and supervise just about every financial aspect of a client's life, including:

- Financial, tax and estate planning
- Insurance (life, health and property)
- Banking (lines of credit, account transfers)
- Bill payments
- Accounting (personal and corporate)
- Employment contract negotiation

Some have even purchased cars for their clients and arranged for snow shovelling while the clients were on holiday in Hawaii!

MONEY MANAGER PERFORMANCE

As a conclusion to this chapter and a prelude to the next, I want to make two points regarding the performance of money managers. They are that:

1. All money managers are not created equal.
2. Good and not-so-good money managers exist everywhere.

The first of these is fairly straightforward — some managers are better than others. Investment analysis is a complex information-processing activity with hundreds of variables to consider, most of which are constantly changing. It requires talent and discipline to stay ahead of the game. And some managers, from time to time, appear to be more skilled at the task. But the manager who "gets it right" today may not do so tomorrow, perhaps not for want of skill but because her philosophy is out of favour with current market sentiment. Should she then abandon her fundamental approach to investing or would you, as one of her clients, want her to remain consistent to the theme that attracted you to her in the first place? If you've chosen wisely in the beginning, I hope you'd take the latter view.

Oft-quoted studies attempt to challenge the validity and the value of professional money management by showing how many managers fail to outperform the market. To me, that is like saying that all doctors who graduated in the bottom half of their class aren't good doctors, because they were below average. Is that true? Of course not! Clearly, some managers have superior long-term track records and we should have more confidence in them than those with poor long-term performance. In the next chapter, I'll give you my formula for evaluating investment managers but remember that the margin between "good" and "not-so-good" in the money management business is narrow.

Second, I want to make sure I haven't misled anyone into thinking that superior money management comes only at the highest level of client service. To be sure, firms handling the financial affairs of high net worth individuals can often attract very talented money managers because they can afford to reward them well. But so can and do "everyday" mutual fund companies. Some of the most reputable portfolio managers in the world are responsible for many of the mutual funds we almost take for granted today. These funds got to be household names through superior performance and service and they will continue to have a major share of the market so that any investor can have access to them.

Summary

* Managed money is likely the best investment choice for most Canadians and represents the fastest-growing segment of the financial services industry.
* Managed money evolved from three basic investment strategies:

- pooling of assets,
- diversification, and
- professional management.
* Pooled funds offer the advantages of
  - liquidity,
  - diversification among assets, assets classes and managers,
  - variety of funds for every objective,
  - flexibility of investment options and payout plans
  - full-time management, and
  - short- and long-term track record.
* Managed money comes in many forms:
  - Mutual funds
  - Segregated funds
  - Wrap accounts
    - Entry level
    - Mid-level
    - Upper level
  - Private wealth management services
* All money managers are not created equal.
* Good and not-so-good money managers exist everywhere.

12 Working With Professionals

If you think hiring a professional is expensive,
try hiring an amateur.
— RED ADAIR, RENOWNED OILWELL FIREFIGHTER

Before we discuss what to look for and how to work with a professional adviser and/or investment manager, we should each ask ourselves the question "Do I need one?" Certainly, the do-it-yourself approach has flourished in just about every area where many of us previously relied on the talents of specifically trained professionals. Now we buy the tools at Home Depot to do our own renovations and repairs; search the World Wide Web for a new house or the best deal on an automobile; bake fresh bread overnight in self-activating machines; publish a quality newsletter from our personal desktop computer; concoct our own private-label wine and beer; and do our banking via touch-tone telephone or over the Internet.

Bookstores overflow with self-help titles, and one of the largest selections is always in the personal finance section. Newspapers are filled with advertisements from direct sellers of so-called no-load mutual funds and the ravings of more than a few journalists to "Avoid the fees!" for financial products and services. Repeatedly we are told that most managers fail to outperform the market and that most financial advisers are more interested in their personal welfare than that of their clients. So the question "Do I need a professional?" is not surprising.

Before we get any further along, let me disclose my bias (if it has not already become obvious). I believe in the *value* of *good* professional *service*. Note the emphasis on three words: *value*, *good* and *service*. I am willing to engage others to do things for me that I don't have the time, interest or ability to do myself, provided:

- I receive something valuable from them (advice, a product or needed service) at a fair price.
- They are competent and knowledgeable about whatever they are providing to me.
- Their service meets a reasonable standard of timeliness, accuracy and personalization.

ADVANTAGES OF DOING IT YOURSELF

With this in mind, let's look at the advantages of the do-it-yourself approach to financial management. I see them falling into three areas:

1. *Cost* — There is no argument that many financial products, such as mutual funds, can be purchased directly from the manu-

facturer — that is, a fund company — or through a whole-saler/retailer, such as a discount broker, at little or no sales charge or commission. If you know exactly which funds you need and want or are willing to go along with the pre-packaged portfolio the seller offers to everyone in circumstances similar to yours, this probably makes sense. I caution you to keep two things in mind, however. First, watch out for the less obvious charges for set-up, annual renewals, transfers and/or early with-drawal. All mutual funds have management expenses that are shared by all investors but many so-called no-load funds do assess fees and charges for certain transactions or events. Second, the advertisements and past performance numbers that may attract you to a particular fund in the first place can be alluring but may not reflect the future or even the current reality. They may have encouraged you to *buy* but they will seldom tell you when to *sell*. Holding on to the wrong investment too long or selling too soon can be disastrous. As Red Adair, world-famous Canadian oilfield fire-fighter remarked when asked why he was able to charge such huge fees for capping an out-of-control oil-well fire, "If you think hiring a professional is expensive, try hiring an amateur."

2. *Superior skill* — To accept this as an advantage, you must be convinced that by intellect, information, intuition, insight and interest, you are better than the pros. If that is the case, I congratulate you! Successful financial planning and investment management are complex. The vast amount of information to be integrated into the decision-making process is made even more daunting by the constantly shifting sands of the environment. Economic, political, taxation, interest rate, fiscal, monetary and psychological factors are in constant flux so that evaluating them all simultaneously and coming to a conclusion about an appropriate strategy is quite an accomplishment. Which brings

me to my caveat in this debate — *don't confuse information with knowledge.* Remember that even the most successful investment managers admit they are right only slightly more often than they are wrong. That marginal rate of victory ultimately translates into a return advantage for their clients, but it is achieved only by combining extensive experience, sophisticated research, determined discipline and a little bit of luck! Bear in mind as well that if you decide you can compete with the pros, you will at least occasionally be on the opposite side of the table from them, either in choosing specific securities or forecasting market movements. Do you really want to play high-stakes poker with the world's best players?

3. *Personal pleasure* — Remember my story of Mr. B. from the previous chapter? He was the one who had accumulated a $1.2-million portfolio and then decided, as he aged, to hand the bulk of it over to professional money managers to invest on his behalf. You may recall that analyzing investments and playing the market had been his hobby — his passion, in fact — for more than 50 years, occupying 20 to 30 hours a week of his time. Clearly, Mr. B. got considerable *psychic reward* from his avocation in addition to the investment results he achieved.

There is another lesson in Mr. B.'s tale, and it becomes apparent when we recall that Mr. B. was going to give the professional money managers $1 million of his $1.2-million total portfolio and retain control over the $200,000 balance so that he could continue to play the market. I think that is a great strategy for someone who wants to take the do-it-yourself route but doesn't want all the risk. At the very least, you'll have something against which to compare outcomes. If your personal results consistently exceed those of the professionals (over an extended period), you may well be blessed with unusual talent or more than your share of good luck. Take advantage of it! On the other hand, should your skills not measure up to those of the pros, you will not have risked your entire portfolio to find that out.

Having looked at the "plus" side of the ledger for the do-it-yourself position in this debate, let's consider some of the reasons the majority of people choose *not* to take that approach. We have already covered several of them in the previous chapter on managed money. I won't repeat them all here. Even so, this additional list of disadvantages is somewhat longer than the list of advantages.

DISADVANTAGES OF DOING IT YOURSELF

1. *Complexity of choice* — With more than 2,500 mutual funds, literally thousands of stocks and bonds and countless other investment options available to us, there are simply too many places to put our money. It is easy to become overwhelmed by the choices. As a consequence, many of us take the path of least resistance and invest only in those things with which we are most familiar, running the risk of ignoring investments that offer the greatest prospect of helping us meet our objectives. Conversely, because we know we are missing out on some great opportunities (even though we aren't sure what they are), we'll often be tempted by a good "story." That means we may find ourselves the proud owners of shares in some long-defunct gold mine–turned–Internet provider or vending machines that were supposed to dispense freshly cooked pizza slices but kept burning up in heaps of melted cheese.

   This is not to say that we should expect our professional advisers to consider every conceivable investment opportunity on our behalf. Their job, however, is to narrow the field of choices. In spite of the above dig at mining companies, professional advisers can be likened to gold miners in that they start with the largest rocks they can handle, filter them through a series of increasingly fine-mesh screens until they ultimately end up with pure gold. This sifting-and-winnowing process is one of the most valuable activities we pay for when we hire a professional money manager or investment adviser.

2. *Information overload* — The complexity of choice described above leads to another responsibility that must be accepted by the do-it-yourselfer — the need to keep track of what's going on with your financial and investment program. If there are individual securities in your portfolio, that means watching the markets, interest rates, trading volumes, prices and news re-leases to ensure that those investments remain appropriate for your needs. Alternatively, if you have included some type of pooled funds, it means keeping tabs on the managers you chose. Are they still performing as expected? How do they compare to their peers? Are the same people, in fact, still involved? Have they remained consistent to the philosophy and strategy they had when you first selected them?

   Additionally, there is all the paperwork that accompanies doing everything yourself. There are purchase and sale confir-mations, tax reporting and the important matter of ensuring that the portfolio continues to reflect the asset allocation you desire. As noted previously, portfolios can drift from their original weightings easily and need to be regularly reviewed and, per-haps, rebalanced to maintain the desired risk/return profile.

3. *The illusion of success* — This notion is often expressed other ways in investment lingo. One goes like this: "A rising tide lifts all ships." Here is another, slightly less polite version: "Don't confuse a bull market with brains." The inference is clear — investment success can come *despite* an individual investor's decisions rather than *because* of them. When this occurs, it is

often difficult to give credit where it is due, and the individual investor frequently and unconsciously develops at least a modest sense of invincibility. I recall an old university chum at a reunion proudly boasting that he was earning 22 percent on his bond portfolio. The fact was that he had *always* invested exclusively in bonds, sometimes earning less than T-Bills! It wasn't his insight or unique skill that rewarded him with such great returns. His chosen investment vehicle just happened to be at the top of its price cycle at that time.

This sense of invulnerability also manifests itself when individual investors are "hot" — for example, when they pick winning stocks or sectors several times in a row. In those instances, the underlying risks are often ignored because the investors believe they have such great insight into the market or a particular security that either *market* or *business* risk is no longer an issue. Almost inevitably, however, the winning streak fades and the portfolio often ends up in poorer condition than it was before the "winners" were brought on board.

4. *Emotional push and pull* — The latest scientific study in the field of investing is called behavioural finance (or behavioural economics). We have discussed some of its findings and theories already in this book when we examined the psychology of investing. The underlying premise of this research is that *people do not always behave rationally under conditions of risk*. And since investing invariably has some element of risk associated with it, we can expect investors to do things that they would reject as inappropriate behaviour under less stressful circumstances. This is one area where the experience and objectivity of a professional adviser can be most valuable because while your heart might be in the right place, your stomach may not.

It is at the time when markets or individual investments aren't behaving as anticipated that investors are most vulnerable to straying from their planned strategy. That's when they have the greatest tendency to sell too low or buy too high, act on rumours and "hot tips," are susceptible to the preachings of so-called investment gurus and respond emotionally rather than logically. The professional adviser's role, at that point, is to get the investor back on track, remind him or her of the core strength of the strategy, ensuring that it continues to meet the client's long-term needs.

5. *Avoiding serious mistakes* — In a much earlier chapter we discussed how to win by not losing. We looked at the rates of return required to catch up when an investment program loses money in the early years. This also points to one of the major advantages of using the services of professional financial planning or investment advisers — they seldom take such large bets that a decline in any one sector or security will seriously damage the prospect of meeting a long-range objective.

As I think about this, I am reminded of one of my favourite pastimes, watching professional golfers at work. It never fails to amaze me how on any given day, any golfer can win a professional tournament. These people are good! Even the newest rookie can put together a couple of good rounds and end up in contention for the championship. More often than not, however, in such situations, one of the seasoned veterans will magically appear near the top of the leader board, apparently from nowhere, having slowly, quietly, methodically worked his or her way up from somewhere back in the pack. The neophyte front runner is suddenly challenged by the presence of one of the big-name players and frequently crumbles under the pressure, attempting shots that are beyond his or her limited expertise and changing the game plan that up to that point was successful. Meanwhile, the veteran continues with proven strategy, avoiding mistakes, gaining stroke after stroke and ultimately takes first place. The analogy to investing is this — professionals win points; amateurs lose them.

So my bias is clear — I endorse the use of professional advisers. The next question, then, is "How do I find the one that is right for me?" To answer that, we first have to differentiate between two professional management approaches; that is going to lead us into one of the investment world's never-ending debates — which is better, *active* or *passive* management?

ACTIVE VERSUS PASSIVE MANAGEMENT

Let's start with definitions. *Active* management proponents believe:

- There is an art and a science to security selection.
- Professional money managers can do better than individual investors due to knowledge, skill or technology.

Passive management supporters, on the other hand, contend:

- Investment markets are so "efficient" that prices reflect all available information and adjust too quickly for active security selection to add value.
- After transaction costs, active managers cannot "beat the market."

In simpler terms, *active* management requires the manager to have a hand in what is happening, trying to gain advantage by buying and selling the correct securities, rotating the portfolio from one sector to another or shifting the asset mix. *Market timing* would be considered an extreme form of *active* management. *Passive* managers are perceived as just "going along for the ride." That isn't quite accurate because *passive* managers often do make active trading decisions. However, they respond to widely known information about individual securities and market or economic conditions rather than trying to outguess the markets.

Index Funds

The most extreme form of *passive* management is *indexing*, which is the practice of buying or mirroring a major market index, like the TSE 300 Index or the Dow Jones Industrial Average. There is no active security trading, so without those costs indexers should have returns very close to those of the markets themselves. (There are some management expenses that must be covered in any circumstance.) Index mutual funds are one of the fastest-growing categories of investment vehicles. In my opinion, that's because markets have been generally going up over the past few years, sometimes substantially. Therefore, there is a strong case to be made for using lower cost index funds to participate in the upswing. The real test for these funds will come when markets decline for some extended period, as they inevitably will. Then the index funds will fall correspondingly. I wonder if most index investors are psychologically prepared to stand back and watch that happen?

Which Is Better?

This debate will never end, simply because the investment world is too dynamic. When markets are climbing, the argument shifts in favour of *passive* management. Why pay the extra costs of active management when so many managers fail to outperform their respective indices? When markets start to tumble, however, many investors want the expertise of a professional *active* manager to cushion the fall. In fact, this is the most frequently cited argument in favour of active management — managing risk — and isn't that what this book is all about? So you can probably guess on which side of the table I sit. I am a believer in active management because:

- It offers potentially better downside risk management.
- The number of passively managed investment products is very limited in comparison to those that are actively managed. Consequently, it may be impossible to achieve the level of diversification considered necessary in a portfolio or to incorporate all the desired asset classes, sectors, specialty securities or management styles (growth versus value, for example).
- There is a legion of good money managers who have consistently outperformed their respective indices. Their expertise is only available through actively managed products.

And finally, but perhaps as important as anything else, is the fact that we are human beings, which means we bring emotions into the investment arena with us. There are psychological rewards that come from using active management services:

- We feel more involved in the process.
- We feel more comfortable that someone is doing something when things go awry.
- We have a sense of hope and optimism that we *will* beat the market sometimes.

Here then is my summary advice on how to deal with the "active/passive" debate — *take an active role in manager selection and a passive role in security selection.* I believe that will give you the best of both worlds.

HOW TO CHOOSE AN INVESTMENT MANAGER

There is a natural tendency, when evaluating professional money managers, to focus solely on *rate of return* as a measure of their ability. For instance, many mutual fund companies urge us to do so with their advertising or through the emphasis they place on performance when they meet with the investment advisers who represent them, who, in turn, pass that information on to us. I am happy to say that many investment management firms are now recognizing the heightened sophistication of their prospective clients and have shifted the theme of their promotion to other benefits of their products. That having been said, I like to scrutinize potential money managers from four perspectives: *results*, *risk*, *rank* and *resources*.

Results

In the previous chapter, I made the point that the availability of a long-term track record was one of the advantages that *managed money* products had over other investments. I now need to add a caveat to that statement, which is to use *cumulative* performance as a preliminary screen only. It is essential to look at *year-by-year* results to accurately assess a portfolio manager's prowess and his or her suitability for you in view of your personal risk tolerance.

Let me illustrate with a simple example using a couple of mutual funds so that I can apply actual performance data to show how this works in real life. I have rounded off the numbers for clarity.

Suppose you had the chance to invest $10,000 in either of two funds with the following results:

	Fund A		Fund B	
	% Gain	$ Value	% Gain	$ Value
Year 1	+40%	$14,000	+10%	$11,000
Year 2	−20%	$11,200	+13%	$12,400
Year 3	+25%	$14,000	+12%	$13,900
Year 4	+ 4%	$14,600	+14%	$15,900
Year 5	+20%	$17,500	+ 8%	$17,500

On a cumulative basis, both funds would be worth exactly the same after five years and, consequently, their five-year performance would be listed in the various financial information sources as identical. However, look at the different tracks taken to get to the same result. Fund A did four times as well as Fund B in the first year, twice as well in the third and two-and-a-half times better in the fifth. That would have been exciting! On the other hand, Fund A also lost 20 percent of its value in the second year. That, too, would probably have gotten your heartbeat up a bit! I can imagine typical headlines (and advertisements) in the financial press at the end of Year 1 — "Hottest Fund in Canada Quadruples Results!" — then in Year 2 — "Has Fund 'A' Lost Its Magic?" — to be followed in the third year by something like "Fund 'A' Is Back!" This is an obvious lesson in the danger of looking at short-term performance, *good or bad*, because as illustrated, there would be no dollar difference if you were in either fund for the full five years.

But what if you sat on the sidelines through the first year until the media hype convinced you that Fund A was the place to put your money? You might have jumped in at the beginning of the second year, just in time to watch your investment shrink by 20 percent! Or suppose you had to redeem your fund at the end of the second year. Fund A would have generated a net return of about 6 percent annually while Fund B yielded more than 11 percent average per year. And finally, you would have to ask yourself, "Was the excitement of the good years worth the psychological roller-coaster ride that came along with it?" I'm not certain that it is, so my clear preference is to avoid funds with inconsistent performance. For your convenience, I repeat here the chart from Chapter 2 showing the recovery time necessary to get back on track in a five-year time horizon.

Annual Gain Needed Next 4 Years to Meet Target		
First-Year Loss	10% Target	15% Target
10%	16%	22%
15%	17%	24%
20%	19%	26%
25%	21%	28%
30%	23%	30%
40%	28%	35%
50%	34%	41%

Risk

To summarize this discussion, when looking at the performance of money managers, do so from three angles: long-term *cumulative* returns as a preliminary assessment of their expertise; *year-by-year* results as an indication of volatility; and *consistency* to give you some notion of the degree of risk associated with that volatility. The investment industry has developed a number of ways to measure and report on *risk-adjusted* returns. Many financial information sources and most investment advisers should be able to evaluate your prospective money managers on the basis of a specific measurement called the Sharpe Ratio, which was developed by another Nobel Prize winner, Bill Sharpe. This statistic uses the same components of standard deviation that we discussed in Chapter 5 and calculates the amount of additional return an investor should expect to receive for every additional unit of risk assumed. Confusing? Think of it as a "reward-to-volatility" ratio. How much more return should we get for taking on extra volatility? The actual calculation yields a decimal number, such as 0.55, for example, which would mean that I should be rewarded with a 0.55 percent increase in return for every 1 percent increase in volatility. Obviously, then, the higher the Sharpe Ratio, the better the tradeoff is between risk and reward. A ratio of 0.80, for example, suggests more incremental return for each additional unit of risk than a ratio of 0.55. Don't worry too much about the calculation. It is being more widely published in newspapers in the mutual fund performance columns so you can look it up if you want to. It is a useful piece of information but you can also get a general sense of what it measures by simply studying year-by-year performance, comparing returns and volatility.

Rank

The statement was previously made that "all money managers are not created equal" and, particularly when it comes to generating returns, all portfolio managers are not blessed with the same talent. Therefore, you must look beyond absolute performance to improve your chances of picking the best managers for your needs. You must consider the *ranking* of investment managers *relative to their peer group*. It's great to have a manager who has a track record that gives you confidence in his or her ability to generate the rate of return needed to meet your long-term objectives. But if that performance is substantially lower than other managers with similar funds are achieving, you are taking on more risk than is necessary. If your target rate of return is 10 percent and the manager you choose achieves that level, you might be satisfied until you discover that most other managers of similar funds are earning 14 percent. That would mean you were exposing yourself to the same risk for a 10 percent return as your neighbour would be for a 14 percent return. Here's the rule: "All other things being equal, if the risk is the same, choose the investment with the greatest expected return."

As mentioned earlier, there are no "all-weather" managers who perform well under every market condition. Although there are several hundred mutual fund managers to choose from in Canada, there isn't one who has ranked in the Top 10 of the performance charts for each of the past one-, three-, five- and ten-year periods. But let's look at a fund with a good 10-year track record that often placed near the top of its peer group. Following are the actual results for 10 years by that manager:

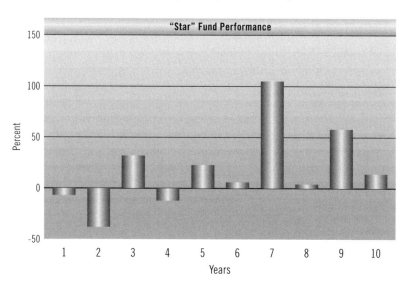

Had this fund been in your portfolio, the first two years would probably have tested your patience as you lost 7 percent and then 38 percent. Being a long-term investor, however, you stayed around for Year 3 and were rewarded with a first quartile (top 25 percent of all managers) return of 32 percent. Unfortunately, you gave some of it back in the next year but recovered again in Year 5. The next

12 months were relatively quiet with a 6 percent gain but then the big payoff — an industry-leading 105 percent more than doubled your money! Memories like that would surely keep you in through the next year, even with a meagre 4 percent return. And a good thing they did because the fund shot back up again by almost 60 percent before settling down in Year 10 to a more sedate 14 percent gain. What a ride!

During this period, this fund had a 10-year average annual return of more than 13 percent, which placed it in the top quartile of its peer group (which happens to be Canadian equities). Its three- and five-year numbers were even more impressive, at 25 percent and 32 percent respectively. On that basis, then, if Canadian equities were an appropriate asset for your portfolio, you might have chosen this fund because of its relative ranking. This example emphasizes the importance of studying year-by-year returns. The volatility of this fund was very high and should have been weighed against personal risk tolerance. Some investors wouldn't have minded the instability because they enjoy the thrill of extraordinary annual returns, even if they are sporadic. Others would have been quite uncomfortable with that kind of volatility and they would have looked for other ways to get slightly lower but more stable year-by-year returns. On the next page are the results of another fund, which also ranked high, although not at the top of the Canadian equity peer group.

The 10-year average annual return for this fund was slightly less than the 13 percent for the previously illustrated one, but the volatility was less than one-third — only ±11 percent compared to ±38 percent. Take your pick — the leader or someone near the top who might not be as spectacular but provides more consistent, above-average returns. Portfolio managers must be ranked according to their risk as well as their returns.

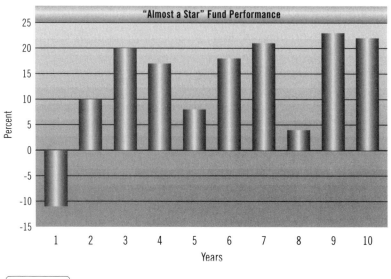

The final criterion addresses the ability of the manager to provide you with the level of expertise and service you require. The first of these, expertise, merits special attention.

If you are going to use performance as a guide to picking a professional investment management firm, you must ensure that the *portfolio manager* in place at the time you choose that organization is the same one who was responsible for the rates of return that attracted you in the first place. Portfolio managers do, from time to time, change companies, although many are also often significant shareholders in their own firms, lessening the likelihood that they will leave. However, it does happen that good managers retire, die or are attracted away by competitors. This is less of an issue if a committee rather than an individual manages the fund in which you are interested. In either case, however, you must determine who is responsible for the fund's track record and whether he or she is still in charge. You should be able to obtain a portfolio manager's performance history over at least five years, even if some of that time was spent managing money elsewhere. If you are look-ing at the track record of a manager while he or she was managing another fund, try to compare the type and mandate of the previous fund with the one you are considering. If they are substantially dif-ferent, you may not want to rely on the manager's past success being carried forward to the new environment.

The second consideration is *service*. Assuming you select your managers carefully, one would hope that they would be part of your investment strategy for many years. Therefore it makes sense to deal with an organization that can give you the level of service you desire. In the previous chapter on managed money, I discussed how some firms provide every imaginable service to their clients while others scrape by, barely meeting regulatory requirements for reporting and so on. Like most things in life, you generally get what you pay for, so if you think you'd like toll-free telephone numbers, regular portfolio updates, "no-fee" transfers, Internet access to your account or the simple convenience of walking into a bank building to do business, quiz the firms you are considering as to their capabilities and practices in these areas and any others that are important to you. Not one of these services is, by itself, critical to the success of your investment program. In evaluating professional advisers, however, it makes sense to consider the whole package.

SHOULD I HAVE MORE THAN ONE INVESTMENT MANAGER?

There is no standard answer to this question because the size of your portfolio, combined with your investor personality and risk tolerance, will have an impact on the decision. Consequently, what's right for you may not be for your neighbour. It would be reasonable to say, however, given some of the things we have covered in this book regarding diversification, that the greater the diversity among the managers, the more likely it is that you will be able to avoid major losses in overall portfolio value. It also seems prudent to respond to the increasing volatility of markets with a broader range of investments, which may mean using multiple managers to obtain the varied and specific expertise needed.

To simplify this discussion, I will assume that your entire portfolio is made up of mutual funds even though, for most readers, that will not be so. If that were the situation, as a minimum, you should have all three major asset classes represented by different funds, which would require you to own at least three funds. The alternative is to buy a balanced or asset allocation fund and have it represent all three classes for you; if your portfolio isn't too large or if you have a "passive money manager" personality, this may be just the thing to do. The shortcoming of those types of funds, as we discussed, is that you would be relying on the strategy of only one manager and the mix may be predefined, eliminating the possibility of tailoring your portfolio to suit your preferences.

On the other hand, if your portfolio is sufficiently large or you want to take a more active role in the management of your money, even three funds may not be enough. Let's say you elected to have 30 percent of your portfolio in Canadian equities. If you used only one manager and he or she had a bad year, 30 percent of your portfolio would suffer. Why not diversify among two or three Canadian equity managers so that if one underperforms, for whatever reason, only 10 or 15 percent of your assets will be affected? If you were going to do this, you would obviously want to look for two or three Canadian equity managers with different philosophies, strategies or market emphasis. Otherwise, the benefit of diversification would be minimized.

Can you own too many funds? Certainly you can, for a number of reasons, the most important being the potential for duplication of investments. There is little value in owning three bond funds that are all invested in the same bonds — there would be no diversification effect. This can be a problem with large Canadian equity funds, which are restricted to owning no more than a certain percentage of any one company (usually 10 percent) and no more than, say, 5 percent of the fund invested in any one stock. When those two constraints are combined and applied to multi-billion-dollar funds with mandates to invest primarily in Canada, the list of companies that qualify for investment narrows considerably. Consequently, most large Canadian equity funds have at least several of the same names in them, such as BCE, Nortel, Magna and Bombardier. As a general rule, look at the top 10 holdings in each fund, and if you see more than a 25 percent overlap, think about consolidating the funds or substituting a manager with a different mandate or outlook. Fortunately, in the Canadian mutual fund industry, many of the management companies have become huge complexes unto themselves and now offer up to 100 funds internally. It is quite possible, therefore, to stay within one fund family and still achieve good diversification. This may make transfer among fund types more efficient. But don't exclude some of the smaller, more specialized management firms from your search.

TERMINATING A MONEY MANAGER

The decision to "fire" an investment manager should not be an easy one nor undertaken without good reason. From time to time, all investment managers will underperform. Discarding a manager too quickly for poor performance has obvious consequences:

* The long-term plan may be disrupted.
* A new manager has to be found, who may or may not turn out to be better.
* There may be transaction costs or taxes to be paid.

We have already described the four criteria for selecting a money manager in the first place: *results*, *risk*, *rank* and *resources*. These are the same measures that should be used in determining whether to stick with a manager who appears to be falling short of your expectations. Ask these questions:

- For what period of time has his performance been below my expectation? Depending on your investment personality, what you think of as "too long" could be two months or two years.
- Is my manager *consistently* underperforming her peer group? Is this a one-time anomaly or has it happened before?
- Has there been any change in the organization? Is "my guy" still managing my money?
- Has there been any change in management style? Is the manager adhering to the original philosophy that attracted me to choose her in the first place?
- Am I aware of anyone who could do better?

Ironically, professional money managers do not often lose the loyalty of their clients due to poor performance exclusively. Most investors have come to appreciate that markets fluctuate and investment styles fall in and out of favour; they are willing to stay with a manager through the ups and downs for a while *provided* the manager is doing a good job of communicating what is happening and why. The lesson is to seek out a manager who keeps investors informed and thus minimizes the risk of alienation through what could be a temporary downturn in performance.

HOW TO CHOOSE AN INVESTMENT ADVISER

The title of this chapter is "Working With Professionals" and most of the discussion so far has centred on selection of a money manager. Now let's consider one of the other professionals you may want to include on your team — that is, the financial planner or investment adviser. Almost all the comments made previously with respect to money managers can also be applied to these pros, along with some additional thoughts. And while I have distinguished between a financial planner and an investment adviser, in many cases they are one and the same. Members of each group may specialize and not cross over to the area of expertise of the other, but increasingly, financial planners are becoming more involved in investment management and investment advisers are developing portfolio strategies only after taking their clients through some sort of financial planning process. For our purposes here, I will treat them as equally important and subject to the same selection standards. Here is one of my core beliefs: *investment recommendations should be made only in the context of a well-developed financial plan.* The investment strategy is a tool — the vehicle for getting you to your financial destination. The financial plan is the roadmap that tells you how far it is, what direction you should take and how long the journey will be.

I like to apply the following criteria when assessing professional financial planning or investment advisers:

1. *Competence* — Are they good at what they do? Do they have the required credentials for the level of expertise you require?
2. *Commonality* — Do you share a similar investment philosophy? If you are a passive money manager and he or she is an active market timer, the potential for disagreement and ultimate discord may be considerable.
3. *Comfort* — An amiable "warm and friendly" adviser may not garner or maintain the confidence of a no-nonsense Type A investor or vice versa.
4. *Communication* — Are you a "Here's my money — call me when I'm rich" type or do you want to have regular updates on your progress, including face-to-face meetings with your adviser?

5. Compensation — Are you aware of how your adviser is paid and are you comfortable with that arrangement?

If you are not already familiar with an adviser you respect and trust, ask your friends and colleagues for a recommendation, just as you would if you were seeking a new lawyer or doctor. You may also want to contact one of the industry's professional trade organizations such as the Canadian Association of Financial Planners (CAFP), the Canadian Association of Insurance and Financial Advisors (CAIFA), the Mutual Fund Dealers Association (MFDA), the Investment Funds Institute of Canada (IFIC) or the Investment Dealers Association (IDA). Other professional groups, including the Canadian Institute of Chartered Accountants (CICA), are also becoming active in the financial planning field. Any of these organizations will be pleased to provide you with a list of their qualified members in your area.

I also encourage you to read up on the subject yourself so that you can judge whether the adviser can bring true value to the relationship. Once you have identified an adviser whose services you would like to engage, ask that person to demonstrate his or her competence, for example, by showing work completed for others, by outlining the steps followed in the process and describing how specific investment recommendations were arrived at. In return, be prepared to disclose the details of your financial circumstances as they are today and communicate your thinking about the future. If you are honest with each other, by the end of an initial meeting, you'll know whether you can be a team.

Some caution is warranted here, however, because regrettably the financial services industry is not an easy one to sort out when you're trying to determine who does what. As noted previously, some advisers sell products only; there is nothing wrong with that if all you are looking for is an investment product specialist to carry out your self-designed plan. Product specialists may work for a bank, in which case they are normally compensated by salary, or as mutual fund representatives, stockbrokers or insurance agents, all of whom are usually compensated by commission. At the opposite end of the spectrum from the product specialists are the "fee only" financial planners, who perhaps make no product recommendations at all or who will, after completing your financial plan, refer you to a product specialist. As the description implies, these practitioners are paid for their time, on an hourly or flat-fee basis. The most frequently cited reason for hiring a fee-only adviser is that you want independent advice, unbiased toward any particular product because you believe the adviser is compensated by the client rather than by the product supplier. This may or may not be the case in fact. At the end of the day, whether one gets good value from a relationship still comes down to the integrity and competence of the adviser.

I have seen both good and not-so-good plans prepared by advisers under every conceivable compensation arrangement. I believe it would be accurate to say that, across the country, the majority of financial and investment plans have been prepared by advisers who are paid on a commission basis or perhaps on a fee-plus-commission basis. This is likely due to the simple fact that, historically, there have been many more people in the financial services industry working on a commission basis than working for fees or salary only. That balance is beginning to change, however, as the number of people entering the field increases. In particular, the banking industry has been very aggressive in introducing financial and investment planning services to their customers.

The "commission versus fee/salary" debate will probably persist forever so let me tell you where I stand. I would want an adviser who stood behind *both* the plan and the product because, as noted earlier, they are interdependent. I believe it is somewhat irresponsible to attempt to make intelligent asset allocation decisions without *first* considering an overall financial plan, and the plan will be worthless unless it is implemented through the judicious use of well-chosen investments.

A final comment now on the use of professional advisers, be they money managers or investment or financial planning specialists. Hiring one of these pros to guide or assist you through the maze of organizing and managing your financial affairs does not relieve you of the responsibility for what happens to your money. As stated when I introduced the investment pyramid much earlier in this book, defining your risk parameters and setting your objectives are the foundation to a successful investment plan. These cannot be delegated to anyone else. In fact, many professional advisers with whom I have spoken say one of their greatest challenges is getting their clients to be thoughtful or specific enough about what they need or want. Without a good understanding of what is motivating their clients, advisers cannot fully employ their skills. They then have to compromise and seek some middle ground in their recommendations. So, in dealing with any professional financial or investment adviser, consider carefully and completely what it is you are trying to accomplish and where your "comfort zone" is and be candid in your description.

THE PROFESSIONAL INVESTMENT POLICY STATEMENT

In Chapter 6, I introduced the notion of an Investment Policy Statement that was derived from our four-part investment pyramid. I indicated that later we'd look at a "professional" Investment Policy Statement (IPS) such as you should hope to receive if you engage a private wealth-management firm. It seems appropriate to include one in this chapter on working with professionals. The sample shown should not be considered in any way perfect or all-encompassing. For clarity, I have omitted most of the "boilerplate" text that is part of many investment policy statements to focus on the relevant points. Firms providing these services all have their own formats and clients will decide how valuable the IPS is to them, based on their own needs and preferences. So I'll be generic in my comments and recommend that this sample IPS be viewed as just that — a sample. Even if you are not involved with a firm that produces a detailed IPS for its clients or you are a do-it-yourselfer, you may find the sample useful as a guide to your own thinking.

Why a Formal Investment Policy Statement?

We can think of an IPS as a letter of understanding between the investor and the investment manager or adviser. Its benefits are as follows:

1. Provides a written description of the investment decision-making process from objective setting through implementation and ongoing monitoring of progress toward the goal
2. Is a model against which to measure performance
3. Provides a framework for evaluating new investment opportunities as they come along
4. Serves as the non-emotional tether that investors can use to ground themselves when markets are misbehaving and the temptation to act impulsively or irrationally is high
5. Can be made part of the financial or estate plan. This could be particularly important for older investors who have built sizeable portfolios. When the investor dies, the executors won't have to second-guess the intended investment strategy of the portfolio. It can be left intact for the heirs for many years if that was the deceased's wish. This might be desirable when the heirs are minors or have spendthrift habits.

Contents of an Investment Policy Statement

The IPS is both a planning tool and an expression of philosophy. It should, therefore, touch on all four steps in the process described back in Chapter 6:

1. Philosophy (Risk Tolerance + Personality)
2. Objectives (Growth, Income and/or Liquidity)
3. Asset Allocation
4. Security Selection

In addition, it should describe the monitoring process and the conditions under which it will be formally reviewed.

Looking at the sample at the end of the chapter, we see that the IPS is set out as follows:

1. *Purpose*
   a. Why the IPS was written — by whom, for whom, when
   b. Who has responsibility for what

2. *Objectives*
   a. Projected financial needs — how much and when
   b. Present asset allocation — where you are today?
   c. Risk tolerance and time horizon of the investor
   d. Risk profile and investment time horizon of the portfolio

Note that a well-written IPS will also contain several qualitative objective statements such as:

+ To be "reasonable and prudent"
+ To seek returns that are commensurate with the investor's risk tolerance

- To control costs of managing the portfolio
- To minimize taxes

3. *Investment Policy*

    a. The "rules" by which the investment strategy will be implemented

    b. Acknowledgement of the uncertainties of investing

    c. Investor preferences for asset classes or securities

    d. Desired rate of return

    e. When and how to rebalance

4. *Security Selection*

    a. Criteria for choosing securities

    b. List of types of securities *not* to be included in portfolio (e.g., tobacco, alcohol)

    c. List of types of transactions *not* permitted (e.g., leverage, options, commodities)

5. *Manager Selection*

    a. Results — Cumulative and year-by-year

    b. Risk — Volatility vs. return (Sharpe Ratio)

    c. Rank — Peer group performance

    d. Resources — Who's running the show? Services?

6. *Monitoring*

    a. Monthly — Current holdings, market value and transactions

    b. Quarterly — How is the portfolio doing against the benchmark? How is the manager doing against his or her peers? Is the asset allocation being followed?

    c. Annually — Review investor's risk tolerance, desired rate of return, asset class preference and time horizon to major disbursements. Analyze expenses and fees paid.

Summary

If the investment policy is well written, almost anyone reviewing the portfolio should be able to follow what was done. Guidelines should be specific enough to make it clear what was intended, yet give whoever is charged with implementing the strategy authority to actively (but prudently) manage the portfolio. The thoughtful drafting of a comprehensive IPS ensures that all responsibilities, assumptions and measurements are spelled out. However, it is not a do-it-once-and-forget-it exercise because the investment markets and our attitudes toward them change along with our objectives and needs. In the framework of wealth management, however, it can be a most valuable tool for both investors and their professional advisers.

INVESTMENT POLICY STATEMENT

for

Mr. and Mrs. Wealthy Client

Prepared by
HNW Wealth Management Inc.

Prepared on February 27, 2000

I. Purpose

The purpose of this Investment Policy Statement (IPS) is to guide HNW Wealth Management Inc. and Mr. and Mrs. Wealthy Client in effectively implementing and supervising a strategy for managing the Clients' investment assets. This is accomplished by:

* Describing the Clients' attitudes, expectations and objectives.
* Outlining the various asset classes, allocations and management styles to be used to yield the desired rate of return with full regard for the Clients' risk preferences.
* Providing guidelines for investment policy and security selection.
* Establishing criteria to evaluate and monitor manager performance.

II. Investment Objectives

Having completed a comprehensive review of the Clients' current and future financial requirements, it was jointly agreed that the objectives were:

a) *Liquidity* — To have sufficient liquid assets to pay all known current obligations and to have an allowance for unexpected expenses.

b) *Income* — There is no income requirement at this time. Income will be required beginning in Year 6 of the plan.

c) *Growth* — To achieve growth in overall portfolio values equal to the rate of inflation plus five percent (5%) on an after-tax, after-fee basis. This is to be accomplished by the application of "reasonable and prudent" investment strategies, controlling costs of managing the portfolio and minimization of taxes.

III. Investment Policy

1. *Time Horizon* — The strategy is based on a long-term perspective of ten (10) years or more. Consequently, short-term market fluctuations should not require deviation from the plan.

2. *Risk Tolerance* — The Clients recognize that investment markets fluctuate and that some short-term volatility must be accepted in order to achieve the long-term objectives. The Clients have described themselves as "moderately risk-tolerant" and expressed an ability to manage a loss in overall portfolio values of up to 20 percent in any 12-month period and 30 percent in any 24-month period.

3. *Performance Expectations* — As stated in the Objectives, the desired rate of return is "inflation plus five percent" on an after-tax, after-fee basis. Minimum acceptable three-year return is 15 percent before tax. These rates have been based on the assumption that future returns will approximate those historically earned on the types of assets to be included in the Clients' portfolio. The Clients acknowledge that past performance may not be indicative of future results and that a real return of 5 percent

may not be realistic under some market conditions. Therefore, additional performance benchmarks are outlined in Section VI (Monitoring), to be applied in those situations where expected long-range returns are not being realized.

4. *Asset Allocation*
The Clients have reviewed the long-term performance of various asset classes and, based on a balance of acceptable risk and reward, have chosen the following asset allocation:

Asset Class	Current	Desired	Minimum	Maximum
Canadian Equity	70%	40%	30%	50%
U.S. Equity	0%	20%	15%	30%
Global Equity	0%	15%	10%	20%
Canadian Bond	30%	0%	0%	0%
International Bond	0%	15%	10%	20%
Real Estate	0%	10%	5%	15%

5. *Rebalancing*
The Clients recognize that occasionally market conditions may shift the asset allocation, rendering the portfolio out of balance. To avoid unnecessary transaction costs and possible tax consequences, each asset class will be permitted to vary by up to 10 percent from its allocation. Variations greater than 10 percent will necessitate rebalancing according to the above limits. Additional contributions that the Clients may make from time to time should be allocated proportionately to maintain the asset mix in effect at that time.

IV. Security Selection
The following guidelines should be applied to the selection of securities:

1. *Equities*
  • No more than 10 percent of the portfolio's equity component may be invested in any one company (or related companies).
  • No more than 30 percent of the portfolio's equity component may be invested in any one economic sector.

2. *Bonds*
  • No more than 10 percent of the portfolio's fixed income component may be invested with any one bond issuer.
  • All bonds shall have a rating at least equivalent to a "BBB" as ranked by a recognized rating agency.

The following securities are not acceptable investments:
  • Companies directly involved in the tobacco industry
  • Companies operating for less than two years

The following transactions are not permitted:
  • Short selling
  • Lending cash or securities

V. Manager Selection
HNW Wealth Management Inc. will select money managers who are:

  • Registered Investment Counsellors.
  • Able to provide historical performance data for the five previous years.
  • Able to provide written statements of their investment philosophy, policies and procedures.
  • Able to report on a monthly, quarterly and annual basis.
  • Free from any pending legal or regulatory entanglements.

VI. Monitoring

a) Money Manager Responsibilities

   i. To manage the Clients' assets according to the IPS.

   ii. To inform HNW Wealth Management Inc. of any material changes that might affect the management of the Clients' assets.

b) Performance Benchmarks

   i. In addition to the performance criteria stated previously, the following benchmarks will be used for peer group evaluation:

Asset Class	Benchmark
Canadian Equity	TSE 300 Composite Index
U.S. Equity	Standard & Poor's 500 Index
International Equity	Morgan Stanley World Capital Index
International Bonds	Salomon Brothers World Bond Index
Real Estate	National Association of Real Estate Investment Trusts Index

VII. Reporting and Review

a) Monthly

On a monthly basis, each money manager shall provide an accounting of all transactions, current holdings and market value.

b) Quarterly

HNW Wealth Management Inc. and the Clients will meet on a quarterly basis to review:

- Money manager performance
- Consistency with IPS

c) Annually
At each fourth-quarter review, HNW Wealth Management Inc. and the Clients will review the Clients':

- Risk tolerance
- Desired rate of return
- Asset class preference and
- Time horizon to major disbursements.

Expenses and fees paid will also be analyzed.

VIII. Money Manager Review
Money managers will be placed under review if:

a) their performance is in the bottom half of their peer group in any quarter or annual period.
b) their five-year performance is in the bottom half of their peer group.
c) there is a material change that might affect the management of the Clients' assets.

Summary

- "If you think hiring a professional is expensive, try hiring an amateur."
- Don't confuse information with knowledge.
- Professional advisers can be likened to gold miners in that they start with the largest rocks they can handle, filter them through a series of increasingly fine-mesh screens until they ultimately end up with pure gold.
- Disadvantages of "doing it yourself":
  - Complexity of choice

- Information overload
- The illusion of success
- Emotional push and pull
- Avoiding serious mistakes
- *Active* management proponents believe:
  - There is an art and a science to security selection.
  - Professional money managers can do better than individual investors due to knowledge, skill or technology.
- *Passive* management supporters contend:
  - Investment markets are so "efficient" that prices reflect all available information and adjust too quickly for active security selection to add value.
  - After transaction costs, active managers cannot beat the market.
- Evaluate money managers from four perspectives:
  - Results
  - Risk
  - Rank
  - Resources
- Evaluate financial planners and investment advisers by their:
  - Competence
  - Commonality
  - Comfort
  - Communication
  - Compensation
- Think of an Investment Policy Statement as a Letter of Understanding between the investor and the investment manager or adviser.

Conclusion

Remember — the future comes one day at a time.

We have come a long way together and I congratulate you on completing the journey. I hope, as a result, you have greater confidence in your ability to achieve investment success than when we started. Let's take a brief look back at the path we followed.

We began our voyage by learning how we, as individuals, can use knowledge of our personalities, behaviour and attitudes toward money, in addition to the inherent concerns we all have about risk and volatility, to improve our chances for investment success. Of course, understanding how we think, feel and behave as investors is just the beginning. We also need to acquire knowledge about investing. And here, the problem is not a scarcity of knowledge, but too much of it. Sorting out what is relevant and appropriate for us individually requires discipline and, probably, the assistance of others. Consequently, we presented the research and wisdom of successful investment professionals and the financial academic community, including several Nobel Prize winners. Who better to listen to?

By combining a sense of who we are with a deeper understanding of sound investment principles, we saw how to prepare an intelligent and personal investment policy statement. Despite the apparent straightforwardness with which we did that, I know that "easier said than done" applies. It is one thing to intellectually understand the concepts presented and quite another to implement and adhere to principles that, over the long term, periodically place you at odds with much of the investing public, not to mention human nature itself.

Now it is up to you. Just as investment planning is not a "do-it-once-and-forget-about-it" proposition, I don't expect you to remember everything we have discussed and apply it completely throughout your investing experience. So keep this book handy for future reference and skim through it periodically to remind you of where we have been. If you have made it this far, your probability of success is very high. Thanks for making the journey with me.

Index

Index

interest rate risk, 16
interest rates, 14–16, 58
effect of, 39
fluctuations in, 54
and leveraging, 107
long- and short-term, 41–42
Internet
access, 259
on-line trading, 52
stocks, 30, 44
inverted yield curve, 42
investment advisers, xii, 267. *See also*
professional advisers
selection of, 263–66
investment analysts, 34
Investment Dealers Association
(IDA), 264
Investment Funds Institute of
Canada (IFIC), 264
investment income, 20, 21, 188–96
investment managers, 11, 267. *See
also* money managers;
professional advisers
discarding, 261–62
ranking of, 255–58, 269
selection of, 251, 252, 269
investment objectives, 103–4, 119,
120, 216. *See also* growth
objective; income objective;
liquidity objective
and asset classes, 110–11
in Investment Policy Statements,
268
in Investment Statements, 98–100,
145, 171
and life stages, 105–6, 108–10
and risk tolerance, 120
visualization of, 122–24
investment personality, 79, 262
determination of, 83–84, 91–96
in Investment Policy Statements,
268
in Investment Statements, 171
investment philosophy, 78–79, 216

in Investment Policy Statements,
268
in Investment Statements, 96–101,
171
of professional advisers and
managers, 207, 262, 263
investment policy. *See* asset allocation
Investment Policy Statements (IPS),
170, 237, 266–76
investment pyramids, 98–99. *See
also* Investment Statements
Investment Statements, 97–100,
145–48, 266
Level 1, 100–101
Level 2, 123–24
Level 3, 153–55
Level 4, 167–72
and monitoring, 187
and portfolio adjustments, 186
investment strategy, 10–11, 57, 66,
207–8
changes in, 4 (*see also* style drift)
investor expectations, 52–53, 114–16
involvement, 83–84, 92–93, 96–97

Las Vegas, 129
lawyers, 11
leveraging, 106–8, 120, 269
life expectancy, 21–23, 24
Life Income Funds (LIFs), 192
Lipper, Michael, 6
liquidity, 48, 209
liquidity objective, 104, 105, 106,
109, 147. *See also* investment
objectives
loans, 48, 80, 111. *See also* debt assets
locking in, 231

managed money
defined, 197
managed money products, 138
benefits of, 209–16
classifications of, 198
disadvantages of, 217–18

284

precious metals, 52, 111. *See also* equity assets

preferred shares, 111. *See also* debt assets

price-to-earnings (P/E) ratio, 43–46

private wealth management services, 138, 198, 237–38

professional advisers, 170, 241–42, 249, 266. *See also* financial planners; investment advisers; investment managers; money managers
  role of, 245–46, 248
  value of, 120, 178, 247

professional management, 212, 214
  as principle, 198, 206–8

psychology of investment, 3–6, 27–28, 29, 31, 40, 57, 247–48, 251
  and stock prices, 2–3, 43–44

purchasing power, 20–21. *See also* cost of living
  and inflation, 188, 189, 193
  loss of, 24–26, 73

real estate, 8, 17, 42, 52, 80, 96, 111, 140–41, 160, 161. *See also* equity assets

real estate mutual funds, 210

real returns, 57–58, 73

real value, 2

rebalancing, 175, 177, 183–86, 269

Registered Pension Plans (RPPs), 224

Registered Retirement Income Funds (RRIFs), 192

Registered Retirement Savings Plans (RRSPs), 108, 224
  asset classes in, 178, 179
  foreign content in, 210
  and mutual funds, 221, 222
  re-allocation of, 177–78, 179

retirement, 63, 109, 122–23, 194
  age of, 21–23

return of capital guarantee, 229–31

returns. *See also under* asset classes; *specific asset classes*
  and asset allocation, 128–31, 132–34, 144
  components of, 73
  expected, 75, 132, 139, 141, 149
  long-term average, 69
  nominal, 57
  real, 57–58, 73
  vs. risk, 119, 139, 151
  risk-adjusted, 254–55
  total, 38, 46
  weighted average, 131, 149

Richards, Dan, 16

risk. *See also* business risk; market risk; volatility
  and asset allocation, 131–32, 133–34, 139, 141–44
  defined, 12
  of loss of capital, 13–17, 25–26
  of loss of purchasing power, 24–26
  vs. returns, 119, 139, 151
  total, 34

risk assessment, 234

risk management, 251

risk premiums, 73

risk tolerance, 12, 61, 78–79, 89, 119, 216, 257
  and asset allocation, 147, 152
  determination of, 79–83
  factors in, 13
  and investment objectives, 120
  in Investment Policy Statements, 268, 269
  in Investment Statements, 96–97, 171
  and leveraging, 108

RRSPs. *See* Registered Retirement Savings Plans (RRSPs)

Rule of 72, 189, 230

savings, 47

security selection, 216, 251
  effect of, 134–35, 157

George Hartman's 25-year career in financial services spans both the insurance and investment industries.

George has an MBA from Wilfred Laurier University. In 1976 he received his Chartered Life Underwriter designation and was awarded the Dunstall medal as overall top student in Ontario. George has also taught economics, business administration and marketing at Mohawk College in Hamilton, Ontario.

In 1985 George joined The Universal Group, a Toronto-based investment fund manager, as VP, Marketing. During his six years in that role, the assets of the firm grew from $70 million to more than $600 million.

In 1991 George formed his own financial services consulting firm, Hartman & Company Inc. Areas of expertise included investment portfolio design, financial planning, sales management, product development and marketing.

In recent years George has become well known for his research on asset allocation as an investment strategy. He is a highly sought-after speaker and trainer, having conducted workshops and seminars for more than 50,000 investors as well as numerous investment dealers, financial planning organizations and educational institutions. He appears regularly on radio and television talk shows and was a contributing editor to *Canadian MoneySaver* and a frequent special columnist for *The Globe and Mail*'s "Report on Mutual Funds." George is on the editorial advisory board of the personal finance magazine *IE: Money* and for three years hosted Vancouver's popular weekly radio show *Money Matters*.

In 1992 George published *Risk Is a Four Letter Word — The Asset Allocation Approach to Investing*, which reached Canadian bestseller status, selling more than 50,000 copies. Both professional advisers and individual investors praised the book for its melding of technical information with practical advice on implementing investment strategies.

Readers wishing to contact George are encouraged to visit his web site, www.mostlymoney.com.